Firms as Political Entities

When people go to work, they cease to be citizens. At their desks they are transformed into employees, subordinate to the hierarchy of the workplace. The degree of their sense of voicelessness may vary from employer to employer, but it is real and growing, inflamed by populist propaganda that ridicules democracy as weak and ineffective amid global capitalism. At the same time, corporations continue untouched and even unremarked as a major source of the problem. Relying on 'economic bicameralism' to consider firms as political entities, this book sheds new light on the institutions of industrial relations that have marked the twentieth century, and argues that it is time to recognize that firms are a peculiar institution that must be properly organized in order to unshackle workers' motivation and creativity, and begin nurturing democracy again.

Isabelle Ferreras is a tenured fellow of the National Fund for Scientific Research (FNRS, Brussels, Belgium), a professor of sociology at the University of Louvain (IACCHOS-CriDIS) and a senior research associate of the Labor and Worklife Program at Harvard University.

T0371056

Firms as Political Entities

Saving Democracy through Economic Bicameralism

ISABELLE FERRERAS

Tenured Fellow, Fund for Scientific Research (FNRS, Brussels)
Professor, University of Louvain
Senior Research Associate, Labor and Worklife Program,
Harvard Law School

with

MIRANDA RICHMOND MOUILLOT

Translator and Editor

CAMBRIDGE
UNIVERSITY PRESS

CAMBRIDGE
UNIVERSITY PRESS

University Printing House, Cambridge CB2 8BS, United Kingdom

One Liberty Plaza, 20th Floor, New York, NY 10006, USA

477 Williamstown Road, Port Melbourne, VIC 3207, Australia

314-321, 3rd Floor, Plot 3, Splendor Forum, Jasola District Centre, New Delhi-110025, India

79 Anson Road, #06-04/06, Singapore 079906

Cambridge University Press is part of the University of Cambridge.

It furthers the University's mission by disseminating knowledge in the pursuit of education, learning and research at the highest international levels of excellence.

www.cambridge.org
Information on this title: www.cambridge.org/9781108402521
DOI: 10.1017/9781108235495

First published 2017
First paperback edition 2018

A catalogue record for this publication is available from the British Library

ISBN 978-1-108-41594-1 Hardback
ISBN 978-1-108-40252-1 Paperback

Cambridge University Press has no responsibility for the persistence or accuracy of URLs for external or third-party internet websites referred to in this publication, and does not guarantee that any content on such websites is, or will remain, accurate or appropriate.

In memory of Janek Kuczkiewicz,
in the name of his union brothers and sisters,
ardent defender of citizens *at work*
in the North and the South, in the East, and the West,
gone too soon but never forgotten

Labor is prior to and independent of capital. Capital is only the fruit of labor, and could never have existed if labor had not first existed. Labor is the superior of capital, and deserves much the higher consideration. Capital has its rights, which are as worthy of protection as any other rights. Nor is it denied that there is, and probably always will be, a relation between labor and capital producing mutual benefits.

Abraham Lincoln (1861)

A civilization that uses its principles for trickery and deceit is a dying civilization.

Aimé Césaire (1972)

I have no doubt that many people will immediately reject the idea of extending the democratic process to business firms as foolish and unrealistic.

It may therefore be helpful to recall that not long ago most people took it as a matter of self-evident good sense that the idea of applying the democratic process to the government of the nation-state was foolish and unrealistic.

Robert A. Dahl (1989: 328)

Contents

Figures

Acknowledgments

In 2004, as I was working on my Masters Thesis at MIT (Ferreras 2004), two of my professors, Joshua Cohen and Michael Piore, encouraged me to explore an analogy I had imagined in the course of my doctoral study of supermarket cashiers (Ferreras 2007). Their strong intellectual and moral support has been invaluable to me over the years, and I am eternally grateful to them both. I also would like to express my gratitude to Elaine Bernard, Richard Freeman, Chris Mackin, Joel Rogers, Michel Serres, and Philippe Van Parijs who, while offering their doubts and their critiques, blessed my work with their encouragement during those first years, and ever since. The support of these extraordinary minds has been one of the most precious gifts of my academic life.

I am tremendously grateful to the institutions who have funded and hosted my research since 2004: first and foremost the Belgian National Fund for Scientific Research in Brussels (FNRS-FRS), the University of Louvain (CriDIS-IACCHOS), and the Labor and Worklife Program at Harvard, which have provided me with continuous support since the beginning. Over shorter periods, I am grateful for the support of the Minda de Gunzburg Center for European Studies at Harvard, the MIT Department of Political Science, the Hanse Wissenschaftkollege in Delmenhorst, the Graduate School for Social Sciences of the University of Bremen, and the Wage Indicator Foundation in Amsterdam. All of these institutions have made it possible for me to practice a kind of "slow science," of which this book is one of the fruits.

I was invited to present this work in seminars or conferences. I would like to thank the organizers for having offered me these opportunities to discuss my work: the University de Montréal (Daniel Weinstock),

the University of Québec at Montréal (Idil Boran), the Louvain Work-
place Democracy Workshop (Axel Gosseries), the University of Bremen
(BIGGGS) (Karin Gottschall and Steffen Mau), the Hanse Wissenschaft
Kollege, as well as the Harvard Labor Theory Workshop (Alex Gourevitch), the Lovanium Doctoral Seminar on Ethics and Public Policy at the
University of Louvain (Philippe Van Parijs, Nicholas Vrousalis, and Toon
Vandevelde), the CAPRIGHT network (Jean De Munck, Claude Didry,
Annette Jobert, Serafino Negrelli, and Robert Salais in particular), the
members of the Network K 'Law and the Social Sciences' of the Society for
the Advancement of Socio-economics (Alvaro Santos and Kathy Stone)
during its meetings in Costa Rica (2008) and Madrid (2011), the Center
for the Sociology of Organizations at Sciences Po-Paris (Pierre François,
Olivier Borraz, and Henri Bergeron), the Interuniversity Research Centre
on Globalization and Work (CRIMT) at the University of Montréal (Gre-
gor Murray, Christian Levesque, Nicolas Roby), the Académie royale
des Sciences, des Lettres et des Beaux-Arts de Belgique-Collège Belgique
(Philippe de Woot and Isabelle Cassiers), the International Seminar on the
Constitutionalization of the World-Power System, Collège des Bernardins
(Jean-Philippe Robé and Stéphane Vernac), the Max Wéber Centre at the
Université de Lyon (Christian Thuderoz and Bernard Baudry), Séminaire
interdisciplinaire CLERSé-LEM at the Université de Lille (Nicolas Postel
and Richard Sobel), the Political Theory Workshop at the Department of
Political Science, Yale University (Hélène Landemore), the Département
de philosophie et d'éthique appliquée at the University of Sherbrooke
(Allison Marchildon and André Lacroix), and the Louvain Hoover Chair
of Economic and Social Ethics 2016 Conference on "Utopias for our
times" (Philippe Van Parijs).

Numerous organizations also invited me to discuss my work. I want
to thank them, in particular various labor unions and political parties,
particularly in Belgium (CNE, CSC, SETCa, FGTB, Ecolo, Parti social-
iste), the European Trade Union Confederation/European Trade Union
Institute (Philippe Pochet), and think tanks: Ligue des droits humains,
Brussels (Alexis Deswaef and Véronique van der Plancke), Philosophy
& Management (Laurent Ledoux and Roland Vaxelaire), Association
Syndicale des Magistrats (Manuela Cadelli), SAW-B-Brussels (Quentin
Mortier and Barbara Garbarczyk).

I would like to thank the many people who supported me and helped
this book come into being. All my colleagues, in particular at the Center
for Interdisciplinary Research on Democracy, Institutions & Subjectivity
at Louvain and at the Harvard Labor and Worklife Program should be

warmly thanked. I wish to express special gratitude for (critical) exchange and, or support to Jean De Munck, Matthieu de Nanteuil, Julien Charles, Suzanne Berger, Jonathan Zeitlin, Philippe De Villé, Albert Bastenier, Philippe Coppens, Thomas Périlleux, Melanie Adrian, Dominique Méda, Jennifer Amadeo-Holl, Christian Arnsperger, Lorette Baptiste, Alex Bryson, Isabelle Cassiers, Priscilla Claeys, Sabine Wernerus, Philippe Corcuff, Emeline De Bouver, Mathieu Berger, Geoffrey Pleyers, Philippe De Leener, Bernard Francq, David Grewal, Eric De Keuleneer, Marc Verdussen, Armand Lawson, Aristide Mukeza, Constantine Mukaneza, Patrizia Nanz, Russ Muirhead, Paulien Osse, Kea Tijdens, Barbara de Radiguès, Jean-Philippe Robé, Denis Segrestin, Jack Trumpbour, François Eymard-Duvernay, Olivier Favereau, Laurent Taskin, Olivier Jégou, Philippe Barré, Thierry Amougou, Xavier Baron, Géraldine Thiry, Hadrien Coutant, Lionel Casterman, David Grewal, Maya-Merida Paltineau, and Erik Olin Wright. Thinking of your role in my work is a source of gratitude, and if anyone has slipped my mind as I write this, please forgive me, it has been a long road since 2004.

I would like to express my special thanks to Robert Dreesen and the team at Cambridge University Press who believed in this project. Thanks also to Lew Bateman of Cambridge University Press and Michael Aronson of Harvard University Press, as well as to Monique Labrune of Les Presses Universitaires de France, all of who helped sustain this project along the way. My deepest thanks as well to the two anonymous reviewers whose close readings for Cambridge University Press, which came with detailed notes, objections, suggestions, and comments, were invaluable to the completion of this manuscript. Any faults remaining in the present text are surely my own, while its merits owe much to their contributions.

The members of The Endicott/Dictate.me.not Society (Robert Fannion, Pierre François, Paulin Ismard, Hélène Landemore, Auriane Lamine, Liam McHugh-Russell, Benjamin McKean, Sanjay Pinto, Virgile Chassagnon, and Miranda Richmond Mouillot) have been a great source of inspiration, each in his or her own way. Their willingness to seriously reflect on and debate the hypothesis of firms as political entities has been very precious to me. We have a lot on our plate going forward.

One of the aforementioned individuals deserves special mention. Miranda Richmond Mouillot has been working with me tirelessly since 2012. She gave me my voice in the English language, expressing better than I ever could have the essence of ideas that were at times difficult even for me to formulate in my mother tongue. Miranda is not a translator. She is an interpreter, an intellectual partner, a midwife practiced in the art of the live birth of ideas. If you appreciate the reading, I have Miranda's interpretive powers to thank for it.

I shall end by expressing my deep deep gratitude to my family and friends for their support through the high and low points of those years, and above all to the larger-than-life Grégor Chapelle – and to Pam and Olga Chapelle Ferreras – for their support, faith in me, and loving patience.

Introduction

What about the Workers?

This book addresses a fundamental tension between capitalism and democracy, a tension so great that it has the potential to lead our democratic societies to the brink of collapse. It begins with the observation that life in Western democratic society has created an expectation of voice in the economy and the workplace, which cannot be fulfilled by the arbitrary way in which most firms are run. To be a citizen and to be an employee today is to live with a great contradiction between the democratic culture of our times and the reality of the work experience. Our democratic culture gives citizens a hunger for a voice in the way their lives unfold, while their experience in the workplace is one in which they are reduced to mere production factors. *Capital investors* truly are "more equal than others"[1] within contemporary firms – specifically, more equal than the employees who *invest their labor* in those same firms. Capitalism grants capital investors *despotic* power – in the original sense of that term[2] – over

---

[1] "All animals are equal, but some animals are more equal than others"; George Orwell, *Animal Farm* (1946).

[2] The term "despotic" comes from ancient Greek (*despótēs*), which means master, owner, lord. For Aristotle (350 BC), the ideal type of despotic rule was the master-slave relationship. Aristotle believed this relationship was justified in this specific case alone because he believed that slaves were by nature lacking in deliberative faculty, and therefore in need of a "natural master" to look out for them and direct their actions (Book I). Despotic rule should take place in the realm of private life, according to Aristotle; in the political domain, it is a symptom of corrupt government: constitutions "which aim only at the advantage of the rulers are deviant and unjust, because they involve *despotic* rule, which is inappropriate for a community of free persons" (Book III). The term *despotic* as it is used in this book, therefore, refers us to the realm of the private sphere, in which some rule over others in a fundamentally unequal way – a type of rule wholly unfit for our contemporary economy, as we shall see.

I

labor investors, who, in a capitalist economy, are considered to be elements in the means of production. This runs counter to the democracies in which capitalist firms have flourished, and this contradiction has necessarily affected contemporary workplaces: employees today struggle with a range of problems, from lack of motivation and absenteeism to depression. It affects the world outside the workplace as well: the financial, environmental, social, and political crises we now face all press us to examine the role and structure of the firm as an institution within the context of our *democratic* societies. This book offers such an examination, and its conclusion is unambiguous: firms are better understood as political entities, and not mere economic organizations. Economic organizations they are, but they are much more than that as well, and it is time to acknowledge this fact. If democratic societies do acknowledge this, they will be called to begin to treat firms like all of society's other institutions: not only endowed with rights, held accountable for discharging specific responsibilities. As political entities, it is crucial that firms be made compatible with the democratic commitments of our nations – in other words, democratized.

The political project that organizes our lives in Western democracies is driven by a democratic ideal. By this we mean "a compelling normative idea, requiring that people be treated as equals in the process of collective decision-making" (Cohen 2009: 6). This entails that the government be a government "of the people, by the people, for the people," according to Abraham Lincoln's Gettysburg Address in 1863. Despite the physical, material, intellectual, and cultural differences of our members, we as societies have declared all citizens to be equal, and organized our institutions in ways intended to help us perceive and treat each other as equals. As Article 1 of the *Universal Declaration of the Human Rights* affirmed in 1948, we are born "free and equal in dignity and in rights" – equal, and therefore fit to participate in choosing the collective standards that order our lives. But as this book will argue, these assertions are not taken seriously in the world of work. As the level of inequalities within and among nations reaches historic levels (Piketty 2013, Milanovic 2016), people around the world are increasingly impatient with the failings of democracy. They are aware that their life prospects and those of their children differ drastically depending on whether they are born rich or poor – and what clearer violation of the standard of equality underpinning the democratic ideal could there be? Of all aspects of contemporary life, the world of work would seem to be the last great holdover from a bygone era in which despotic and plutocratic rule was the norm.

The unsettling cognitive dissonance to which this state of affairs has given rise is plain: in their everyday lives, citizens are enjoined to behave as responsible members of their democratic society. As electors, they are presumed capable of coming together to decide important political questions such as "Who should be president of this country?" or "Should this country leave the European Union?" And yet these same citizens, when they arrive at their jobs, become the subjects of a despotic corporate government in which profitability is the main criterion for all decisions. This criterion of profitability is just as ill defined: Whose profit? To what end? According to what terms? Over how long? In my work as a sociologist, I have observed that employees today live with a contradiction that I, reading it from a Marxian perspective on capitalism, have identified as the *capitalism/democracy contradiction*. It raises significant questions: What are the limits of the current confrontational coexistence of capitalism and democracy? And, in practical terms, how are we going to reconcile, escape, or end this confrontation? What can be done moving forward to solve the contradiction? Essentially, the road diverges ahead, and we must choose: more capitalism or more democracy. The former will grant more arbitrary power to those who own capital, giving "capitalist despotism" freer rein in our work lives and beyond. The latter leads toward a reinvigorated version of democracy, in which the political rights granted to working people are at least the same as the political rights accorded to capital owners.

To offer a concrete example – not to say an ideal type – the United States has, for the past four decades, been on the path toward *capitalist despotism*. Corporate money provides limitless funds to electoral candidates; the U.S. Supreme Court's *Citizens United* ruling declared that corporations are to be considered as people with the right to free speech; and a significant proportion of social and cultural life has come under the influence or even the direct leadership of corporations, from prisons to sports arenas. In January 2017, as this book is being completed, Donald Trump, a billionaire corporate leader with a track record as a capitalist heir, is about to be sworn in as the country's president, showing just how far down the path of capitalist despotism the United States has gone. For the time being, and perhaps for the foreseeable future, the United States appears to have resolved the *capitalism/democracy contradiction* by choosing more capitalist despotism and less democracy.

Yet, what analysts have referred to as a populist revolt against the establishment in the November 2016 election expresses nothing so much as a deep "hunger for democracy" (Ferreras 2007b). People raised as citizens in a democracy aspire to have some agency over the course of their own lives, and the past decades have shown them with aching clarity that this aspiration to agency is little more than a dream.[3] It seems clear that the time to explore the alternative route is now. The path of more democracy, as a project of *deepening and extending democracy* (Olin Wright and Rogers 2015), is a long, historic avenue, the one down which social justice and progress have advanced. It is the long path of emancipation, distinguished by the enfranchisement of different categories of people previously considered unequal. If we are to continue down it today, we must dare to look closely at the specificities of the world around us. This book does just that, and offers a map for the next step, which is the democratization of the corporation. If we fail to take this step, we will be forced to a standstill, from which we will see capitalism eat up what is left of political democracy. To forge ahead – and we can – we must keep moving toward more *productive*[4] institutional arrangements in the firm. This book, then, offers a way out of the impasse of "capitalist democracies" (Cohen and Rogers 1983) in which we now live, in which the standards organizing our – capitalist – economies are set by capital investors, while the purportedly egalitarian standards organizing the rest of our – democratic – political life are set by all.

In the West, our age-old understanding of the economy as private in nature has worn away to the point that it must be reconsidered. What should be considered private has changed considerably with time: our economy began as agrarian, became industrial, and is now service-based. More and more employees now work in full or partial view of the public, meaning that the economy, considered since antiquity to be *private* (the term *economy* being derived from the Greek *oikos-nemein*, or the management of the household), is now experienced by many of those contributing to it as part of the larger *public space*. Service employees greet their fellow citizens as customers face-to-face, over the phone, and through the tentacular world of the internet; even those not in direct contact with customers are constantly reminded of their importance and presence. Beneath the constant gaze of citizen-customers, the corporation-household, once intensely *private*, has slowly moved into the *public*

[3] For a vivid account of the situation in the United States, see Arlie Russell Hochschild's (2016) monograph on citizens in the destitute South who turned to the Tea Party in an attempt to win back economic opportunity and influence over their lives and the future of their children.
[4] The use of the term emphasizes a conception of democracy committed *at the same time* to both efficiency and justice, as in Rogers's (2012) conception of "productive democracy."

sphere. This is a shift the full impact of which has yet to be measured. In advanced democracies, we take as given that the public sphere should not be dominated by the power (*kratein*) of a single (*auto-*) person, nor by a small group of individuals, valiant, intelligent, or rich as they may be (*aristo-* or *pluto-*). Democratic societies have agreed that the public sphere is a space through which people – the *demos*, all the members of the democracy – should express their sovereignty, both as individuals and as a society. If this is so, and if the workplace has shifted into the public sphere, then shouldn't our reference point for its government also shift from the household (*oikos*) to the people – *demos*? Analyzing the experiences of those who invest their labor in the firm, I have found that it is impossible to ignore the ways in which they are steeped in notions of democratic justice. Work, for those who do it, is a fundamentally *expressive* experience. This is, in fact, one of the fundamentals of my argument, that those who invest their labor in firms are motivated by *expressive rationality*. By this I mean that the work experience resonates with meaning that is constructed by those doing the work, and that this meaning is derived by mobilizing concepts of what is just and unjust in the life of a community – what political philosophers generally refer to as the "political."

Although it is hardly surprising that traces of democratic culture should be perceptible in the workplaces of democratic societies, this reality has remained strangely invisible. I will mobilize research in corporate and labor law (among other fields) to argue that this is because the idea of the corporation has managed to eclipse the idea of the firm, allowing corporate shareholders to maintain all power over it. As I will explain, the dominant *economic theory of the firm* reduces the firm to a mere *corporation* at the center of a *nexus* of contracts, including labor contracts. In this sense, it practices what I call a *Reductio ad Corporationem*: it folds the firm into the corporation, despite the fact that the latter is merely the legal vehicle that structures capital investments. It does this by pretending that the fundamental qualities of a firm are identical to those of a corporation. This occludes an immense portion of the firm's reality. In this way, the *economic theory of the firm*, while claiming scientific neutrality, has in fact upheld and validated a very narrow approach to the firm (and even to the corporation, as we shall see in Part II) – one that has helped shareholders maintain an excess of power. The scientific task pursued by this book is to initiate the development of a *political theory of the firm*[5] as an alternative

---

[5] A first statement was provided in French in Ferreras (2012). Since the financial crisis of 2008 and its damaging consequences, one should notice the appearance of the term

to this *Reductio ad Corporationem* by shedding light on the dense reality of the firm not captured by the description and institutional design of the *corporation*. It will examine the actual relationship *between* the corporation and the firm, rather than ignoring or obscuring that relationship. This alone is a vast project. This research agenda cannot possibly be addressed without a dedicated collective effort. A great deal of research into this topic already exists. Unfortunately it has so far remained isolated in different corners of the social sciences. This research needs to be drawn together – and, I believe, deployed – through the hypothesis put forth in this book: to consider firms as political entities. To do so requires addressing three dimensions of the *political theory of the firm*: the substantive, the descriptive, and the normative. The *political theory of the firm* mobilizes analytical categories coming from the body of literature in political analysis and political theory to look at the life of the firm. Its evaluative and critical aspects – the normative dimension of the theory – will flow straightforwardly from the substantive and descriptive dimensions.

In the interest of giving life to this new research landscape made of the many existing, scattered contributions that the author of these lines could not possibly hope to know of, and cite, this short book contains a proposal that draws practical conclusions from the analysis it provides, as a lens for looking to the future. The imperative of efficiency conditions economic life today, and the imperative of collective freedom conditions public life in Western democracies. The continued growth of our economy and our society demands that we identify a viable compromise between the two. As current events constantly remind us, the grave risks posed by the shock of these two imperatives are inescapably present, and the need for compromise inescapably important. We as citizens are facing big questions, and our democracies cannot afford to shy away from them. Can efficiency and justice be reconciled? How compatible are capitalism and

"political" in analysis from various fields attempting to account for the behavior of the corporation or of the business firm. Calling on the Rawlsian theory of justice, Neron (2010, 2013) proposes that the business firm be taken seriously as an object of the "political theory of the business firm," and contrasts this perspective with Corporate Social Responsibility literature that claims to be "political" (Whelen 2012). Ciepley (2013) developed an impressive contribution to the "political theory of the corporation," which combines political analysis and history. It is centered on the history of the corporation, in the legal sense, and shows how the corporation can be accounted for entirely through political analysis. This demonstration speaks only to the corporation, and not to the whole of the firm, as the present work aims to. Yet, by offering a political reading of the corporation, it makes a substantial contribution to a *political theory of the firm*, which includes the corporation, as we shall see.

democracy? Can capitalism be democratized? My own research into the workplace led me to these questions – and then to the observations and to the proposal put forth in this book. I have written a text intended to inject new life and new energy into an often shopworn and anxiety-inducing debate. The ideas I offer in the pages that follow are the beginnings of my own attempt, as a scholar and a citizen, to seriously and pragmatically envision a sustainable future for our democracies threatened by financial global capitalism, and more specifically by the current confusion of the corporation with the firm.

I am a labor sociologist and a political scientist, but the work I present here is strongly interdisciplinary, as is required by such vast questions. Because this is a book about the future of democracy and capitalism, I have grounded my analysis in the past, which is, after all, an indispensable reference point if we are to look ahead. Specifically, I have grounded it in political history: although the transition is arguably still in process, over the long term our Western societies have progressed from absolutism (in the form of autocracies or oligarchies) to democracy. For this reason, in my thinking about the government of the firm, I chose to draw inspiration from political revolutions, since the central issue that caused them is the same one now faced by the capitalist firm: how power ought to be shared. As I will explain, in the history of Western democratic revolutions the transition from absolutism to democracy occurred through a specific institutional innovation. Although it varies from country to country and from context to context, this transition has always involved what I call a *bicameral moment*. In modern history, England may be considered as having given birth to this compromise: faced with the prospect of losing it all, the king of England realized it was necessary to share his power. British bicameralism was his tactic for avoiding fatal revolution, a compromise with the people in the form of a partial democracy that seated landed aristocrats in the House of Lords and the representatives of the people in the House of Commons, with an executive branch accountable to both. The king's government had to win the majority in both Houses to pass a law. Today's workplace bears a more than passing resemblance to a pre-democratic state, with upper management holding the place of the pre-democratic executive branch of government. It is an institution governed by a property-owning minority that profits from the labor of the majority. The parallel is arresting: What would you think of an England governed by the House of Lords alone?

Bicameralism was a radical idea because it was so simple. This book seeks to inject the same radical simplicity into the debate over governing and democratizing capitalism – not to oversimplify the questions we face as societies, but rather to offer solid foundations for that debate. It begins with the observation that work has shifted from the private to the public sphere; that employees are suffering from the tension between their aspiration to greater voice in the workplace and the authoritarian power structures that continue to hold sway there; that the formerly "private household" of the economy has evaporated under customers' gazes and left employees with a work experience that takes place in the public space of the service economy. Then, drawing inspiration from the political history of Western societies, it conveys the notion of bicameralism, the institutional innovation that spurred the process of democratization, into the government of the firm.

The point of democracy is to serve all; my proposal here is no exception. Lately, business rhetoric has become more and more imbued with the idea of corporate social and environmental responsibility, and with the questions of how to sustainably secure the innovation capacities of firms' "human resources" while promoting efficiency and avoiding lack of motivation, depression, and, in extreme cases, job-related suicide. The proposal that follows is based on the pragmatic observation that the investment of labor in firms is at least as necessary and legitimate as the investment of capital, and that firms would be better served if all its investors were represented in their government. After all, as political history has shown, power sharing is preferable to confrontation, gridlock, or even collapse. Sharing, not relinquishing: to each set of investors its own house, bound to govern together in the interest of all through a representative government they both designate. A Capital Investors' House of Representatives and a Labor Investors' House of Representatives with an executive branch – or top management – whose laws must be consented by a majority in both houses; in other words, by at least 50% + 1 vote from the Representatives elected by Capital Investors and 50% + 1 vote from the Representatives elected by Labor Investors.

What historical analogy is most appropriate to understanding and imagining a revolution in the government of the firm? Is Economic Bicameralism desirable? What institutional design does it require? What organizational issues are at stake? When it comes to it, what is a workplace? Can capital and labor be considered as instruments? And is the firm really a *political* entity? Would a bicameral firm be a Rube Goldberg machine? Would it sap away firms' crucial competitiveness? Or would it be proof of respect – of capital investors, and of society in general – toward the people who invest their labor in the economy, their motivation and efficiency, their mental and physical health – all determining factors in a high-performing knowledge economy? Would Economic Bicameralism be the first step in an unacceptable power grab by workers, or, to the contrary, would it be nothing more than a shameful compromise with capitalism? Or, in the end, would it be a *bridging* institution, the step toward making the firms that wield such influence over our globalized times into fit members of our democratic society, therefore making it stronger and sustainable? This book opens the door to these questions. You decide.

OVERVIEW: AGAINST THE REDUCTIO AD CORPORATIONEM

This book is structured in three sections that will critically examine work, and how it is governed – that is the firm in Western capitalist democracies, proceeding chronologically from the past through the present, and into the future. Our goal here is to present our subject along lines as clean as possible – to not only open the door on a new possibility, but to turn on the light and invite readers and scholars in to think and to contribute. To this end, to paraphrase C. B. Macpherson (1977), we have chosen simplicity and brevity over a welter of detail.

Part I will offer a critical history of the government of work and of the position of the economy in society under Western capitalist democracies. It will highlight the slow transition of the economy, and of the government of work, from the domestic to the public sphere of democracy. Having sketched out this background, the book will explain in Part II how, in the present era of financial globalization, the vehicle structuring capital investors we call the *corporation* has managed to take over the *firm*, whose fundamental logics it will then identify. Having exposed the confusion of the firm and the corporation, Part II will then identify the dimensions of research with which a more reliable account of the firm may be built, both substantively, and descriptively, and propose that such an account be the domain of the *political theory of the firm*, and in so doing help to initiate the latter as a field of academic study in its own right. Part III will use the past to look to the future, and to offer a proposal. It will examine the history of Western societies in order to identify moments in the past when power shifted from a small group or faction that had previously dominated a majority with an equally legitimate claim to self-government. Observing that shifts took place in "bicameral moments" of compromise in which a new institutional structure was put in place to transfer rule from the few to the many, Part III applies this idea to the government of the firm. To this end, it re-categorizes the firm as a political entity where the corporation is the structure through which capital investors' interests are represented, and grants labor investors their own channel of representation as well. This would transform firms' top management into a legitimate executive power answerable to the firms' two constituent bodies, capital investors and labor investors.

Background

Many innovative forms of firm governance were imagined and invented over the course of the nineteenth and twentieth centuries, a fact that is often forgotten today. Over the years, democracies have debated intensely over ways to govern capitalism, the corporation, and the firm, its flagship institution. Despite this, the firm remained only vaguely recognized and ill-defined, with its definition evolving slowly alongside our models for economic and political development. This evolution continues, and calls for new thinking about the firm as an institution of democratic society. Our economy today has become a knowledge economy, dominated by the service sector. Experts agree that "human capital" drives innovation more than any other factor. Our archetype of the worker as humble manual laborer, busy at his factory assembly line, is entirely out of date – as is that of the farmer, who was a figurehead of the economy from the Neolithic era through the end of the Second World War. Currently, more than 75% of jobs in Western economies are in the service (or tertiary) sector. The archetype of the Western worker today is a supermarket cashier, a call center employee, an app developer or a bank teller – someone who serves customers, builds relationships, and produces knowledge. In an economy increasingly powered by information technology and artificial intelligence, workers who are not knowledge producers risk rapidly being replaced by automation and robots (Frey and Osborne 2013, Ford 2015). This means that the employees who remain can no longer be considered to be a mere "production factor" among others, like machines, raw materials, or money. Although they are clearly much more than that, their perspective and understanding still count for little in the government of the firm.

Today, we face a grave, multilevel crisis – one that is environmental, economic, social, and political: the very credibility of our democracies hangs in the balance. In light of these facts, it is obvious that solutions at many levels are required. This book will tackle firm government as a hot point for those problems, and their solutions. It seeks to help renew the tradition of firm innovation in order to offer a path marked by the expanded sense of social justice needed to consolidate and reinforce peace, sustainability, and prosperity – to help, in short, with the work of keeping our democracies meaningful. This book contains three parts:[6]

Part I. Critical History of Power in the Firm: The Slow Transition of Work from the Private to the Public Sphere

The observation that workers aspire to more voice in the workplace and that the concrete experience of work is informed by a culture that favors democratic justice is not new or surprising. As Part I will explain, workers' expectations today are infused with a long history of struggles for political freedom in the form of both individual and collective rights; the challenge they now face is how to achieve collective self-determination in a workplace that has become part of the public space of our democratic societies. Part I of this book will turn back to the beginnings of our modern capitalist democratic societies, as democratic culture is rooted in the individual's quest for dignity and freedom, which has a history far older than that of capitalism. This book therefore opens by explaining the progressive transition of work from the private sphere to the public in the history of capitalism in democratic societies. Highlights of this transition include the institution of a labor code separate from the *Code du Commerce* at the end of the nineteenth century; the emergence of unions and collective bargaining rights; social welfare policy piloted by labor-management coalitions; works councils and workplace health and safety committees; the National Labor Relations Act of 1935 in the United States, the establishement of codetermination (*Mitbestimmung*) in large German firms after WWII; and, most recently, European works councils. All of these institutions may be seen as bearing witness to work's progressive transition to the public sphere of our democracies. One function of Part I, therefore, is to offer an argument for the necessity of experimenting anew, with new and more promising institutions capable of rendering our democracies more socially and economically productive.

Part II. What Is a Firm?

Part II opens by asking and answering a very simple but very powerful question: What is a capitalist firm today? This question is a powerful one

---

[6] Central as it is to my long-term research agenda on the capitalism/democracy contradiction, this book offers ideas entirely revised and updated, which were first outlined in French through two monographs, Ferreras (2007) and Ferreras (2012).

because so many people – particularly members of economic elites such as company heads, shareholders, investors, mainstream economists, and their political allies – would like to believe that it has a simple answer. A firm? Nothing more than an organization that seeks (maximal) return on capital investment. An organization that exists to make a profit. End of story.

Part II of this book pushes past this simplistic view by examining the two classic approaches to the firm: *liberal economic theory of the firm* – which mistakes the corporation for the firm, and the Marxist understanding of the firm – which shares the remarkably similar view of instrumental rationality, defined in this context as the belief that the firm is nothing more than an instrument to generate returns on capital investment. Here, we will show that this narrow understanding of the firm actually mistakes it entirely, confusing it with the corporation in what we have named the *Reductio ad Corporationem*. As legal scholarship reminds us, a corporation is a legal entity, a vehicle used to structure capital investments. In fact, as the first section of Part II will show, no model whose understanding of the work experience relies solely on instrumental rationality is sufficient to describe what a firm *is* – in other words, to describe what happens in such an organization, what is lived out there, what human and social realities exist there.

Indeed, we have failed to take into account that our economy is ever more tertiary, and the service model is expanding across all economic sectors. With this in mind, the second section of Part II will explain why work deserves to be analyzed as an experience whose logic is *expressive, public*, and *political*, and as such, a logic that is driven by an expectation for democratic voice (Ferreras 2007) – what I call the *intuition of democratic jutice*. We will name the logic driving labor investors *expressive rationality*. We will then attempt to lay the groundwork for what we have called the *political theory of the firm* by providing a more satisfactory account of the firm as a political institution that must balance two intertwined types of rationality, the instrumental and expressive, which drive their two constituent groups, investors in capital and investors in labor. The *political theory of the firm*, as this section explains, must offer both a substantive account of the firm, and an analytic, descriptive account of the precise, factual dimensions informing such a definition of the firm. Part II draws upon many fields in the social sciences, including law, sociology, psychology, economics, industrial relations, and philosophy. While each of these fields has sought to account for one particular aspect of the complexity of the firm, this book's interdisciplinary perspective intends to give a more comprehensive view logic of the firm as a political institution. Labor is the living embodiment of the firm. With no one to work in it, a firm does not exist. Even if its functions were filled almost entirely by robots, a firm would still need human work; at the very least it would need one engineer to fix and maintain them. Indeed, as the world becomes more and more automated, it is all the more important to describe and define the institution within which humans are actually still working. The resulting definition conditions the very nature of the power structure assigned the responsibility of governing work, and, by extension, the responsibility of legitimately governing (or not governing) the capitalist firm.

This section closes with the idea that, because a firm is necessarily a place in which workers *invest* themselves and their labor, it cannot be taken as its capital investors' *res; it is not a belonging they are free to dispose of as they wish*. This book subscribes to the idea that the people who invest their labor in it *constitute* the firm at least as much as those who invest their capital. Despite this fact, the firm continues to be governed by capital investors as if it were nothing more than a *corporation*, when the latter is in fact nothing more than the vehicle structuring their own capital investments. The *political theory of the firm* logically contains a third, normative dimension, which will be covered in Part III. Its evaluative and critical aspects will flow straightforwardly from its substantive and descriptive dimensions, that is, the analytical categories established from the body of literature in political analysis and political theory used to give the account of the firm that emerges earlier in Parts I and II.

Part III. Looking to the Future: From Political Bicameralism to Economic Bicameralism

In light of the foundations for the *political theory of the firm* laid out in Part II, the way in which firms are currently governed – by corporations whose authority rests on the fact that they are conflated with firms – no longer corresponds to their institutional reality. Firm government today is *illegitimate*, because it represents only one of the firm's two constituent bodies. It is *unreasonable* in that it allows all power to be deployed in the interests of a single group of actors, a firm's capital investors.[7] Finally,

---

[7] History supports the idea of the hegemonic tendency on the part of any group in power to eliminate any hint of counter influence. Thus, depending on what the legal context allows, firms actively fight even workers' vaguest attempts to form coalitions – not to mention unions – which they perceive as threatening their interests. Union-busting techniques – all too familiar in the United States – as well as the intimidation, blackmail, firing, and

common sense leads us to doubt that such a government would manifest any great measure of *intelligence*. The scope of these observations is broad, reaching to the very core of what propels growth in Western economies. Its point is simple: the monocameral capitalist approach to the government of the firm, led almost entirely by the corporation, deserves to be questioned, if only from the perspective of pure efficiency.

In light of this, Part III looks for possibilities in the future by reaching into the past. It opens with a historical study of the solution Western societies have identified to face the demands of democratic self-determination. Although the modalities have varied, Western societies have always transitioned from despotism or oligarchy to representative government through what this book terms a "bicameral moment." For firms, implication of this observation is as simple in analytical terms as it is radical in practical terms: if it is to be governed according to its deeply political reality, the firm as an institution must be founded in both of the rationalities that drive it, and represent both of its constituent bodies. It must cease to favor capital investors over labor investors, in other words. The history of political bicameralism shows to what extent the transition of any politeia from an authoritarian regime to a liberal democratic one depends on the recognition of its internal, dual logic. Part III will review the main defenses of political bicameralism in political philosophy and philosophy of law to show that the government of the firm, and particularly those who hold the executive power within it, ought too to be held responsible to both of the firm's two constituent bodies, its capital investors and labor investors. Part III will follow the logic of bicameral political theory to argue that these two constituent bodies should be represented by elected officials in ad hoc *chambers of representatives* that jointly function as the legislative power; in other words, the firm's parliament. The government of the firm – its *executive management* – would answer to these two chambers. This would transform it into a truly accountable government, responsible for finding productive compromises to help advance the firm in the interest of *both* parties, not just one of them.

even assassination of dozens of union leaders on an annual basis are a clear illustration of this tendency. (See the Annual Survey of Violations of Trade Union Rights by the International Trade Union Confederation.) What happens in politics when the ruling party wins an absolute majority is an interesting point of comparison: if there are no solid, independent system of checks and balances (constitutional, judiciary), the government quickly becomes *unreasonable*, even in situations where the forms of democracy seem to have been respected (elections, respect for term limits, etc.). The case of the Putin-Medvedev government in Russia has provided a clear example of this in the past decade.

Unlike currently prevalent views of the firm, which recognize only the logic of instrumental rationality in the corporation, Economic Bicameralism recognizes the firm as an institution, driven by two types of rationality (*expressive* and *instrumental*). Furthermore, it provides for institutions that are adapted to the challenges of the contemporary government of the firm: it acknowledges that firms should be governed in a manner that respects the instrumental rationality of capital investors and recognizes the *expressive* rationality at the heart of work and the life of the firm. The fruit of this compromise would be a bicameral firm, a capitalist enterprise that bolsters and is bolstered by our democracies. Part III outlines how the bicameral firm would be equipped to meet the challenges of innovation and prosperity in the contemporary world of the service-based economy.

The time has come for firms to evolve. Capitalism has gained the upper hand over states. Globalized corporations enact their own rules, engage in social dumping, and shop around for the legal systems that suit their ends. Governing capitalism can no longer be left in the hands of capitalists alone. Currently, there is no global institution capable of fostering solidarity across nations, and protecting democratic sovereignty, and we cannot effectively foster and protect them if we do not understand the firm for what it truly is – a fully political institution with its own patterns of dominance that has great impact both on the lives of those directly involved in it, and on the wider world. Citizen-workers have high expectations for greater voice in the workplace, and in their life in general. It is time to meet these expectations with a system of powers (and therefore, of checks and balances) that measures up to what philosophers of law and the founders of the modern state once envisioned. In today's service economy, high-performing firms depend on the quality of their collaborators' dedication and hard work. Their success depends on their ability to transform individual skill sets into a collective capability to innovate, in order to respond to the demands of their customers in the best way possible. This book places Economic Bicameralism in the long historical evolution of political and economic institutions within liberal democracies, and proposes it as a solution that meets both the imperatives of democratic justice and the needs of innovative businesses.

At the end of this book, the reader will find a readers' guide that discusses some of the objections that may be raised to the proposal for Economic Bicameralism. Here, however, we wish to address directly a possible misunderstanding: our goal in proposing Economic Bicameralism is to draw a concrete proposal from our analysis of the firm. All too often, scholars hide behind the idea that their role is to offer diagnostics; I believe that we have a responsibility to try to provide concrete proposals as well. Hopefully, this book will improve our understanding of social facts by offering a concrete utopia, a proposal with force enough to open the floor for debate, to push from analysis toward practical applications. That is its goal. Theoretical discussions rarely leave the halls of academia. And then, one day, we awake to find that our political reality has been built on an ill-founded idea, defended by a theory that was never debated in the "real world."[8] By ending the analysis given herein with a concrete proposal for the future, the author hopes to offer a constructive way to bring fellow citizens into the – crucial – debate over how the firm should be governed in a global and democratic context.

* * *

REGAINING CONTROL OF GLOBAL FINANCE CAPITALISM: "IT'S THE CORPORATION, STUPID!"

It seems we are living in times that Karl Polanyi predicted. In his landmark book *The Great Transformation* (1944), Polanyi examined the conditions that led Germany to fall for fascism in the 1930s. Looking

---

[8] Our own epistemological position places our work in the category of *critical sciences* (or *critical theory*) described by Habermas (1971: 301–317). Habermas developed a theory of social sciences that acknowledges the fact that science does not operate outside what he calls "knowledge-constitutive interests." Though it may believe itself to be so, no science can be truly neutral, objective, or independent of its social context. Even the "hardest sciences," which honestly believe themselves to be totally objective, are driven by a specific knowledge-constitutive interest. Physicists and engineers are driven by a desire to control nature, to build a sturdy bridge; doctors by the desire to cure the sick; historians by the desire to understand the motives of Julius Caesar's assassins. Scholars of the social sciences – of contemporary society – would do well to recognize that they are, perhaps above all others, driven by knowledge-constitutive interests too, and could make their choices explicit. Habermas distinguishes among three possible "knowledge-constitutive interests," control (or domination), mutual understanding, and emancipation. Alongside sciences that seek control, and sciences that seek mutual understanding, Habermas calls the long tradition of scientific research organized around the interest of emancipation the "critical sciences." This book is a contribution to the latter field. Critical sciences' contribution to democratic society seeks to increase citizens' capability to understand their historic and social situation, to comprehend the motions of the society they belong to, and to foster citizens' capability to act on it with the goal of helping to increase their collective and individual autonomy (Castoriadis 1975) – as opposed to heteronomy, which is upheld by the approach rooted in the "interest of control," an important one in the social sciences, particularly those in line with the neoliberal agenda, which developed based on the works of some prominent researchers in this field. Through the concrete proposal it puts forth, this work is also a contribution to what Boaventura de Sousa Santos calls the "sociology of emergences" (Santos 2014).

at the economic features of the nineteenth and early twentieth centuries, Polanyi observed that society had reached a point where it could no longer tolerate the effects of the fictitious, laissez-faire, "free market" ideology that dominated policies in nations across Europe. The dominance of "market forces" over society had distinct consequences, including rising inequalities, unemployment, low wages, and worsening living conditions for a growing portion of the population. The seeming unresponsiveness of political elites to these problems led society to choose to protect itself by surrendering – via democratic elections – to fascism. In this setting, Hitler positioned himself as the strongman who would fix the system, and offer the long-awaited protection. Polanyi wrote of how fascism became the tragic solution of last resort in the 1930s, offering an escape from society's subordination to market domination, which was the end goal of free market ideology. Tragically, "the fascist solution of the impasse reached by [neo-]liberal capitalism," Polanyi (2001: 46) wrote, "can be described as a reform of market economy achieved at the price of the extirpation of all democratic institutions."

In the early twenty-first century, political debate and resentment in Western societies have revolved around globalization. For the past two decades, globalization has been the bête noire of workers in the West watching their jobs being offshored, or, for the luckier among them, living with declining and stagnant wages. Financial globalization – that is, the removal of protections in a domestic economy in order to open it to global financial markets – has been pursued since the late 1970s, and is the cornerstone of the neoliberal agenda. No sooner had World War II ended than an updated version of free market ideology was developed by a group of scholars such as Friederich von Hayek and Milton Friedman, who came together in the Mont Pélerin Society in order to advance the neoliberal cause (Mirowski and Plehwe 2009). Now, decades later, history seems to be repeating itself as societies are once again seeking to protect themselves from the damage inflicted by the reign of markets, which began in earnest in the second half of the twentieth century, under President Ronald Reagan in the United States and Prime Minister Margaret Thatcher in the United Kingdom and followed on French President François Mitterrand's failed attempt to resist the pressure of capital mobility. During the 1990s, under the leadership of left-leaning social-democratic parties, the European Union actively promoted financial globalization (Abdelal 2007), while, on the other side of the Atlantic, the Clinton administration reduced the regulation of financial products. From then on, the neoliberal agenda was the new ideological consensus uniting the political class in the West. It even had a name, the Washington Consensus, to refer to the package of policy reforms promoted by international institutions imposed on non-Western, so-called developing, countries. By the mid-2000s, financial globalization was the economy's established reality. But then, in October 2008, came the greatest economic collapse since the 1930s, a financial crisis that left the United States mired in unprecedented levels of deficit as they scrambled to bail out the banks that had led them into the recession.

The crisis struck individuals very unequally. Today, in the United States, "our wealthiest 400 (individuals) now have more wealth combined than the bottom 61 percent of the U.S. population, an estimated 70 million households, or 194 million people. That's more people than the population of Canada and Mexico combined," write Collins and Hoxie (2015).[9] Yet, the working and middle classes have continued to see their wages stagnate over the past decades, or simply decline, and too many were simply left without a roof over their heads (Sassen 2014, Desmond 2016). The concentration of wealth in the top percentiles of the population has continued and intensified, and as this book was being completed in early 2017, financial markets and key financial institutions had returned to their pre-crisis levels of wealth. In the United States, not a single banker was indicted for wrongdoing related to the 2008 recession, let alone sentenced or jailed. And as the crisis went on, governments carried on with secret negotiations of trade agreements between the United States and the Pacific and Transatlantic areas. In 2016, as Polanyi would no doubt have predicted, financial markets profited even as the Western world was rocked by anti-trade and closed-border activism. A xenophobic campaign by the anti-European extreme-right-wing leader Nigel Farage led the British people to vote to exit the European Union, while the demagogue corporate billionaire Donald Trump was elected president of the United States on an "America First" platform that promised to bring jobs back to the United States, impose trade tariffs on Chinese steel, deport immigrants, and seal U.S. borders. As this book goes to press, every country in the West faces some version of a *fascist solution*, to quote Polanyi.

---

[9] We should also factor in the still stunning level of inequality measurable along ethnic lines. More data coming from Collins and Hoxie (2015): "African-Americans overall make up 13.2 percent of the U.S. population, but have only 2.5 percent of the nation's total wealth. Latinos make up 17 percent of the U.S. population and hold 2.9 percent of total private wealth.... What about the divide in median wealth? Typical white households in the United States now hold $141,900 in net worth. The African-American household median: $11,000. The Latino: $13,700."

But in his analysis, Polanyi overlooked one crucial element: corporations. The *free market* might not actually be the core problem. For one thing, it does not really exist: as a comprehensive body of research in the social sciences has highlighted, markets are distinctly "unfree," man-made constructions best seen as institutional arrangements underpinned by extremely complex legal and state-powered infrastructures (see, for example, Hall and Soskice 2001). The underlying problem is rather with the actors that *free market ideology* empowers, without demanding any accountability of them. If, as Adam Smith envisioned in *The Wealth of Nations*, the free market were a place in which simple individuals met and exchanged, it might well be an exchange device of egalitarian logic. But if the supposedly "free market" currently poses the threat it does to the stability of society, not to mention the progress of democracy, it is because it labels a very distinct reality, that of organized financial capital as it moves across borders, controlled and constrained by no power and no interest beyond itself even as it controls and constrains others. And who organizes capital, and how? Corporations do. Corporations are the legal form that structures capital investments, thereby effectively organizing capital; they are the actors that move across markets. They can and should be identified as the actors triggering the phenomenon of social disintegration originally identified by Polanyi. The "free market" is a smokescreen, behind which lies the brutal, despotic power of corporations.

Identifying the corporation as key actor in this phenomenon is crucially important for the descriptive power of our analysis. It is equally important if we are to envision appropriate responses to the challenge Polanyi identified. Stated briefly, the following analysis is based on the observation that the problem with laissez-faire ideology in general, and neoliberal financial globalization in particular, is less a problem of the *market* than a problem of the *corporation*. It is less a problem of mobility than it is a problem of what is actually moving, and with what forms of power, and what kind of impact. If one understands the problem of globalization as a problem of markets, then the logical political response is to close off borders and prioritize the people "at home" (hence the success of the Brexit or the Trump campaigns in 2016). But doing so would not fundamentally alter the dynamic of the free market at home, as identified by Polanyi, nor slow the social collapse that it threatens to spur. If, on the other hand, it is a problem of those acting *in* the market, then the appropriate political response is to confront those actors – that is, corporations. Because previous analyses have failed to properly emphasize the critical nature of the role of the corporation in the corporate-driven financial globalization we currently face, the solutions put forth thus far have been inadequate – at best – to meet the challenge. This book seeks to map out a path to that challenge, over the long road of human emancipation, by proposing a means to democratizing the corporation, in the hopes of offering a viable and realistic alternative to what Polanyi identified as the "fascist solution of the impasse reached by [neo-]liberal capitalism" (Polanyi 2001: 46).

Emancipate[10]

From the Latin emancipare: 'to free a slave'

derived from *e-manu-capare*: to cease holding by the hand

Origin: in the Roman Forum, one signaled intent to purchase a slave by taking his hand.

Meaning: to release from slavery, guardianship, domination, alienation, or from physical, moral, intellectual, or other constraints; that is, *to set free.*

By extension: to grant a given category of a population the same rights as all others, rights hitherto recognized for others of which this category had been deprived.

Examples: to emancipate a slave, a colony, an ethnic group, women ...

to emancipate ... *workers.*

---

[10] Picoche (1983: 212).

PART I

CRITICAL HISTORY OF POWER IN THE FIRM

The Slow Transition of Work from the Private to the Public Sphere

If we read the history of Western "capitalist democracy" (Cohen and Rogers 1983) as the progressive departure of labor from the *domus* to the public sphere, and identify this shift as a desirable one, a transition that should be pursued to completion, then we must understand its origins and scope[1]. The shift – a process of emancipation – occurred over three major historical periods, beginning slowly in the eighteenth and nineteenth centuries with the industrial revolution, when workers physically departed from the domestic arena, leaving farms and households for factory jobs. It continued through the twentieth century, when work was slowly recognized as a vehicle for membership in society and even for citizenship, structured by the ad hoc establishment of labor law. This evolution was not inevitable: rather, it came about through considerable efforts to restructure power dynamics, the fruit of a social, intellectual, and political struggle in the Western capitalist democracies that involved the mobilization of workers through unions and organized labor movements. By the close of the nineteenth century, labor law in Western European countries was its own branch of law, considered separate from private law. Major institutional innovations continued throughout the twentieth century, the most significant of which was the invention of collective bargaining. The right to collective bargaining and union representation, benefits agreed upon by employee-management negotiations, works councils, workplace health and safety committees, and, most recently, European Works Councils, may all be understood as incremental movements away from the private sphere in the twentieth century, from a regime of domestic

---

[1] This thesis was first developed in Chapter 1 of Ferreras (2007), and is here expanded.

subordination to a regime answerable to the norms of the public sphere within our democratic societies –where, at the very least, power cannot be arbitrary and is held accountable; where, ideally, those subjected to norms participate on an equal footing in determining these norms. Today, as I will show, the increasingly predominant role of the service industry in the economy is shifting labor even further into the public sphere. This, I shall argue, occurs through the mobilization of cultural conventions typical of the democratic public sphere in the workplace. This raises questions about the nature of firm *government*, for despite workers' expectations of democratic justice in the workplace, firms continue to be governed as if the old rules of the domestic sphere still applied – the head of the *domus* rules, and, quite often, can hire and fire at will. At best, these rules define a strict framework within which labor investors may participate in a firm's *management*. They do not (yet) offer the possibility for those who invest their labor in the firm to participate in determining the rules that apply to them, and the ends that they collectively pursue. And yet if we are able to assemble a long-term picture, they indicate a pathway to democratizing the capitalist economy. This slow process of transition is still underway.

I

Stage One

The Workplace and Its Emergence from the Household

As the industrial revolution gathered momentum over the eighteenth and nineteenth centuries, and workers left sculleries and fields for factory floors, work began to depart from the private sphere. Until that time, it had been a domestic activity in both senses of the word: it was both based in the home and subject to household rules[1]. In antiquity, labor was done by slaves; in the Middle Ages, by serfs; in both cases, laborers were subject to the rules of a master, a domestic regime. During the Renaissance, the merchant class established trade relations, commissioning goods from artisans in order to sell them in the marketplaces of nascent cities, in this way pulling power away from the monarchy and the aristocracy. Under this regime, workers were independent production units, but remained economically dependent on the merchants who ordered their goods. They generally owned the means of production (ploughs, spinning wheels, looms, etc.) and managed their own affairs. Their work life, however, still took place in the home, in domestic surroundings. The industrial revolution brought about a dramatic social transformation: many of these small farmers and artisans, once employed in the countryside, left behind their work and life conditions to work in factories as members of the proletariat. As Marx saw it, the creation of this new socioeconomic class was one of the necessary conditions for capitalism to exist as a productive and social system. The gathering of working men and women in the communal spaces of urban factories and workshops, which marked

---

[1] The term "economy" conveys precisely this idea, coming from the Greek *oikos* (home) and *nemein* (the principles of management), "economy" literally meaning *the management, the rules of the household.*

the transformation of the economy's physical dimension, constituted the first stage of work's emancipation from the private sphere. Work, in the form of wage labor, literally withdrew from the home.

Yet this emancipation was only partial: Marx, in writing about it, identified this dramatic transformation, but was hesitant about what status to accord it. On the one hand, he contested the domination by those who controlled the means of production – the capitalists – of the production process; given that he likened their domination to that of a master over his slaves or a lord over his serfs, one might conclude that Marx did not see the industrial revolution as a step forward in the emancipation of work from the private sphere. On the other, his description of the proletarian workers' experience reveals a more complex attitude: Marx held out hope that the proletariat could become a force capable of ending the human "prehistory" that was the advent of capitalism, precisely because the proletariat labored together in shops and factories, giving their class the possibility of transforming itself from a "class in-itself" to an effective "class for-itself" (Marx 1847: 218–220). In his view, this historical transformation depended first on the fact that workers shared the same work conditions, and second on their becoming conscious that this was the case. Sharing the material conditions of work life was what crystallized the proletariat into a working class capable of action. Marx knew that a common experience of deplorable work and living conditions was not sufficient to launch collective action as ambitious as raising the consciousness of a class for-itself, but he deemed it an essential step in the process. It is crucial to appreciate how, even in Marx's view, the physical relocation of work from the domestic sphere via the gathering of the laboring masses into factories unilaterally controlled by capitalists and their foremen represented a crucial step in the historical development of capitalism. From our perspective here, its significance comes from the fact that it was the first step in the emancipation of work from the private sphere.

In *The Protestant Ethic and the Spirit of Capitalism*, Max Weber also noted how the decoupling of economic activity from the domestic space was among one of the key transformations enabling the development of capitalism. He spoke extensively of the spatial separation of places of work from places of residence, and identified "the separation of business from the household," as a decisive step in the rise of merchant capitalism (Weber 1958: 21–22). In the same vein, Weber cited the invention of a distinctive kind of bookkeeping for what would, from then on, be considered two independent economic units, household and business. It was this multilevel separation of home and work, Weber noted, that allowed for the invention of wage labor, a social precondition for the development of capitalism.

ABOUT THE LOCUS OF ECONOMIC ACTIVITIES

During this first historical period, the emancipation of work from the private sphere was only spatial and geographical in nature. At that time, public debate over work, and over wage labor in particular, was drowned out by the debate over the place of commercial activity in society. What this book identifies as the first stage of work's emancipation from the private sphere should be viewed in the context of a more general discussion at that time about the foundational categories of the social. What should be retained, however, is that economic activity, particularly work, was still understood as situated within the private sphere, for reasons related to the fight against political despotism. For in seventeenth- and eighteenth-century Europe, the intensification of trade was envisaged as a solution to the problem of rivalry between nations. In *The Spirit of Laws* (1748), Montesquieu developed his theory of *doux commerce* (gentle commerce), which he described as as a "cure for destructive prejudices" whose "natural effect" was a state of peace generated by trade. Thirty years later, Adam Smith's *Wealth of Nations* (1776) powerfully echoed this view. Each work argued that at the international level, the political logic of confrontation among nations could be replaced by the potentially more appeasing logic of economics. Within the young nations both authors had in mind, the issue of society's foundations was the order of the day: Enlightenment thinkers, in reaction to the governments of princes, despots, and other absolute monarchs, sought to justify the individual exercise of freedom. To this end, Smith, the founding father of liberalism, offered an alternative to the contractualism of his contemporaries Hobbes, Locke, and Rousseau. In Smith's eyes, the market worked in favor of freedom, not tyranny, and was the desirable way to generate social obligation. Smith believed that the market could guarantee a base of social obligation and harmony, which he described with the metaphor of the *invisible hand*.

In his review of Smith's influence, Pierre Rosanvallon argues that his thinking laid the groundwork for a representation of society that offered a new understanding of the foundations of social harmony while renewing the theory of the foundations of the social: "the mechanisms of the market, by substituting themselves for the procedures of reciprocal engagement central to contracts, allowed society to be viewed from a biological

rather than political perspective....It was not in politics, but in economics, that [one] sought the foundations of society" (1989: 46–47). In
view of the risks posed at the time by the public sphere, which was dominated by authoritarian powers, Smith thought liberty could be justified
through the radical innovation of "understanding society as an economic
market and not as instituted through politics" (Rosanvallon 1989: 48).

By generating "social harmony," to use Smith's own words, the great
organizing force of the market, driving exchanges among producers and
consumers, employers and workers, became a practical and intellectual
tool considered comprehensive enough to both organize and reflect on
society. Work was no longer based in the home: it was a good to be
traded in the marketplace and carried out in factories and workshops.
It had, in other words, emerged from private *space*. It had not, however,
been emancipated from the private *regime*. Indeed, this new view of how
society was organized still turned on the opposition between public and
private regimes. Work, as a good like any other to be exchanged in the
market, remained in the private sphere – a sphere that, for all that it had
been enlarged and renewed, was not seen as touched by the political. Nor
did liberal theorists believe it should be: politics in their time was the business of despots. According to Rosanvallon (1989), this was the victory of
Adam Smith's economic thesis: he succeeded in introducing the concept
of a self-sufficient and self-regulating civil society, one that was nonhierar-
chical, and "invisibly" efficient. This meant it was free from the negative
influence of political authority, whose arbitrary power was, at the time,
used to quell individual aspirations to freedom.

Shortly after Adam Smith, Benjamin Constant made the distinction
between "the liberty of the Moderns" and "the liberty of the Ancients."
His work may be considered as the culmination of the delineation in
liberal thought between the private sphere, which for him included economic transactions and constituted the space where individual freedom
could grow, and the public sphere, which he considered as the locus
of tyranny. For Constant, this was not necessarily despotic tyranny; it
could be the tyranny of the community, as well[2]. Constant's was a limpid

---

[2] We are going to see that this vision, as crucial as it was at a time when politics was dominated by despots, becomes problematic when politics is liberalized and democratized.
The confinement of work in the private sphere, once the public sphere has become democratic, will only lead to a serious impasse. It is the Republican tradition in political philosophy that, distancing itself from liberalism and seeing "freedom as non-domination"
(Pettit 2013), worked to rethink the liberty of the ancients in order to reveal how essential
it was to the health of liberal societies. See the works of Pocock, Skinner, and Pettit. In

and influential expression of liberal thought on the separation between public and private spheres in the early nineteenth century. His work consolidated the liberal view that economic exchange took place in the private sphere and sealed the status of labor as an economic good, and therefore as private, too.

For Constant, the liberty of the ancients "consisted in exercising collectively, but directly, several parts of the complete sovereignty; in deliberating, in the public square, over war and peace; ... But if this was what the ancients called liberty, they admitted as compatible with this collective freedom the complete subjection of the individual to the authority of the community. You find among them almost none of the enjoyments which we have just seen form part of the liberty of the moderns. All private actions were submitted to a severe surveillance" (Constant 1819). By contrast, modern man, as a free individual, could carry out his *private* activities at his own convenience. The defining characteristic of the liberty of the moderns was the right to conduct one's private affairs without interference from any government, "to dispose of property, and even to abuse it" (Ibid.). Constant deplored the fact that "among the ancients ... the individual ... was in some way lost in the nation, the citizen in the city" (Ibid.). Not only did Constant view the private sphere as a privileged space in which liberty flourished and modern man could exercise his freedom, he also cast doubt on the benefit an individual might gain from his involvement in public affairs: "lost in the multitude, the individual can almost never perceive the influence he exerts" (Ibid.). Constant pled for a representative form of government that would free most individuals from the worries of government and allow them to devote themselves to their private affairs[3] – which included working and pursuing economic gain.

This liberal view of society, while advancing ideas of citizenship and the individual that underpin modern democracy, also decoupled citizenship from economic life. This separation continues to this day. But the advance of Western democratic society has made it defunct, perhaps the greatest

particular, see Gourevitch (2015) on Republican thought and the advancement of freedom in the economic realm, from the perspective of the workers.

[3] Nevertheless, Constant seems to have a vague sense of the danger posed by a conception of society where civil affairs are entrusted to a group of professionals who operate the machine of the state far from the concerns of individuals: the danger of mutual ignorance. He therefore calls on officials to encourage citizens to share in the exercise of power, without which they risk losing their dearly won freedoms: "the danger of modern liberty is that, absorbed in the enjoyment of our private independence, and in the pursuit of our particular interests, we should surrender our right to share in political power too easily" (Constant 1819).

aporia of the liberal tradition. Constant, at the close of the eighteenth century, valued private affairs over public affairs; a century and a half later, Arendt (1958), discussing the same questions, advanced the exact opposite view, arguing that involvement in the public sphere was the noblest expression of the essence of man, what she calls *action*, which Arendt opposes to *labor* and *work*, which she assigns to the private domain[4]. Beneath her opposition to Constant's values, however, Arendt assumes his posit that the society is based on an opposition between the public and the private domains, with labor and work contained in the realm of the latter.

We see, then, that the eighteenth and nineteenth centuries moved work's physical locus from the private sphere as workers departed farm and household to labor in shops and factories. At the same time, the era's thinkers, as they observed and interpreted the world around them, maintained a distinction between public and private whereby the private sphere was the space in which the individual could hope to enjoy freedom and agency over his own endeavors, while the public sphere was the domain in which the fight against tyranny occurred. At the time, placing work, along with other economic pursuits, in the private sphere of the factories, made it a vector for emancipation as well. And yet, this was only a first step in a slow transition...

---

[4] To Arendt (1958), *labor* was the specific domain of the reproductive functions of life.

2

The Nineteenth and Twentieth Centuries

Workers' Movements, and the Invention of Collective Bargaining

WORK ENABLING PARTICIPATION IN THE PUBLIC SPHERE

Placing this new version of work in the private sphere was, however, only a step: the private space of nineteenth-century factories were spaces of heteronomy, as well. The economic despot had soon replaced the political one. The twentieth-century emancipation of work from the private sphere may be seen as one of the hallmarks of its social and political history. Work transformed in parallel with the public sphere, which was itself in the process of democratization. As early as the 1880s, social movements organized around labor issues and began to effect changes in European society. Collective actors progressively organized in the form of labor unions and mobilized to obtain decent living and working conditions for wage laborers. As Marx had written, the proletariat, massed together on factory floors, in stifling tenements, and at the desolate outskirts of cities, grew aware of its class conditions and began working to change them. As they struggled for the recognition of specific rights (wages, working hours, benefits, health and safety conditions, and so forth), they also mobilized more broadly to influence the direction industrial society would take. Labor unions became active politically, participating in the public sphere and contributing to society's evolution. Since the dawn of the twentieth century, in every European nation, labor unions have devoted resources to set up political branches or even parties in order to represent workers' interests in the political arena.

Georges Friedmann, the father of the French sociology of work, highlighted the ways in which union organizing was an expression of workers' solidarity: "trade unionism is for many workers not only, or even essentially, a defense of their interests but rather a visible expression, a concrete symbol, of solidarity, of a network of human relationships within the industrial jungle" (Friedmann 1956: 79–80). For him as for many of his contemporaries, work in the twentieth century became a platform action – more specifically, for political action – that helped to determine the direction industrial society would take. Touraine (1966, 1973) developed this line of thought, showing how workers' movements were organized through a principle of "historicity" that defined workers' attitudes toward the goals pursued by society. Workers' movements in industrial society, he argued, developed their own views about the future of that society. Through worker organizations, work became a means of participating in the public sphere and its future orientations. At the same time, work was recognized as contributing to social cohesion in Western democracies, and the notion of "social citizenship" was developed (Marshall 1950). This had material as well as political consequences as nations linked employment to the benefits offered by the welfare state (pension, health, sickness, unemployment), which occurred as early as 1880 in Germany.

This led to a second phase of work's emergence from the private sphere, the signal feature of which was the creation of labor law as branch of the law distinct from both property and commercial law. As Supiot (2002) points out, the invention of labor law and the employment contract speaks to the ambiguous status of work: "the invention of the employment contract consisted of moving labor out of the legal category of 'goods,' in order to give it a new legal status, which acknowledged its personal dimension while maintaining its exchange value. The invention of the employment contract perpetuates a complicated rapport with the abstract idea of work as it was defined in the nineteenth century, which continues to dominate economic thinking. On the one hand, the employment contract provides a uniform legal formula for a diverse range of concrete labor and authorizes its evaluation and commercial use; it is in this sense compatible with the abstract concept of work as an accounting unit of the labor market. On the other hand, and unlike a contract for services, an employment contract acknowledges the presence of the worker, and thus opens the way to non-market values, which have a parasitic effect on the abstract notion of work. For this consideration of personhood, the legal recognition of the identity of the worker providing the work, necessarily opens the door to a practical and diversified approach to labor." (Supiot 2002: 256)

Labor law, in other words, opened the door to a liminal, still ambiguous historical period in which workers hovered between the private and public domains.

COLLECTIVE BARGAINING MAKES WAVES, OR THE LIMITS OF ECONOMIC LIBERALISM

By the close of the nineteenth century, pressure from violent labor struggles had helped push Western Europe's economically liberal industrialized nations to grant workers the right to collective representation in the negotiation of work contracts. This innovation decisively challenged the capitalist fiction of the world as a network of contracts among free-willed, equal individuals. The idea that the individual contract was a sufficient framework for understanding what the economic-liberal paradigm already saw as nascent labor markets was revealed as insufficient. From the standpoint of liberal economic theory, however, the right to collective representation was considered heresy. This tension continues to make waves today, and this book argues that this right is a fundamental one, and that employment relations cannot be understood solely as contracts among individuals. At the industry level, the advent of collective bargaining gave rise to what in Europe is known as social dialogue among social partners, in which employees and managers are represented collectively in negotiations over the frameworks that govern employment contracts and conditions. In these "dialogues" employees have voice through elected representatives or labor unions, and employers through their own representative organizations.[1]

Collective bargaining was the bedrock upon which countries in continental Western Europe progressively built a complex system of institutions for labor-management dialogue and bargaining. These institutions are mandated by states to preside over the labor market in their industry, branch, or at the national level. The negotiations they oversee produce labor contracts or collective agreements that are enforced as law, usually by extension to all firms in the same branch or industry. These collective agreements set the ground rules for competition in the labor market (e.g., for wages) as well as developing coordinated strategies that implement solutions that benefit the industry as a whole, but to which no actor would subscribe alone, such as continuing education and training programs.

British sociologists Sidney and Beatrice Webb were pioneers in the study of these institutions. In the first years of the twentieth century, they attempted to account for a nascent phenomenon they observed in England, which was at that time rapidly industrializing. They called it

---

[1] The internal dynamics on the employers' side of these labor-management institutions are far from straightforward, and vary greatly depending on industry and economic sector (see for instance the debates set off by Offe and Wiesenthal (1985).

"industrial democracy." According to the Webbs, "industrial democracy results from the combination of direct [what they called "primitive"] democracy within unions, which are in charge of worker representation,[2] and collective bargaining between these organizations and employers." (Webb and Webb 1902) But the term quickly came to describe a broader concept that covered employee involvement in the management of all parts of the economy, both within the firm and beyond, as well as that of employee representatives and union organizations. Alternatively, the term *social democracy* has been commonly used to describe this strategy.[3] Collective bargaining is a foundational concept and practice that has exerted considerable influence within the labor movement and conditioned its participation in the political realm.[4]

In 1935, in the midst of the Great Depression, the United States passed the National Labor Relations Act, also known as the Wagner Act. Its principles were similar to the industrial democracy described by the Webbs. The Wagner Act aimed to address the "inequality of bargaining power between employees who do not possess full freedom of association or actual liberty of contract and employers who are organized in the corporate or other forms of ownership association."[5] Specifically, the right of employees to join a union through which they could engage in collective bargaining was recognized: "employees shall have the right to self-organization, to form, join, or assist labor organizations, to bargain collectively through representatives of their own choosing, and to engage in other concerted activities for the purpose of collective bargaining or other mutual aid or protection."[6] Following a world war and two decades of opposition from employers, the Act was revised and further restricted by the Taft-Hartley Act of 1947. Businesses in the United States progressively succeeded in resisting the European trend of "social

---

[2] Through union democracy, the Webbs wrote, very optimistically, "they [trade unions] have solved the fundamental problem of democracy, the combination of administrative efficiency and popular control. In each case the solution has been found in the frank acceptance of representative institutions" (Webb 1902 iv).

[3] The concept has been used broadly. Of the concept of "industrial democracy," scholars have written that it refers to "forms of employee representation in the firm, to their right to information, to protection, to being included in various ways in decisions regarding the firm or relations with the firm's managers. It illuminates the vast arena in which capital and labor, managers and unions, may confront one another – not to mention the universe of politics and that of social struggles" (Giraud, Tallard and Vincent 2007: 39).

[4] The Webbs went on to found the Fabian Society, which was responsible for creating the British Labour Party.

[5] United States Code, Title 29, Chapter 7, Subchapter II, § 151.

[6] United States Code, Title 29, Chapter 7, Subchapter II, § 157.

dialogue" and collective agreements jointly bargained at the industry level. By the 1960s, labor contracts were set on a firm-by-firm basis. in a diminishing number of industries[7].

By the end of the Second World War, the architecture of market economies in continental Western Europe varied in name and mode of implementation depending on the country but its aims were roughly the same: to structure the conditions of collective bargaining and to guarantee the status of labor within this process through collective rights and representative bodies. Roughly, this architecture includes the negotiation of collective labor agreements between labor and management organizations at the firm level, generally with union delegates;[8] at the industry level (also known as the branch or sector); and at the national level. Since the 1980s it has also included the European level, if rather timidly, through labor-management consultations and the creation of European Works Councils for larger companies[9]. However, the objects of these negotiations are limited. Depending on the level at which they take place, they may address compensation, vacation time, working hours, workplace health and safety, and training. Furthemore, as at the European level, they are only consultative, and not binding. Yet, they are concerned with potentially interesting new developments for workers in particular via their involvement with so-called transnational company agreements (Lamine 2016).

The state may take an active role in negotiations, or may serve as an arbitrator. It may also act as a sort of guarantor by extending the scope

---

[7] Except for the public workers, who retained the right to bargain collectively at the state level, which could be equated to the industry level. For the recent, adverse evolution in collective bargaining in the United States see Freeman and Hilbrich (2013).

[8] This is the case only in systems of dual representation, such as those in Germany, Belgium, and France. In these countries, employees have two "channels for representation": union delegates negotiate collective labor agreements, and personnel representatives sit on company works councils. Each channel has its own specific goals and purposes, and delegates or representatives may work in both, or be forbidden from doing so, depending on the context. Other countries have very different systems. Italy, for example, has only one channel for union and employee representation, through which issues of compensation and workplace organization are dealt with together. See Rogers and Streeck (1995).

[9] In 1994, a European Directive commanded that a European Works Council be created to inform and consult employees in companies present in the European Union with a presence either in two countries with at least 150 employees in each, or in one with at least 1,000. Source: Directive (revised version) 2009/38/EC of the European Parliament and of the Council of 6 May 2009 on the establishment of a European Works Council or a procedure in Community-scale undertakings and Community-scale groups of undertakings for the purposes of informing and consulting employees (Recast) OJ L 122, 16.5.2009, p. 28–44 (EUR-Lex – 32009L0038).

of such agreements, or translating them into law for equivalent firms in the same industry, even in cases where these firms are not present or not represented in the bargaining process.[10]

The strategy the Webbs identified was a powerful one, and calls for three observations: two regarding the effects of industrial democracy, which are of particular interest to this book, and one of a dead end it could not avoid, which will be discussed further on.[11]

The first of the two effects is conceptual: industrial democracy, with collective bargaining as its emblematic institution, demonstrated the limits of the liberal economic understanding of society as contractual, as the mere sum of individual exchanges and agreements. The reality of industrial democracy, in which collective actors produce a framework designed to stabilize the conditions in which economic exchanges take place, revealed that this individualistic view of the economy, and particularly the labor market, was a fiction (De Munck 2000). Significantly, the existence of collective bargaining, both as a set of rights and as an institution, is proof that parliamentary representation, although a central feature of liberal democracies, is not the only institution responsible for determining the context in which the economy unfolds. The de facto role played by collective bargaining raises the question of what institutions are necessary to ensure that democracy is being comprehensively practiced by a society: its existence contradicts the standard liberal belief that democratic representation belongs in a narrowly defined political arena, in which economic relationships are "preserved" from political *interference*. The advent of the right to collective bargaining has opened the

---

[10] This is known as the "coverage rate" of signed agreements, and explains why France, which is one of the Western world's least unionized countries, has over 90% coverage of the workforce, which offsets the effects of low union participation. In the United States, this mechanism for extending agreements does not exist (Rogers 1995). Its effect is stark: less than 7 percent of the private sector is unionized, with great disparities among industries, and among firms within the same industry. The number of firms covered by collective bargaining agreements is small. In the United States, "about 7.2 million public sector employees are union members, approximately the same absolute number as that of private sector workers. On a percentage basis, however, public employee union membership is five times greater: 36 percent, compared with 7 percent in the private sector. This brings the overall level of union membership in the United States to 11.3 percent – again, however, with large regional differences. New York, California, Pennsylvania, Illinois, and other states have union membership approaching or exceeding twice the national average, while Texas, Florida, North and South Carolina, and other states had less than half the national average" (Compa 2014: 97).

[11] French *paritarisme* is the logical continuation of this heritage. Given its peculiar application in the French context (to which we will return further on), we will not use this term, as we wish to discuss this point on a purely conceptual level.

frontiers of that political arena, suggesting that meaningful democracy requires a complex architecture of rights and institutions, not a shell of rights applied to a narrow portion of the human experience.

The second effect of industrial democracy is a practical one: labor and management organizations participate in the production of the norms governing the economy; ipso facto, this demonstrates that participation in the government of the economy through means other than parliamentary representation can be effective and efficient. The effects of industrial democracy were strongest during the three-decade period of economic boom in the West from 1945 to 1975, when unions played an active and decisive role in the representation and organization of the working population in Europe as well as in North America. Yet, in the United States as in the other liberal market economies (Hall and Soskice 2001), policies were driven by the (neo)liberal preference for individualizing economic relationships as much as possible managed to weaken the role of collective bargaining and institutions of industrial democracy. Not only does this policy stance ignore the advantages gained through "social democracy,"[12] it narrows very sharply the definition of who participates in the affairs of the public sphere, which, this book argues, is central to the growth of democratic justice. Recently, and tellingly, two International Monetary Fund economists challenged this neoliberal consensus. Jaumotte and Buitron (2015) identified a strong correlation between falling unionization rates and rising inequality measured as the concentration of private wealth in the top 1% of the population. The data demonstrated that unionization is a vector for income equality. Joining his voice, Krugman (2015) concluded in his reading of the study that its results suggest that "a strong union movement helps limit the forces causing high concentration of income at the top." Particularly after the publication of Thomas Piketty (2013)'s sweeping work on the topic, inequality being identified as a major economic problem, as well as a social and political one, has resulted in a renewed interest in the right to collective representation in the economic realm.

---

[12] See Freeman and Lazear's study in Rogers and Streeck (1995) of the economic impact of works councils. Germany, with its social market economy (*Soziale Marktwirtschaft*), can be considered as the success story in this regard. It has been held up as an example to the rest of Europe, particularly since the 2008 financial crisis, when it enjoyed a remarkable situation: a heavily "coordinated" European economy, where unions are strong and play a powerful role, which translates into higher growth rate, a less unequal wealth distribution, and lower unemployment figures that those of the United States, the flagship of "non-coordinated" economic liberalism, to borrow Hall and Soskice's typology (2001).

With all that in mind, the development of collective bargaining and industrial democracy as highlighted by the Webbs also leads to an impasse: the role of union representation has been defined in such a way that the attention is focused onto certain bargaining points (wages, working hours, etc.). It does not question nor contest the scope of managerial power. For the most part, against the wage security provided by the employer, workers and their unions accept the principle of subordination as defined by labor law in employment contracts. While some workers may indeed experience the subordinate relationship established under the employment contract as reassuring, society is currently changing in a way that has called this strategy into question (Piore and Safford 2006). Indeed, here we contend that the "capitalist democracy" has become a contradiction in terms. On the one hand, workers expect increased *voice* in the workplace while contemporary management contends that individual responsibility makes work more effective and more innovative. On the other hand, employees do not have any meaningful say in the institutional system to which they are subordinate as employees of a firm. Put another way, the democratic ideal – which requires that people be treated as equals and included in decisions that affect their own lives, and which helped lead to the establishment of collective bargaining – has yet to exert its full influence on the firm. Collective bargaining, which came about through the labor struggles of the nineteenth century, gave substance to the idea that labor standards must be arrived at via agreements reached through the organized expression of the wills *of* both labor and capital, *by* them and *for* them. This idea underpins this book's central claim – that the firm must be understood and defined as the encounter between these two bodies, and therefore should be *governed* as such, in a way that represents its two constituent bodies, its capital and labor investors. Its proposal that firms should be governed by Economic Bicameralism must be understood in light of the historical background previously presented.

3

The Twentieth Century and the Ambiguities of Institutional Innovations in the Capitalist Firm

The shock of the Second World War sparked significant changes in the way employees participated in the capitalist firm.[1] After the war, political discourse centered on offering compensation to all citizens for their wartime efforts. It was a watershed moment for most European countries, an opportunity to update the *social contract* upon which they had been founded. One major advance in equality was made for women: across Europe, women were granted suffrage, a right men had secured decades earlier, as a "reward" for their war efforts; women in the United States gained this right in 1920, through a movement galvanized in part by the First World War.

The feeling of concord prevalent at the dawn of the postwar growth period known as the *Trente Glorieuses* is epitomized by Belgium's *Pacte social*, signed by labor and management organizations in 1946. The pact officially sanctioned the idea that workers' contribution to productivity (and therefore to social harmony) ought to be compensated by a fair share in the benefits reaped by that productivity (Reman 1994, Arcq and Blaise 1999, Mabille 2000). Across Western countries, the broader context of the Cold War pushed employers to make concessions to workers' demands. The perceived threat of communism cannot be underestimated as a decisive factor in the recognition of new labor rights at that time. A *Pacte social* was passed in France as well, and a works council law was passed in 1946 (Rouilleault 2010). New labor provisions, which were rarely put into practice, called for the presence of two to four employee

---

[1] See Rogers and Streeck (1995) for a systematic study of the impact of the works council on six European countries and in North America.

representatives with an advisory role in firms' board of directors (or boards of overseers) (Rouilleault 2010). With variations from country to country across Western Europe, these changes all carried the same ambiguity, which may be said to characterize this historical period: labor was progressively emancipated from the private sphere throughout this period, but in a way that expressed a tension. On the one hand, capital investors sought to maintain their absolute power over the firm; on the other, they needed to secure their employees' long-term interest, and implication in firm productivity, and to give firm governance more legitimacy by sharing power with them. In his writing on this period, Wolfgang Streeck (2001) looked beyond the specific institutional options chosen at that time in each country to identify a universal ambiguity evident in the way countries went about building industrial relations, one that was intensified by union strategy at the time: whatever their specific orientation, the question of the role workers and their unions ought to play in the advance of capitalism was hotly debated among unions. For some unions and union members, capitalism remained a force they wished to combat, however much power it placed in their hands.

OPTIONS

The following sections will sketch out the various institutional innovations brought about in the twentieth century to give employees and union representatives – what this book calls labor investors and their representatives – power in the capitalist firm. It begins with the observation that the struggle to wrest workplace government away from the domestic regime typical of the private sphere has been gradual and ambiguous, and may be divided into two categories. In the first, capital investors are considered as having exclusive control over firms. Any worker participation in decisions regarding life in the firm takes place within a framework set by the corporation's representatives: this we define as participation in firm *management*. In the second category, workers' investment through their labor is considered as giving them the same authority in the firm as capital investors have, and the same status in deciding on the firm's strategies and end goals; this we define as participation in *government*. Later on, I will argue that the future lies in a decisive shift away from firm *management*, which excludes labor investors from strategic decisions, and toward a new era, of *government*, in which capital and labor investors decide jointly. Before that, however, I will explain the emergence of these two classes of innovation.

After the Second World War, Western European countries faced two contradicting impulses. On the one hand, the normative intuition that workers ought to be included in firm government grew more and more pervasive; after all, in 1948, the Universal Declaration of Human Rights had proclaimed all people equal "in dignity and rights." On the other hand, the classic capitalist idea that labor was a mere production factor did not imply that workers should be given any special status: labor required far more care than a machine or a closet full of office supplies, but had no more reasonable claim to govern the firm than either of the latter had. This tension is central to capitalist democracies. The first idea implies the inclusion of employees in a *deliberation* process, one that included *bargaining* over the terms of economic exchange, and discussion over ends and means. Logically, this meant granting workers a significant place in the *government* of the firm. The second idea implies only participation in management through *bargaining*; government, or deliberation over ends and means, remaining in the domain of employers alone.[2] In a deliberation, the terms of the exchange are *political*, they deal with principles of justice and affect the ends pursued by the activity in question; in bargaining, the terms are quantified and quantifiable: concessions in the form of salary, work hours, schedule, and work pace are compensated and exchanged against subordination, productivity, and social cohesion. As normative concepts in this context, we refer to *government* as it plays out in the democratic public sphere, where, in choosing their own representatives, citizens have equal bearing on the norms to which they are subjected, and, in turn, the representatives they choose are held accountable to the polity, while *management* takes place in the private sphere, within which those with power –the masters- may impose unilaterally their conditions on the terms of the exchange. Participation in *government* involves decisions on ends as well as on the practical pursuit of those ends, i.e. the means; while participation in *management* simply refers to getting involved with the implementation of the means necessary to pursue a predetermined framework deliberated over beforehand and elsewhere. In the context of the corporate firm, decisions about ends are made by the board of the corporation, which is legally empowered to make these decisions. The board of the corporation thus operates as the de facto firm's government.

---

[2] Here, we use the analytical – rather than practical – distinction we elaborated with Jean De Munck among the three components of the "democratic exchange": deliberation, bargaining, and experimentation (De Munck and Ferreras 2012).

If labor is to be fully emancipated from the private sphere, institutions must be created to help labor investors participate fully not only in management but in the *government* too, that is the government of the firm, which commands their own (working) lives. This step was taken very little in the twentieth century: nearly all known institutions co-opted labor investors into corporate firm management, rather than firm government – *comanagement* has been the hallmark of twentieth-century firm government, always within a framework set by capital investors. What follows is a brief survey of the history of employee participation, which, while it is far from being exhaustive, offers the evidence necessary to give substance to our argument.

PARTICIPATING IN MANAGEMENT

This account of the institutional options available so far for governing capitalist firms begins with the one that is weakest from a labor perspective. It also highlights one of the key differences between American and European "varieties of capitalism" (Hall and Soskice 2001). Labor history in the United States reveals almost no ambivalence about the choice between the two ideas cited earlier; throughout it, capital investors have fought to maintain or regain total control over government, while labor unions were unable to avert that[3]. The United States might indeed be considerate as the ultimate "capitalist democracy" (Cohen and Rogers 1983). The country's only significant concessions to employee involvement were through firm-level collective bargaining, which was first implemented with the Wagner Act in 1935 and continued into the 1970s (Weiler 1990), and through collective bargaining in the public sector, where it has been in steady decline for the last three decades (Freeman and Hilbrich 2013). Innovative forms of worker representation predated this – including one set up by a cigar maker as early as 1833 (Rogers 1995b: 390)[4], and despite

---

[3] Forbath's historical analysis confirmed Rogers's (1990) assertion that "the constraints on action forged by the legal order may render rational the pursuit of a narrow trade union strategy: yet this strategy may yield a weakened labor movement in the long run" (Forbath 1991 xi.).

[4] A notable experiment took place in a garment factory in Cleveland, Ohio, from 1914 to 1918. Described by O. F. Carpenter (1921) in John Commons's collection on *Industrial Government*, the experiment conducted by the Printz-Biederman Company implemented ideas developed by John Leitch, a promotor of "Industrial Democracy" (1919). He convinced the stockholders of a garment factory to organize it as if it were a "little republic": "Industrial Democracy was the organizing of a factory into a little democratic state with representative government having both legislative and executive components" (Ebert and

a larger, aborted attempt in the 1920s to set up deliberative bodies within companies under the so-called American Plan – an "open shop" system of shop committees and factory boards (Piore and Sabel 1984: 124–130) – efforts to involve employees in management institutions within the American capitalist firm were never more than incidental, and were generally undertaken to prevent workers from unionizing (Rogers 1995b). The rise of the American labor movement in the 1930s was bitterly contested by employers. With the support of the Roosevelt Administration, collective bargaining was implemented following the Second World War, but only at the company level, and often only at the level of the plant (Rogers 1995b: 397). Significantly, anti-trust laws in the United States made it difficult for industry associations to bargain over wages; that is, representative bodies for employers at the industry or sector level were prevented from engaging in collective bargaining. Indeed, wage bargaining at the industry or branch level, which is common in European countries, was considered in the United States as a form of monopsony in the labor market to be combated actively in the name of free market ideology. The fact that American employers had no collective seat at the bargaining table meant that, contrary to what happened in social-democratic European nations at the same time, there were no collective "political exchange" (Pizzorno 1978) possible between employers and employees.

In contrast to the United States, European countries wavered throughout the twentieth century between involving employees in firm government or in firm management. In the interwar years, the French Popular Front government sparked debate when it sought in 1936 to require employee representatives in all companies with more than ten employees. During the Second World War, the French Resistance adopted a project called the *Programme National de la Résistance Française*, which called

Monschein 2009: 19). However, Carpenter noted that there were considerable differences between the experiment "and the United States Government. The latter is made up of representatives from one body – the citizens of the Republic. Representatives, Senators, President, all come from and represent the same great constituency, while in industry there are capital and labor to be represented. Leitch met this dualism by giving the employees a house of representatives and by giving the management a Senate and cabinet" (Carpenter 1921: 87). It is unclear if the powers of this house were greater than that of a works council; nevertheless, this experiment appears to be an ancestor of the proposal for Economic Bicameralism (see Part III). The experiment was short lived, however: in 1918, the International Ladies' Garment Workers Union had established a branch in Cleveland that fought and ultimately defeated the Leitch plan at Printz-Biederman. According to Carpenter (1921: 91), the union won workers over by convincing them that they would gain more advantages through collective bargaining.

for "worker participation in the direction of the economy," and works councils were put in place in France in 1946, although only in companies with more than fifty employees. It took until 1982, after the French Left swept Socialist President Mitterrand into office, to consolidate the authority of French works councils, through a set of laws - known as the Auroux laws.

These changes to employer-employee relations sparked heated debate in France. Before the Auroux laws, in the 1960s, President de Gaulle sought to revive the *Programme National de la Résistance*,[5] and in 1963, François Bloch-Lainé published an argument for "reforming the firm" that sowed panic among employers (Bloch-Lainé 2000: 7). Bloch-Lainé, a high-ranking civil servant, noted in a sophisticated sentence that "among large *firms*, the democracy of *corporations* is a fiction" (1963: 14), and proposed that the "government of the firm" take the form of a "peer-led" management system that brings capital and labor representatives together in a *commission de surveillance* (supervisory board) that would oversee a *Collège des directeurs* (executive committee). His proposal was inspired by the German system of *Mitbestimmung*, to which we will return further on. A decade later, a report on "reforming the firm," again, prepared by Pierre Sudreau (1975) for President Giscard d'Estaing, proposed a number of ways to give employees more power in the firm; chief among them that one-third of the seats of company boards be filled by employees. Although he proposed only that these seats be for information and oversight purposes, his report met with opposition from employers' associations – and from a certain number of labor organizations, as well.

These reforms and policy proposals caught unions on the horns of a dilemma, pushing them to choose whether to fight for the right to participate in firm government or remain satisfied with pushing for a stronger

---

[5] "There is a third solution: it is participation, which changes the condition of man in modern civilization. As soon as people work together toward a common economic goal, for example, to make an industry function, by contributing either the necessary capital; or executive, managerial, or technical capability; or labor, what happens is that they form a firm together, a firm whose productivity and proper functioning are the interest of all, the direct interest. This implies that a portion of what the business makes and invests in itself through its gains should be attributed to each person by the law. It also implies that everyone ought to be adequately informed of the firm's workings, and able, through representatives they have all freely named together, to participate in the firm and its boards and councils, to have their interests, opinions, and proposals heard. This is the way I have always considered to be right. I have already taken several steps in this direction; for example, in 1945, when, with my government, I instituted works councils; when, in 1959 and 1967, I opened the way to profit-sharing. That is the path we should take" (Charles de Gaulle' speech in 1968, cited in Bourdin and Schillinger 2011: 205).

role in firm management. Serge Mallet's work on this question is emblematic of the debates that animated French labor unions during the *Trente Glorieuses*. His *Nouvelle Classe Ouvrière* (1963), published the same year as Bloch-Lainé's *Pour une réforme de l'entreprise* (1963), argued for a new "worker policy" – what today would simply be called union strategy – adapted to the changes he observed in the capitalist mode of production at the time. Mallet pointed to the emergence of a "new" working class in automated work environments (at the time, the assembly line industries), which he called "organization capitalism." In it, he identified two categories of employee: the workers in charge of production, distribution, and monitoring inside automated production plants; and, outside these plants, the more numerous engineers, researchers, and other technicians from commercial partners and contracting firms both up- and downstream from production operations. Mallet positioned himself firmly as a technological evolutionist: "through the jobs it creates, automation – if it totally eliminates man's relationship to objects – destroys the division of labor and reconstitutes, at the team level, and even at the collective level, an integrated vision of multidisciplinary work. Production units shrink and human relations among groups of workers become more frequent and are less anonymous than those observed in the Taylor-style factory." (Mallet 1963: 85)

In other words, technological complexity was catalyzing a sea change: the uniformity of working conditions it created in offices and shop floors also created the conditions under which a body capable of collective action might emerge, making possible a kind of unionism for which the firm was the appropriate context of action. This was the basis for Mallet's central thesis: if automation led this new working class to organize from within their firms, the labor movement would have to adapt accordingly, and orient its demands toward "demand for a say in the firm's management, regarding both the technical conditions in which production occurs (tools, work organization) and its economic conditions (type of investments, market orientation, etc.)" (Mallet 1963: 87).

This "new working class," because it constituted a new and autonomous political force on the firm level, opened up a new battleground in the struggle between capital and labor. Mallet's intent was not merely to point out the radical nature of such demands for control over the management of firms, however. He also wished to show the impact of the firm's changed role in modern industry. Because firms were thought of as the locus of job security, he argued that they had become "the privileged location from which the worker could integrate within an economic society from which he is otherwise excluded," an exclusion he defined as "the total absence of worker control over the management of the firm and its development." In his conclusion, Mallet argued for "the expansion and institutionalization of the power of firm unions to control the firm's economic orientations" (1963: 242). In the 1970s, the newly unified French Socialist Party took up this theme under the leadership of Michel Rocard. Its platform included the idea of worker self-management, popularized by experiments in Yugoslavia.

As previously mentioned, more than three decades after the idea of works councils for firms with more than fifty employees was first proposed in France, the Auroux Laws of 1982 consolidated the establishment of works councils, and effectively stimulated their creation. Drafted by Labor Minister Jean Auroux, the spirit of these laws may be summed up in his own words: "They are citizens in the *polis*; workers must be citizens in their firms as well" (Auroux 1981: 4). Between the spirit and the letter, however, was a significant gap. The Auroux Law of August 4, 1982, put an end to employers' absolute hold on power in the firm by proscribing the sanction or termination of any employee on the basis of his or her political opinions, union activity, or religious belief, and the Law of December 23, 1982, gave employees the right to refuse work that placed them in grave or imminent danger. Such measures merely moved work away from the harshest version of the domestic regime in place in the private sphere, however much Auroux had sought to advance the cause of citizenship in the workplace. Particularly since the role of works councils was purely advisory, they remained no more than a basic recognition of the idea that labor should be included in firm management. The Auroux law of August 28, 1982, makes this very clear: it specifies the tripartite composition of works councils, which must include the company head, personnel delegates, and union representatives. Though created to advocate "on a permanent basis for [employees'] interests in decisions relating to management and to economic and financial changes, to the organization of work, to professional training, and to production techniques,"[6] works councils have little binding say in firm management, let alone firm government. They are party to a significant amount of economic and financial information related to the life of the firm, and must be consulted in certain matters such as work organization or layoff plans, but their opinions remain non-binding.

---

[6] Excerpted from the *Loi Auroux* on the institution of works councils, Parliament of the French Republic, October 28, 1982.

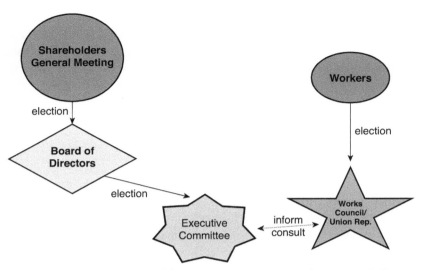

FIGURE 1. The Government of the Corporate Firm in Social-Democratic Europe

France, despite public discourse in its favor, has never created an institution that fosters true citizenship within the firm. A number of recent
initiatives have included the concept of citizenship, such as "corporate
social responsibility" or "corporate citizenship." Their focus is outward,
on firms' relationships with the wider world, such as efforts to improve
environmental impact, or hews to traditional hierarchies and *human
resources management*. In general, initiatives in the latter category seek
to treat employees as co-contributors to the firm as a means to improve
motivation and increase productivity. Dannon, for example, has publi-
cized its employees' involvement in choosing the recipients of the firm's
charitable giving, with the rationale that this improves employee motivation by adding meaning to their work and increasing their sense of
belonging to the firm (Riboud 2007). Other firms have gone much further, allowing employees to take personal initiatives that extend beyond
the scope of their job descriptions, even to include personal projects that
serve no immediate purpose beyond the pleasure of research and innovation. Carney and Getz (2009), as well as Laloux (2014), have studied
firms whose efforts to "liberate the firm," or "free [their] employees" have
been rewarded with higher profits, increased customers' satisfaction and
employees' motivation and innovation capability. Such initiatives help to
leverage growth in an era where the worker's added value makes innovation possible. Firms with "flat" hierarchies, some of which have gone

so far as to eliminate their human resources departments, will eventually have to face the question of whether employees should participate fully in their decision-making processes, even when it comes to highly strategic decisions. Will autonomy at work and innovation be enough for employees? Will they continue to be content to help manage their firms without a say in their government? These questions point to the much broader question of the legitimacy of firm government as it currently exists.

COMANAGEMENT

If the idea of comanagement (also known as *co-gestion* or *paritarisme*) alarmed French employers, they were not alone: labor organizations often regarded them with ambivalence, or even hostility. Here, again, the distinction made earlier is a useful one: comanagement is about *management*, not *government*. Seen in this light, union opposition to the idea was only logical, and we will return to the reasons for it. But as the German system shows, it is harder to see why it alarmed French employers so greatly.

The German institution of *Mitbestimmung*, or codetermination, is the twentieth century's most notable instance of employee involvement in the *government* of capitalist firms, and has justly been described as the most advanced example of a "social market economy" (*soziale Marktwirtschaft*). The system has two distinct levels of codetermination, one at the plant or site level and one at the level of the firm (Milano 1996). At the first level, employees help manage production and workplace organization through a *Betriebsrat*, a council elected by employees, similar to a works council. At the second level, employees are involved in the firm's strategic decisions through the supervisory board. Comanagement at the plant level uses methods for including employees in company management similar to those in France, which were described in the previous section. This section will therefore focus on comanagement at the firm level – that is, the participation of employee representatives in German companies' supervisory boards.

We begin by noting a crucial fact: Germany's most advanced form of *codetermination* – which is also the oldest, and the only one that gives workers a stake equal to that of capital investors in the *government* of firms – has all but disappeared. Discussed in between the two world wars, this radical innovation was only voted into effect by the *Bundestag* in 1951. As Stephen Silva (2013) recalls, the law required joint-stock corporations in the coal, iron, and steel industries with more than 1,000

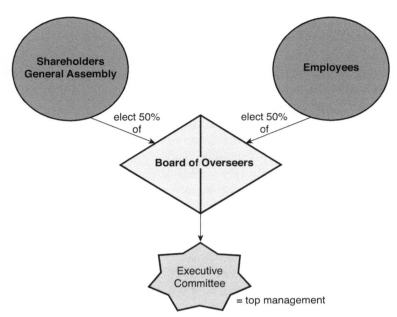

FIGURE 2. Original post-WWII Co-Determination German Firm

employees to have supervisory boards composed of five shareholder representatives and five members delegated by workers, employees, or unions. These boards were presided over by an independent arbitrator elected by all ten of their members.

This legal framework was tied to the historical circumstances that followed the Second World War in Germany (Silva 2013: 43–82), when the Allies demanded the restructuring of industries that had contributed significantly to the power of the Nazi regime. Indeed, strong unions in these industries were threatening revolutionary overthrow; the USSR, Germany's next door neighbor, menaced from the east; and the country's industry leaders had lost legitimacy through their collaboration with the Nazi regime. If stability was to be maintained, the government of firms in this sector had to be reordered. The 1951 law was applicable only to firms in the coal and metalworking industries in Germany – industries whose economic significance has done nothing but dwindle since that time – and while *Mitbestimmung* was applied in other forms in other areas of the German economy, it never involved employees in firm government to the extent it did in its original form. *Mitbestimmung* as it was applied beyond these industries allowed for employee participation in firm *management*, not in firm *government*. No other forms of *Mitbestimmung* have provided for truly joint government in firms.

Indeed, despite attempts by German unions to expand the principle of codetermination, the German economic landscape was largely over-taken by what Franz Gamillscheg (1979) has referred to as "false parity." In 1976, the *Mitbestimmungsgesetz* Act maintained the requirement of equal employee/shareholder membership for supervisory boards in companies that employed more than 2,000 people, but stipulated that the boards be presided over by an additional member chosen by the group of shareholder representatives, who was given voting rights. This means that shareholders hold the effective majority in German firms, and are thus assured that board decisions will be made in their favor.[7] Despite this limitation, the system remains the most advanced form of *comanagement* ever to be implemented in the corporate firm. Under it, employees and their representatives participate actively in the comanagement of the firm and its branches or plants through works councils (*Betriebsrat*). However, they do not have the power to oppose decisions, and remain obligated to cooperate with the decisions made by capital investors, who may or may not be willing to hear their opinions.

It is easy to see how German codetermination benefits capital investors: firms need access to employee knowledge of the products and services they sell in order to optimize production and better meet customers' needs. Involving employees and their delegates in the internal decision-making process is an intelligent way to obtain this valuable information.[8] This "pro-competitive" argument – to use Wolfgang Streeck's term (1992) – was advanced by Jean-Louis Beffa, the former CEO of Saint-Gobin, in testimony before a French Senate Commission in 2010 as he recommended for France that in "companies of significant size, twenty to twenty-five per cent" of supervisory board members be employee delegates (Beffa 2011: 552). Similarly, a German government commission appointed by Chancellor Gerhard Schroëder, led by Kurt Biedenkopf and charged with investigating the modernization of the codetermination system at the firm level, argued that "in competing with others, companies can and should make use of the productivity that comes from cooperation" (Biedenkopf 2006: 20).

---

[7] The situation of de facto majority enjoyed by shareholders has made it very tempting for shareholders to corrupt employee delegates in order to ensure broader majorities in their boards. Volkswagen, Siemens, and other large German firms have been rocked by such scandals in recent decades (Müller-Jentsch 2008).
[8] See Müller-Jentsch's study (1995).

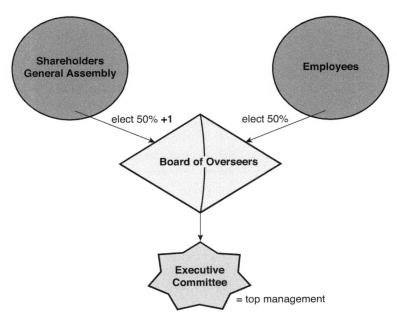

FIGURE 3. Today's Co-Determination Monocameral German Firm

Although employers have often argued the contrary, employee participation in these modes of management and comanagement contributes
to economic performance and has proven to be a unique asset to the
firms that apply them. Or, as the Biedenkopf Commission prudently
concluded, "there is no proof that employee involvement has a negative
economic effect" (Hans-Bockler-Stiftung 2007: 3). Despite the complaints
of employer representatives involved in the Commission, the Commission's academic members have confirmed that codetermination "does
not diminish the competitiveness of production sites, that it is not an
obstacle to foreign investment, that there is no proof of diminished stock
market performance in companies in which codetermination is present"
(Id.). Academic studies analyzing worker participation through various
institutional or financial frameworks have confirmed this observation
(Rogers and Streeck 1995, Freeman and Lazear 1995, Kruse, Freeman
and Blasi 2010).

Economically speaking, involving employees in the *management* of
firms is in the interest of capital investors. As German Chancellor Angela
Merkel declared, "codetermination is a crucial and proven element of
our social market economy" (Hans-Bockler-Stiftung 2007: 7). Therefore,
employer opposition to it seems ideologically, rather than empirically,

motivated. Debate over codetermination and its institutional devices in Germany's case contains an important question at stake in this book: Do firms belong in the public sphere of our democracies, or do they belong in the realm of private exchanges? The response of the Biedenkopf Commission: "the necessity of codetermination is not an economic question.... The goal of the codetermination law of 1976 was not to increase the competitiveness of firms, but to give employees the possibility of participating democratically in firm decisions that concerned them" (Id.). The Commission added that codetermination should be seen "as a consequence of the perception of the firm as a social institution in which owners, firm executives, and employees collaborate to achieve common goals" (Id.).

As German employers cited the advance of globalization and competitive pressure on the economy as reasons to "reduce codetermination" (more specifically, to reduce the percentage of seats held by employee delegates on governing boards to one-third) – the Commission's academic members argued that "democratic participation through codetermination seems to remain a persistent necessity" (Hans-Bockler-Stiftung 2007: 3). The "false parity" of German codetermination is only a small step forward in advancing democratic participation, though. As previously explained, it allows employees to participate only in the firm's *management*. The president's additional vote on the firms' supervisory board means employees are always 1 vote short of a majority, depriving them of the power necessary to oppose a decision, and thus to have true voice in the firm's *government*. Undeniably, employees in major German firms have greater influence than employees in other countries with lesser "capability to deliberate."[9] Employees in either case, however, retain the capability to *bargain*, but rarely have the full capability to *deliberate*, meaning that they have no control over the conditions in which bargaining takes place, and therefore no say in the firm's critical decisions.[10]

---

[9] For comparison, the case study of the restructuring of the Volkswagen factory in Brussels is enlightening. See De Munck, Ferreras, and Wernerus (2010) and De Munck and Ferreras (2013). Through the IGMetall union, German Volkswagen employees had more say in the firm's decisions and were able to protect workers' interests through the codetermination decision structure in Germany, while the firm's Belgian employees, though massively unionized, were reduced to bargaining over the layoff packages or salary proposed by management in Brussels, which itself was following directives from headquarters. In other words, there was *deliberation* in Wolfsburg, and only highly constrained *bargaining* in Brussels.

[10] To return to the distinction made earlier between deliberation and bargaining, in certain situations, even the "false-parity" variant of codetermination gives German workers

German codetermination, like French *paritarisme*, and, more generally, like works councils, expresses an ambivalence over whether firms should be governed by labor and capital investors on an equal basis, or whether capital investors' reign over firms should be preserved. Just as it is easy to see why capital investors would prefer the institutional inventions previously described, which co-opt employees into firm *management*[11] using a framework of their own devising, it is hardly surprising that labor unions have expressed mistrust over or even rejected such schemes.

UNION REACTIONS

Two major labor traditions have been highly influential in Europe and beyond: the Christian labor movement, with its strong and largely voluntary involvement in comanagement institutions; and the socialist labor movement, which has avoided promoting these structures and focused on obtaining "workers' control." Ernest Mandel (1973), a high-profile

---

access to a certain form of deliberation, in which they can negotiate the framework in which the firm's activity takes place. As in the case of Volkswagen, where the IGMetall union was able to convince the state of Lower Saxony, Volkswagen's second largest shareholder, to vote with the union on a specific decision, thereby reaching a majority on the board. In these highly specific cases, it is accurate to say that employees have real voice in the firm's government. (see De Munck and Ferreras, 2012)

[11] See the practice of making labor investors into capital investors through policies that award stocks or shares to employees in order to ensure that their interests are aligned with those of capital investors. It is interesting to remember that Karl Marx himself saw reason for hope in the development of the first joint stock-holding corporations. Marx's analysis in the third volume of *Capital* of the first shareholder companies in the nineteenth century is rather perplexing. Somewhat blinded by his axiom that property ownership determines class, Marx expresses hope and surprise over this separation of ownership and control, which would become a pillar of the capitalist system in the twentieth century (Berle and Means 1932, Chandler 1977). As Dahrendorf (1957) highlighted, Marx saw "the joint-stock company as 'private production without the control of private property,' as 'the elimination of capital as private property within the capitalist mode of production itself'" (in Collins 1994: 60). Marx thus concluded that shareholder businesses were "a necessary point on the way to reconverting capital into the property of producers, this no longer being the private property of individual producers but their associated property, that is, immediate social property" (Ibid.). Dahrendorf sums up his thinking as follows: "the joint-stock company...is halfway to the communist – and that means classless – society" (Ibid.). Given the way the capitalist firm has evolved, it is difficult to agree with Marx's predictions, and one of the goals of this book is to shed light on this problem. All the same, with his usual foresight, Marx prepared the ground for the debate that divided the Left at the close of the twentieth century, over what is known as employee stock ownership plans, as well as intense debates about the proper attitude to adopt, within the labor movement, with regard to the management of employee pension funds (Lordon 2000, Fung, Hebb, and Rogers 2001).

proponent of Marxist theory in the European labor movement, maintained that the only demands acceptable to the labor movement must be "transitional demands" that helped gain more "workers' control," in order to bring about self-government, which was, to him, the only acceptable form of production. The Marxist doctrine set "workers' control" in opposition to the "snares and siren songs of 'co-management'" (1973: 12). To this end, Mandel wrote,

> Whether it is a matter of contesting the boss's right to determine the rhythm of the assembly-line, or his right to choose the site for establishing a new factory; whether of objecting to the types of product made by a firm, or of trying to oppose elected leaders to management-appointed foremen or 'managers'; whether the workers are trying to prevent redundancies and a declining volume of employment in an area, or trying to calculate for themselves the rises in the cost of living; whatever they are trying to do amounts, in the last analysis, to one and the same thing: Labour is no longer willing to let Capital be in control of industry and the economy (1973: 10).

According to Mandel, all strategies for including workers in firm management are simply a way "to canalize and deflect...revolt, with the help of the trade union bureaucracy, towards class collaboration and away from class confrontation" (Mandel 1973: 11). He levels his critique at any and all institutions of *management* and *comanagement* in capitalist firms, arguing that employees and labor organizations that do not avoid them risk being "deflected" toward class collaboration, which serves to profit none other than the capital owners themselves (Mandel 1973: 12). This, of course, is the classic Marxist critique of socialist reformers, utopians, and other social democrats: they argue that all these maintain the vain "notion of a gradual achievement of 'economic democracy,' without any previous overthrow of the power of the bourgeois state or expropriation of Capital." (Mandel 1973: 13). The only desirable goal for classical Marxists is self-management – which I prefer to call "self-government," to preserve the distinction between government (of ends) and management (of means);[12] that is, production organized by the workers and for the

---

[12] The following quote illustrates the prevailing attitude of that era, and, I argue, shows how urgent it is to move past the still prevalent monolithic understanding of property rights in order to envision the democratization of the corporation. Rosanvallon wrote (italics are mine): "In the technical terms of the law, the law of the firm does not exist as a unified legal field. The law of the firm is essentially made of property and ownership rights (corporate law is above all personal law) with a certain number of restrictions and regulations set by other branches, particularly labor law. The law, which is still dominated by the Napoleonic Code, ignores the firm's existence as an economic unit of production or a work collective. There is no way out of this oft-cited contradiction, except through *the destruction of property rights* with regard to the means of production. Indeed, it is clear

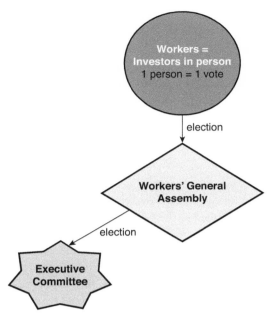

FIGURE 4. The Workers' Self-Governed Firm, a Labor Monocameral Government

workers, with no regard for the constraints of profit imposed by capital. As previously noted, in France in the 1970s, the French socialist party, under the leadership of Michel Rocard, made self-management (*auto-gestion*) a major plank in their economic platform. Yet, what they actually meant was self-government. Following the Yugoslavian model then in vogue (Pateman 1970: 85–103) self-management sought to advance the economy without capital investors, through worker self-determination. Workers were seen as "producer-owners," to use Marx's term, much as they were in the cooperative movement (Laville 1994, Frère 2009). Self-government refers to this institutional structure of government:

Christian-influenced unions were more open to the idea of comanagement, and came to promote it themselves.[13] The papal encyclical *Rerum*

---

that anything resembling the beginnings of firm law could only be erected against property rights. The idea of worker ownership acknowledges this fact in order to organize an adequate legal foundation" (Rosanvallon 1976: 121). On the contrary, this book argues that imagining the law of the firm as its own field does not require the destruction of property rights. Yet, the respect due to property rights should be placed, as historically it has been done with regard to other objects or subjects, within certain limits, which should be openly discussed, and set democratically.

[13] Hallett recalls the strong influence of the Catholic Church, which weighed heavily in the implementation of codetermination in Germany (1973: 13–24).

Novarum, published in 1891, had a decisive influence on the Catholic social teaching, which did not contest the notion of private property. Not without its ambiguities, this tradition recognized the right of capital owners to enjoy their property, so long as they respected workers' dignity. The Catholic Church's social doctrine promoted concord among social classes, seeing the firm as a community rather than recognizing the idea of class antagonism so fundamental to socialist doctrine. As a result, Christian unions often rallied to systems of comanagement.

A number of innovations in the twentieth century have promoted the participation of workers in the steering of the capitalist firm; all of them are marked by the same ambiguity. The overview presented in this section has shown that, with the narrow exception of perfectly balanced codetermination as it was applied in the German mining and metal industry after the Second World War, capitalist firms seeking to include employees in their decision-making processes have never gone further than involving workers and their representatives (if indeed they are represented at all) in firm *management*, within a strict framework set by capital investors. And, as we have seen, participation in the *management* of a firm is not the same as participation in its *government*, particularly as discussions and decisions move from being about means to being about ends. Now, the emergence of labor and its government from the domestic regime typical of the private sphere is reaching a new stage. The time has come, this book argues, to take the next step, to move past the idea of firm *management* (most often referred to as *governance*) into an era of *legitimate, reasonable*, and *intelligent government*.

I wish however to urge that if the large property owner is viewed, as he ought to be, as a wielder of power over the lives of his fellow citizens, the law should not hesitate to develop a doctrine as to his positive duties in the public interest....

History is full of examples of valuable property privileges abolished without any compensation, e.g. the immunity of nobles from taxation, their rights to hunt over other people's lands, etc.

It would be absurd to claim that such legislation was unjust.

Morris R. Cohen (1927: 26)

4

The Twenty-First-Century Service Economy Is Bringing Work Fully into the Public Sphere

Historical and economic conditions today are ripe for work to complete its transition into the public sphere. Industrial society is giving way to service society, and as it does, workers' presence and role in the public sphere is growing. Labor is no longer, and can therefore no longer be considered as, a vehicle or instrument. Nor can work any longer be seen as a mere object of policy, state regulation, and labor-management actions. The *expressive* rationality that characterizes the lived experience of labor must be accepted and accounted for in the institutions governing firms.

TO GOVERN

The idea that workers ought to have the right to participate in governing the institutions in which they experience a significant part of their lives and to which they contribute even more intensively than capital investors is as old as capitalism itself. It has been expressed in the work of thinkers such as Owen, Mill, Fourier, Proudhon, or Ellerman, and experimented with in cooperatives, *kibbutzim*, self-governed companies, worker-owned businesses such as Mondragon,[1] and all the other models that compose today the so-called third or social sector of the economy (Laville 2010, Olin Wright 2010, Defourny and Nyssens 2014, Nyssens and Defourny

---

[1] Mondragon is a cooperative founded in 1956 in Spanish Basque Country, which has become a major international group. In 2014, it counted more than 100 companies and about 100,000 employees working in a variety of industries and countries. The group is managed by its worker-owners through a democratic and representative process by which managers and executives are elected, and is financed by its own bank (Whyte and Whyte 1999, Freundlich 2009).

2015). It is meaningful to keep in mind that this idea has been implemented in numerous, often visionary, and original ways throughout the
world.[2]

But let us maintain our focus on the capitalist firm. Our economic
model, from the manufacturing to the tertiary sector, is changing drastically, and managerial practices are changing with it. The most innovative,
productive firms are looking for new ways to bolster employee participation, since participation determines worker motivation, and thus affects
productivity and innovation.[3] Carney and Getz (2009) describe this as a
"liberated" work environment and the firms that foster them "freedom
incorporated." Yet, the freedom enjoyed by employees is limited: decisions
about the firm's future and strategic options remain in the hands of its capital investors, who alone continue to reap the lion's share of these firms'
added value. It seems reasonable to predict that sooner or later, firm governments that exclude labor investors even as they involve them ever more
strongly in firm management will come to be seen as illegitimate, and that
the contradiction between a work environment built on labor investors'
involvement and responsibility, and their exclusion from the firm's actual
government will begin to have adverse effects on workplace motivation.

Ricardo Semler's experience in Brazil (1999) is emblematic of this
problem and of its solution: Semco, the firm he took over from his father,
grew astronomically when he decided to democratize it. The firm, which
employed a few hundred people in the 1980s, counted a workforce
of 3,000 in 2005, and then became a multinational firm, with similarly
dramatic growth in profits. Semler explains that he could not hope for the
motivation and implication he needed from his employees without giving
them the right to vote on the firm's hierarchy (they also vote on the hiring
of future colleagues), on the development of new projects, to approve
shareholder earnings, and to set their own pay.[4] In other words, he was

---

[2] For a comprehensive account, see Erdal (2011). See also Pinto (forthcoming) or Barreto
(2011).
[3] According to Pink (2009), the main factors driving motivation at work are autonomy,
mastery, and purpose. Echoing Pink, this book is founded on an understanding of work
as animated by an "expressive, public, and political" logic (see Part II), which is driven
by expectations for democratic justice, and which explains motivation at work, hence
potential for innovation.
[4] Another interesting detail: workers make these decisions based on pay scales that include
comparisons to their competitors' pay scales. They must therefore justify any pay raises to
their colleagues, which catalyzes debate, collective learning, justification, and accountability to market competition within a deliberative framework about conceptions of justice
among workers (Semler 1999: 215–220).

moving, if slowly, to include the firm's labor investors in its *government* – this dynamic is what we call the subversive power of the democratic inutition. It should also be noted that Semler gradually did away with the human resources management department. Since his employees were now in charge of their work lives and jointly responsible for the teams in which they worked, there was no longer any need to "manage" them as (human) resources. Semler's experience shows that when workers are given responsibility over their own work, they aspire to participate in all decisions that concern and constrain their work lives, which means in the government of the firm, not in its management alone.[5]

As previously recalled, the Universal Declaration of Human Rights states that all people are equal "in dignity and in rights." If this is so, then why should they not have equal rights in the government of their work lives, just as they do in the government of their lives as citizens? Our Western democracies, whose history is intertwined with the history of economic liberalism, have long hesitated to acknowledge this in the context of the firm. Under the assumption that individual contracts are freedom enough, they have largely left capital investors to treat firm employees as a production factor or a resource, albeit one that must be handled with particular attentiveness. The idea of Economic Bicameralism, which will be introduced in Part III, grew from the observation of this tension, which cannot be remedied through *comanagement* alone, since comanagement allows for bargaining over means, but not for debating and deciding on the ends of the firm. So long as this tension is unresolved, capitalist democracy will remain a contradiction in terms. The knowledge- and service-based economy requires labor investors' intensive involvement in understanding and meeting the needs of the clients, users, patients, and customers they serve. This is true whatever and wherever the labor investment – in schools, stores, law firms, doctors' offices, consulting companies, college classrooms, or collaborative web platforms. Employers and employees everywhere must face this tension at the heart of capitalist,

---

[5] Attention must be given to the "responsibilities" with which the injunction to participate might burden workers. Employees would be all the more capable of shouldering such responsibilities if their say in the *government* of their work were real, rather than fictive, as is the case in most *management* systems currently employed in firms. For a study and discussion of these issues, see Charles (2016). In particular, Charles points out that participating in firm management (as well as in firm government obviously) requires effort, involvement, and consideration from workers, who must do more than simply put in a day's work and go home. He argues that this should be accounted for and supported through appropriate organizational and institutional support.

democratic society: How can labor investors give the best of themselves if they are treated as mere resources[6]? Whether they are seeking to mobilize employees to deliver efficient services to customers or to galvanize them to continue innovating new products, firms must recognize that we stand at the edge of a new phase in the history of the expansion of work into the public sphere. If efficiency and justice are to be pursued in the context of democratic societies, work must continue this expansion in a way that is reflected in the government of firms. The time has come for firms to take labor investors seriously as key partners not only in the management but also the government of the firm. A new chapter must be opened in the history of the government of firms. Having reviewed the history of the role played by labor investors in the government of firms, we shall now examine what work, and the firm, mean today.

---

[6] The critical case, in the methodological sense (Golthorpe and Lockwood 1968), for the argument to treat workers as constituents of the firm – when considered as a political entity – will be that of those working down the supply chain. For an examination of the challenges faced by labor investors so far down the chain that their interests easily disappear from the focus of the capitalist government of transnational firms, see Locke (2013).

Behind every fact is a theory and behind that, an interest.

Frank Knight (1922: 458)

PART II

WHAT IS A FIRM?

What is a firm? Practically and analytically, this is a crucial question, for the way we answer it determines the rights that we as a society grant firms, as well as the responsibilities we expect them to uphold. The dominant understanding of the firm has largely been informed by two paradigms: the liberal economic theory and Marxism. Though diametrically opposed in their views and preferences about the role of the state, the market, and individuals, these two perspectives are, paradoxically, united in their view of the firm as an *organization* that they see as structured and defined by instrumental rationality. The dominance of these two schools of thought has created a form of intellectual hegemony which, in excluding all other types of rationality from the definition of the firm, has prevented us from fully grasping its truly complex nature and has given us an incomplete understanding of its past, present, and future. Since the turn of the twentieth century, however, the dominance of these two paradigms has regularly been challenged, creating what today should be considered a distinct, albeit eclectic, body of work, including contributions by scholars in fields as diverse as sociology, economics, industrial relations, political theory, global studies, and law. These contributions have the potential to creating a new research field that sees *firms as political entities*, and I suggest that a concerted effort should be made to consolidate that field, which might be named the *political theory of the firm*. This field should be developed as a forum to nurture scientific debates that matter to society as well as to the future development of scientific knowledge.

Although we shall give particular attention to this emerging school of thought and the possibilities opened up by the new definition it offers, we must begin with a review of the perspectives of the liberal economic theory and Marxism, the two traditions with the strongest intellectual and political influence over the world's understanding of the firm. Their opposing viewpoints have, as previously mentioned, one thing in common: a highly reductive – not to say flawed and inadequate – definition of the firm's role, which has had the ironic effect of causing these rival views to mutually reinforce each other.

5

Obsolete Vision

Instrumental Rationality as the Firm's Sole Logic

So far as the individual stockholder is concerned, it is in general to be assumed that his interest is solely to obtain the maximum direct return from his holdings of the shares of a particular corporation, whether this be in the form of dividends or of appreciation, or in the short or in the long run.
– Friedrich A. Hayek (1967: 111–112)

ECONOMIC THEORY OF THE FIRM

Liberal economic theory is based on the rather perfunctory idea that the capitalist firm is an organization built to pursue a single goal: to generate returns for capital investors. By this logic, the firm exists because someone has risked capital – not labor – to invest in it, and ought to be rewarded for that risk. Ownership of one or many shares of the corporation gives capital investors specific rights: they become residual claimants with the right to any profit remaining after all contracts signed by the firm have been honored (employment contracts, orders from suppliers, etc.). Investors are motivated by the prospect of earning a return on their investments – that is, a profit greater than the capital they invested. This may occur through added value (the stock or share's –future- value rises) or through dividends (in the form of payments to shareholders). Classic economic theory sees each production factor involved in such a venture – specifically, capital and labor – as "motivated by its self-interest" (Fama 1980: 288). These "facts" are the foundation upon which the influential liberal economic theory of the firm predominant was built. Within this tradition, the firm is conflated with the corporation. In fact, economists use the two words as synonyms to refer to an organization whose end is to earn profit for its capital investors, who are considered to be its "owners." Labor, the other production factor participating in the firm, is supposed to take advantage of the firm to advance its individual interests.

In liberal economics, as just said, the terms "firm" and "corporation" are used interchangeably. This confusion has given rise to the unfounded belief that the *firm* belongs to its shareholders, when in fact, from a legal standpoint, it is merely shares in the *corporation* that are *owned* by shareholders. Legally, shareholders do not own the corporation, let alone the firm – they simply own shares or stocks in the corporation (Robé 1999, 2001, 2011). Confusion between the *corporation*, a legal entity set up by shareholders as a collective vehicle for their financial investment, and the *firm*, a much broader entity to which, as Robé has illuminated extensively, no specific field of law is devoted, has been a constant since the corporation was invented. The absence of any systematic consideration of the firm as an institution in its own right, as we shall see, is of service to some and of disservice to others.

Until now, the firm's legal existence has been dominated – and even eclipsed – by two often adversarial branches of the law: corporate law and labor law. This fallacious assimilation of the firm to the corporation has led to the proliferation of a few simple but – as we shall see – extremely powerful ideas.

The Firm as Instrument of the Capital Investor

In a capitalist economy, private ownership of capital accords capital investors two sets of rights (Cohen and Rogers 1983: 165): first is the right to choose where, when, and how these owners choose to invest it. Second, once they have chosen where to invest it, capital investors retain the right to control how it is used – to control the production process, in other words. From a sociological standpoint, one can understand why liberal economic theory perceives capital investors as "owners" of the firm: by deciding to invest their capital in a given business, capital investors invest in the contents of that business; investment is assimilated to ownership, which is assimilated to control, meaning that their authority over the assets of the corporation, which is mobilized for such purposes as the signature of contracts in the corporation's name, extends to government of the machines and the people working in that corporation. By the same logic, this control extends to any "surplus" the tools of the corporation produce – the profit remaining once all contracts (including employment contracts) have been honored. According to this straightforward logic, a capitalist firm is an organization whose sole raison d'être is generating return on investment for the corporation's shareholders – its capital investors, who are considered to be its sole investors.[1]

This view underpins the economic theory of the firm, which developed more refined theoretical tools as the economy evolved over time. By the close of the nineteenth century, the shareholder model had begun its ascendancy in the United States (Dunlavy 2008). Around the First World War, as "giant corporations" gained a prominent role in the American economy, Berle and Means (1932) published their seminal study of the power of professional managers, in which they described this new era of *managerial capitalism*. They used the concepts of ownership and control to explain the tension underlying manager-shareholder relations, deploying them as a descriptive apparatus to show that while shareholders *own* shares in a firm, actual *control* is in the hands of professional managers, who participate daily in the life and strategies of the organization. Aglietta and Rebérioux recalled that Berle and Means recommended that limits be set "on managerial power, in other words that it be exercised not in the interests of those who wield it but in the interests of those affected by it." They concluded from this that "managers should no longer be accountable solely to the shareholders; they must be made accountable to all the stakeholders in the firm" (Aglietta and Rebérioux 2005: 27). In their view, the firm should begin to be understood as an *institution*, as it was "no longer an object of property" owned by its shareholders (Aglietta and Rebérioux 2005: 27). As Berle and Means understood it, the firm therefore required appropriate control mechanisms.

Aglietta and Rebérioux (2005) recall that the tremendous impact of Berle and Means' study was intensified by the context in which it appeared: in 1932, the year their book was published, the United States

---

[1] That profit be the prerogative of capital investors has also been justified by asserting that capital investors are the only ones to take risks in a firm, since work is carried out under contract and compensated by wages in a relatively stable manner. The soundness of this assertion is dubious, as employees clearly assume risk in signing contracts with firms. Their participation in the life of the firm deserves to be understood as an investment of specific skills and knowledge. Such an investment, once made, often cannot be transferred to another firm with the same ease as a shareholder may sell his shares and transfer his capital to another firm. See Cohen's classic discussion of this question (G. A. Cohen 1982, Landemore and Ferreras 2016).

was in the early years of the Great Depression. Their work was immediately taken up for political ends, and sparked a counter-movement to limit the influence of managers and to grant more power to shareholders. Two schools of thought developed in the ensuing decades, whose combined influence would be unrivalled: the ascendancy of the shareholder value theory in the 1990s may be traced directly back to these two schools. Founded on the pivotal work of Coase (1937, 1960), the "transaction costs" theory gave rise to the field of law and economics, with major works coming from Demsetz (1967), Alchian (1969), and Williamson (1985). At the same time, "agency theory" in economics was developed: using rational choice theory, thinkers such as Jensen and Meckling (1967, 1976) and Fama and Jensen (1980) developed the framework of principal-agent relations.[2] This entire field, which shall be identified here as the *economic theory of the firm*, sought to affirm the legitimacy of shareholders' authority over the *corporation*, and by extension over the *firm*'s other actors. This perspective reduced the firm to the corporation, an intellectual move we call the *Reductio ad Corporationem*. Although it is descriptively inexact, this reduction has had tremendous practical consequences.

The Nobel Laureate Milton Friedman may be considered the greatest spokesperson for the *economic theory of the firm*, as he was particularly influential in establishing this reductionist view of the firm as a corporation. Although legally inaccurate, the view of the firm he helped to legitimize was a kind of self-fulfilling prophecy, and spread rapidly.[3] As he

---

[2] Their work seeks to elaborate on an idea of the firm being "in the exclusive service of its shareholders" because the latter are considered to be the weak link in a firm's chain of command, building on the idea that firm managers should be "considered as the agents of the latter [the shareholders]," conceptualized as principal, and must have as their "single objective the maximization of return on capital" (Rebérioux 2003: 85). But Rebérioux notes that an honest attempt to use the concepts elaborated by the economic theory of the firm necessarily leads to an impasse; as the incomplete nature of contracts can only get deeper (Rebérioux 2003: 91–92), the firm's singleness of purpose becomes a chimera, or, at best, a kind of forced construct. It becomes clear, Rebérioux writes, that "since cooperation cannot come from the exclusive pursuit of individual interests, it can only be brought about through the establishment of institutional mediations" (2003: 97).

[3] Jung and Dobbin described the dynamic of the economic theory of the firm as follows: "They purported to describe the world as it exists but, in fact, they described a utopia, and their piece was read as a blueprint for that utopia. We take a page from the sociology of knowledge to argue that, in the modern world, economic theories function as prescriptions for behavior as much as they function as descriptions. Economists and management theorists often act as prophets rather than scientists, describing the world not as it is, but as it could be. And when new theories take hold, people tend to perform the roles economists script for them" (2016: 293). "Evidence of self-fulfilling prophecies in economic theory produce a conundrum for economic sociologists and sociologists of knowledge. In the

wrote,[4] "in a free-enterprise, private property system, a corporate executive is an employee of the owners of the business. He has direct responsibility to his employers. That responsibility is to conduct the business in accordance with their desires, which generally will be to make as much money as possible while conforming to the basic rules of the society.... The manager is the agent of the individuals who own the corporation." The Nobel Laureate's description of shareholder behavior indeed became fact, a trend reinforced outside the firm by the growing importance of institutional investors starting in the 1980s and the development of complex financial products in the 1990s. Within firms, "good practices" such as stock options were promoted in order to align the interests of top managers with those of shareholders in order to maximize shareholder value. Here, we must recall Friedman's assertion that "the manager is the agent of the individuals who own the corporation." Although legally unfounded, this assertion came to be accepted as reality. The consequences of accepting this unfounded claim have intensified as the economy has become increasingly financialized, and capital transnationalized.

Looking past the various technical nuances and improvements wrought in the fields in which the *economic theory of the firm* has been perfected and deployed, the theory has systematically and erroneously conflated the firm and the corporation (Robé 1999), defining the firm as an organization driven by 1 very specific type of rationality – instrumental rationality, which sees all action as driven by an end independent from the action itself. The end of a firm, when it is conflated with a corporation, is to promote the self-interest of the entrepreneur, and above all of the capital investor, in the form of a return on investment – in other words, shareholder profit. Using Max Weber's pioneering work on *Zweckrational* (Weber 1971), which may be translated as purposive or instrumental rationality, sociologists studying the spread of capitalism have agreed that this rationality was central in the development of the economy in the modern West. Investment in firms is not pursued because the firm is an end in itself – in terms of the work accomplished, the goods

natural sciences, it is thought that theories only rarely affect the phenomena they depict. But generally in the social sciences, and particularly in economics, theories may produce the patterns they describe when people embrace the theories" (2016: 320). Beckert (2016) offers a masterful demonstration of the power of the self-fulfilling dynamic that characterizes financial capitalism, and of the imagined realities and futures of the economic theories that justify it.

4 Milton Friedman, "The Social Responsibility of Business Is to Increase Its Profits," *The New York Times*, Op-Ed, September 13, 1970. Robé provides a thorough critique of Friedman's *New York Times* Op-Ed (2012).

produced, the service rendered, the production in question – but rather because firms are perceived as the appropriate instruments to generate profit, which may be accumulated by those who invest their capital in it. The firm, in all its vast complexity, is reduced by this theory to nothing more than an instrument. It is a vehicle for profit, as are the managers and workers who labor within it: they are simple instruments, what agency theory calls "agents," and the sole purpose of their presence is to serve the principal –the stockholders- and its earnings.

Work as Instrument Alone

The liberal economic theory of the firm applies this same perspective, "with each factor motivated by its self-interest," (Fama 1980: 288) to a firm's employees. They are the firm's "labor factor" and come to work in pursuit of their own personal interests. According to this view, workers work for wages. Hence, their work is the instrument they need to survive in the world. In the eyes of standard economic theory, workers consider work to be a "disutility," something they would prefer to do without in order to enjoy higher-utility activities outside the workplace, such as leisure and family life (Lane 1992). The logic of this is, quite obviously, analogous to the logic of capital investors: in both cases, actions are driven by instrumental rationality; in both cases, these individuals are pursuing their self-interest through the firm, which is a vehicule for pursuing an end they seek (money). Only the actions themselves differ: employees work in the same way that shareholders make financial investments. An investor seeks maximum profit for minimum investment; a worker seeks to exert the minimum amount of effort required to make a living and pursue whatever life outside the workplace their jobs permit. From this perspective, there is no substantive distinction between capital and labor, since both act according to the same rationality. And if instrumental rationality drives them both, then what we shall call the regime of domestic subordination – in which power is exercised unilaterally by the person who is best positioned to determine the ends and the means to obtain them – is the most efficient mode of government for them both.

The Capital Investor as Optimal Guarantor of Instrumental Rationality

If the firm is a vehicle for the instrumental rationality driving investors in both capital and labor, then it is only logical that power in the firm be held, and decisions made, by those believed to be the best representatives of instrumental rationality. By this logic, the best representative of instrumental rationality within the firm would be the capital investor, who is its ultimate beneficiary. If purely instrumental logic – the goal of earning a return on his investment – drives him to invest in a given firm, it stands to reason that he is in an optimal position to guarantee that the firm follows that logic. Those who invest their labor, on the other hand, might be more personally biased: while also motivated by the desire to maximize personal gain, they necessarily seek to do so with the least possible effort;[5] furthermore, their judgment is potentially "polluted" by considerations, emotions, and affections, which cause them to form irrational attachments to their colleagues and to the firm's traditions and history.[6] Workers, according to this logic, lack the rational judgment required to guarantee the firm follows the pure instrumental logic of return on investment, which is, after all, the reason it exists. This logic also justifies the firm's traditional power structure, which may be characterized as *domestic*.[7] The "domestic regime of work" (Ferreras 2007) follows the

---

[5] From the perspective of the employer, it becomes a problem of "individualistically oriented workers whose motivation is diluted by the free rider problem" (Weitzman and Kruse 1996: 294). Employees perceived as being motivated only by the maximization of their individual interests are difficult to manage. As a logical consequence, from the principal's point of view, a set of incentive and disincentive mechanisms must be implemented to extract the best work from employees, who are considered to be inherently lazy and eager to shirk, or seek a "free ride."

[6] This is one of the classic arguments advanced against involving workers in strategic decisions: workers are considered to be incapable of choosing to reduce the workforce in cases where this may be necessary, because the pursuit of their (ill-understood) individual interests would lead them to oppose anything that might lead to close monitoring of productivity or reductions in the workforce. Numerous documented cases disprove this argument (Erdal 2011). As we shall see, workers reason using expressive rationality much more than instrumental rationality, which means that they are able to make political judgments, to weigh different interests, and to engage in precise and detailed discussions of different options and alternate conceptions of justice in order to make decisions.

[7] More broadly, liberal theory – and beyond – sees this domestic logic as being deployed in the realm of so-called private activities, and economic activities are still thought of as being conducted in the "private sphere" (Ferreras 2007). This sphere is opposed to the public domain, which is oriented to the common good and deals with matters that regard all its members. The latter domain is the domain of politics (*polis*), while the former is the domain of the economy (*oikos*). Semantically, in terms of usage, this separation is still very influential: echoing this fundamental distinction – and with an eye to maintaining it – the world of "private enterprise" and "private business," with its references and its logic, is often opposed to the "public" world of public administration and the state. Yet corporations can go "public," a term that underlines the fact that a group of shareholders has chosen to place the firm under their own – public – scrutiny in order to hold it accountable.

model of a family or household in which power is exercised unilaterally by a "head of household," the *domus* in Latin, the *despot*, in our case here the *principal*, whose orders need not be justified, and are executed without question by those working beneath him, be they employees, domestic servants, or slaves. Subordination within the capitalist firm draws legitimacy from the fact that it is standardly considered the most adequate and efficient means of implementing instrumental rationality. This applies all the way down the firm's chain of command: the capital investors name their representatives to a board of directors, which controls the agents acting on its behalf (the CEO and members of the executive committee), who, in turn, establish the way in which these orders will be carried out. Workers, who are just 1 production factor among many, and whose labor has been purchased by contract, are there as instruments to execute the plans established by those higher up in the chain of command. In the end, each link in this chain is the agent of his hierarchical superior, and the principal of his subordinate.

To summarize, in the eyes of the *economic theory of the firm*, the firm is an organization driven by instrumental rationality, and the act of investing in the firm, through capital or through labor, is understood as a means to a specific end – to earning profit or wage. Either way, the investment is considered to be deployed in the private sphere, in which power is exercised unilaterally by the principal, following a model that is considered to be the most effective way of implementing instrumental rationality. We describe this model as "domestic" because it follows the pattern of power relations typical of interactions that, historically, pertained to the private sphere, where the head of household set tasks for domestic servants to carry out. Although the theoretical tools invented and employed by this school of thought disprove their own assumptions (Rebérioux 2003),[8] this vision of the economy nevertheless underlies the legal system in contemporary liberal democracies, and exerts singular influence on contemporary firms. Yet, the only major contribution this dominant tradition has made to our understanding of the firm is its identification of the firm's two key actors: capital investors and labor investors.

Indeed, the classical economic theory of the firm has drawn a parallel we wish to highlight: in its eyes, the firm's two main actors, excluding non-human production factors, share the same status. This view that capital investors and "the labor factor" are driven by substantive, identical – instrumental – logic aligns, somewhat surprisingly, liberal firm theory with the Marxist view of the firm, a point we shall examine more

[8] See note 49.

closely in the next part of our analysis. According to both traditions, two categories of actors are present in the firm: we have called the first category investors in capital or "capital investors"; the second, as they invest their personal labor, we have named investors in labor or "labor investors." According to the economic theory of the firm, these two groups of actors invest in the firm in order to earn returns on their investments, either in the form of profit or of wage. This is the salient point of this section and we will return to it throughout the book: the firm, even when it is conceptualized as existing only in the realm of instrumental rationality, is driven not by one but by two categories of investors – capital investors and labor investors.

MARXIST THEORY IN SUPPORT OF THE IDEA OF LABOR AS INSTRUMENT

The view traditionally seen as opposite to liberal economic theory is Marxist theory. Marx defined capitalism as the private ownership of the means of production, whose end is the appropriation of added value, which gives rise to a number of prerogatives. Laborers are put to work by capital investors under varying conditions of exploitation, a word Marx chose to employ because the profits realized by capital investors come from the activities of their employees. In Marx's view, there would be no surplus or added value without the worker, and therefore no profit for the capitalist shareholder. A capitalist firm, therefore, is a place in which added value is extracted by exploiting workers – a situation that, by its very nature, is irremediable under capitalist conditions.

From the Marxist perspective, workers in firms are inevitably exploited because exploitation is inherent in the capitalist firm. According to Marx, work is the very "essence of man" (Méda 1998) – but only work carried out in complete autonomy, by the worker, for the worker. The exploitative nature of work in a capitalist firm alienates workers from their own essence. Capitalist society perverts this essential activity through the conditions in which it puts people to work. Because employees carry out the wishes of others, in a situation of complete heteronomy, they become strangers unto themselves – alienated, in other words. As Marx wrote,

In my *production* I would have objectified my *individuality, its specific character*, and therefore enjoyed not only an individual *manifestation of my life* during the activity ... and therefore in my individual activity I would have directly *confirmed* and *realised* my true nature, my *human* nature, my *communal nature*.

(1968: 35)

But, Marx adds, "Presupposing private property, my work is an *alienation of life*, for I work *in order to live*, in order to obtain for myself the *means* of life (Marx 1968: 34)." Marx was very clear in this respect: alienation is brought about through the instrumental relationship to work created by the capitalist system. If workers are the instruments of capitalists, then work becomes nothing more than a mere instrument of survival.

Just as in the liberal economic theory of the firm, the Marxist understanding of work in the capitalist system sees the alienated and exploited worker as driven by instrumental rationality: "I work *in order to* live, in order to obtain for myself the *means* of life." The worker hires himself out to the capitalist only because capitalist society has succeeded in offering him no other means of survival. According to Marx, any worker would choose to break free from this system if he were able – and would do so as soon as he were able. Although the Marxist tradition places itself in diametrical opposition to liberal economic theory – where the latter seeks to legitimize the capitalist system, the former seeks to critique and destroy it – the instrumental relationship to work remains pivotal in both schools of thought. Few scholars working on work in the Marxist tradition have sought to build methodological or conceptual tools that allow for any other vision.[9] Worker alienation, according to the Marxist tradition, mirrors the capitalist gesture, perpetuating and extending the instrumental nature of the capitalist investment. In this perspective, the worker's relationship to work is unquestionably instrumental.

Given that their goal was to offer a radical critique of capitalist society – an anti-capitalist vision of the world – it is strange to observe that scholars working in the Marxist tradition maintained the idea of the economic realm as the exclusive domain of instrumental rationality, a vision promoted by the very tradition they sought to combat. In their efforts to critique capitalist society, and the capitalist firm within it, the majority of Marxist thinkers failed to notice that the idea that workers'

---

[9] See Gorz (1988, 1998) and Méda (1998). In response to Méda's critique of this argument (2009, 2010), we should like to draw attention to a logical confusion that should be avoided: the analysis of work upon which the idea of Economic Bicameralism is built does not include an idealized view of work as the source of all human satisfaction. To the contrary, we argue that acknowledging the authenticity of the human desire for autonomy in the workplace itself should not blind us to the needs specific to this desire (needs this book is intended to address), nor to the need for emancipation that people may encounter in other types of activity, including the need to limit or reduce the place taken by employment in a person's life (through the reduction of working time, for instance), and even including the desire to escape employment entirely (through the introduction of a basic income, for instance).

relationship to work was governed exclusively and unilaterally by instrumental rationality was merely an idea – and an inadequate one, at that. Furthermore, it has had the paradoxical effect of validating, or at least bolstering, the classical economic view of work as an instrument.

In practical terms, implementing Marx's analyses meant collectivizing the means of production. Only rarely has this measure been accompanied by any serious contestation of the idea that workers have an exclusively instrumental relationship to work. Nor was the relevance of the domestic regime as applied in the capitalist workplace ever questioned under communist regimes (Pateman 1970). Indeed, Soviet factories were carbon copies of their American counterparts, and in them, assembly line workers labored following Taylor's principles of scientific management, of which Lenin was a great admirer. The foreman may have been a comrade, but he remained a foreman, and his orders were to be followed. Questioning the rationality driving economic activity – capital or labor – was not a priority for those who used Marxist thought to contest or reshape the capitalist system. In a superficial reading of Marx's work, what stands out is indeed his strong critique of the private ownership of the means of production, and this reductive reading shaped Marxist political movements, which focused heavily on the collective appropriation of the means of production. As closer reading shows, however, this is just 1 facet of the alternative to capitalism Marx envisioned. In fact, his writing makes specific reference to a rationality broader than the strictly instrumental one he criticized capitalists for subscribing to, and which, despite his critiques, was taken for granted by many of his followers. As previously mentioned, Marx's understanding of work was firmly rooted in the Hegelian tradition; he saw it, as Méda neatly phrases it, as "the essence of man" (Méda 1998: 93–113). When Marx speaks of "true work," as opposed to "real" or alienated work, he is evoking what this book identifies as employees striving to deploy their *expressive rationality*: true work as he sees it is an activity that makes it possible "to affirm ... my true nature" (Marx 1968: 35). Unfortunately, this facet of his thinking did not end up exerting the same influence on Marxist critiques of capitalism as his writing on the means of production.

To a reader seeking to remain faithful to Marx's original thought, the real communist response to capitalism is therefore fundamentally flawed. Under capitalism, ownership of the means of production is *private*; under communism it is *public* – meaning collectively owned through the state – but those are two sides of the same coin, argues David Ellerman. Marx's interest was in human emancipation, and his aims are betrayed by this enduringly shallow distinction. Ellerman (1992) uses the luminous historical analogy of Sparta and Athens during antiquity to demonstrate how the difference between the way the labor factor is treated under the capitalist and communist systems is largely a symbolic one. As Ellerman explains, in Sparta slaves were publicly owned, by the city, and in Athens they were privately owned, by the individual masters – but both were slaveholding societies in which it was acceptable to hold human beings as property (Ellerman 1992: 2). From the slave's point of view, no matter the system, he remained chattel. To pursue the aim of human emancipation that nourished Marx's critique of capitalism, it is necessary to look beyond questions regarding ownership of the means of production. The critical issue is whether workers are able to participate in decisions concerning the conditions of their labor.

If it is to carry any weight, a critique of capital investors' hegemony over the firm must be fully rooted in the complexities of reality. Accounting for these complexities is the only way to develop a meaningful array of conceptual tools capable of building a rigorous, empirically founded, and relevant critique of the institutions that currently govern the capitalist firm. Our observation that both of these views of the firm, as ideologically opposed as they may be, perceive it as driven only by instrumental rationality, significantly advance us in this task, in two ways. The first is that a firm exists when capital and labor investors are involved in working together toward a common goal. Second, that while instrumental rationality is an adequate way to account for capital investors' relationship to the firm, especially in an age of global financial capitalism, in which capital is highly mobile, it cannot fully explain that of labor investors.

Property, being only one among other human interests, cannot be pursued abso-
lutely without detriment to human life.... The issue before thoughtful people is
therefore not the maintenance or abolition of private property, but the determi-
nation of the precise lines along which private enterprise must be given free scope
and where it must be restricted in the interests of the common good.

Morris R. Cohen (1927: 21)

6

Foundations for the Political Theory of the Firm

Despite their immense impact on society, from the halls of academia to the political struggles that marked the twentieth century and this one, we have just observed the extent to which the two dominant views of the economy, the economic theory of the firm and Marxist thought, were developed using rudimentary and incomplete conceptions of the firm, and continue to perpetuate them. They both view the firm as a mere organization pegged to the corporation, and perceive instrumental rationality to be the only logic driving the firm's two categories of investor – capital and labor. Once the observation has been made that this univocal reading is not borne out in factual reality, it seems almost shocking in its lack of intellectual nuance. It has, nevertheless, contributed in no small part to the conceptual foundations upon which the laws of our capitalist democracies have evolved – an evolution that has, in turn, reinforced these flawed conceptual foundations. To form the beginning of a response to this observation, this section shall offer an overview of a third approach that, while it lacks the tidy coherence of the schools of thought previously examined, provides what we hope is a more accurate and complete account of the firm as it actually exists. To do so requires us to tackle the three dimensions of the *political theory of the firm*: the substantive and the descriptive (covered in Part II) and the normative (Part III). The *political theory of the firm* is interdisciplinary in scope, but sees the analytical categories coming from the body of literature in political analysis and political theory as central in its approach to firms. Its evaluative and critical aspects (featured in Part III) will flow straightforwardly from the substantive and descriptive dimensions covered earlier (in Part II).

A substantive account is necessary to ensure that none of the relevant features to be included in the descriptive account have been left out. For if we, as the two schools of thought previously reviewed have done, suppose that instrumental rationality dominates economic life, we shall, like them, see no more in the firm than a corporation *plus* contracts – a mere *nexus of contracts* – or the pure exploitation of the weak by the strong. The reality of the firm is more complex, and offers equally rich challenges to those who value efficiency and to those who value democratic justice. Scattered across the social sciences are a wealth of intellectual resources, which, when drawn together, will help us to develop an understanding of the firm that reaches beyond corporate, reductionist liberal and Marxist frameworks.

A SUBSTANTIVE ACCOUNT OF THE FIRM: TWO RATIONALITIES MAKE A FIRM

What is a firm? The two schools of thought examined earlier have given us a partial answer: a capitalist firm is, indisputably, a space in which instrumental rationality is deployed, through capital investors, who seek the maximum return on their investments. In this idea of a firm, rational shareholder-employees celebrate rising stock prices even as the firm prepares massive layoffs, and workers are satisfied with recognition through salary alone. However factually relevant this limited vision of the firm may be, we cannot wholly understand the reality of the firm if we do not acknowledge that it is *at the same time* driven by another form of logic, by a rationality we propose to call "expressive rationality." While capital investors in the contemporary global and financial age are highly mobile and can easily arbitrate on rates of return on investment, *labor investors* are for the most part driven by expressive rationality, as they invest their persons, not their capital, in the everyday workings of the firm. The operation of these two rationalities makes possible the activity of the firm. Denying the existence and influence of either one of them poses a grave threat to the robustness of the firm and its future. Identifying the existence of these two rationalities allows us to build a better analytical account of the reality of the firm, which we shall do in the sections that follow.

Instrumental Rationality Sustained by Capital Investors in the Age of Global Finance

We shall begin our exploration of the landscape of the *political theory of the firm* by acknowledging the crucial importance of *instrumental rationality* to the firm's existence, and identify capital investors as its best representatives. This perspective does not imply that labor investors are not also influenced by this rationality in their relation to the firm, only that it is not the central rationality guiding their actions. By the same token, observing that capital investors are principally motivated by instrumental rationality does not mean that they are unaffected by expressive rationality. Quite to the contrary, and perhaps most visibly in the period between the Second World War and the collapse of the Bretton Woods system in the 1970s, when capital mobility was largely limited within national borders, capital investors' interests were tied to multiple non-instrumental considerations, such as serving the local community or the greater good, increasing consumer purchasing power, or generating employment. However, when the Bretton Woods system ended in 1973 and the Western economy began to financialize in earnest, capital investors were freed from considerations other than return on investment. The focus on pure financial return on investment has narrowed and intensified over time through incentive mechanisms such as executive stock options. Mary A. O'Sullivan insists on the fact that "in addition, during the 1970s the quest for shareholder value in the US economy found support from a new source – the institutional investor. The transfer of stock-holding from individual households to institutions such as mutual funds, pension funds, and life insurance companies made possible the takeovers advocated by agency theorists and gave shareholders much more collective power to influence the yields and market values of the corporate stocks they held" (2000: 7).

Exceptions to this remain in the contemporary economy, of course, and some capital investors, typically those in what is known as the social or citizen-sector economy, are motivated by non-instrumental concerns[1].

---

[1] Again, this is not to say that expressive rationality is absent from the standard capital investor's relationship to the firm. The history of entrepreneurship (firms founded by entrepreneurs whose expectations were driven by the expressive dimension of a new venture) and of prominent industrial families (whose histories are linked to the history of inventions, industries, and geographic regions) shows that investors are not purely instrumental in their investments. For recent example, expressive rationality comes into play when firms still controlled by certain historical investors have to make difficult decisions, and choose to favor certain geographical areas or privilege certain fields of activity when they downsize. One contemporary example of this was Volkswagen's clear preference for Germany in its restructuring of the Volkswagen plant in Brussels in 2007–08 (De Munck, Ferreras, and Wernerus 2010, De Munck and Ferreras 2013). Yet, our suggestion is that the ideal type of rationality of capital investors in the current era of financial globalization is largely instrumental. In cases where corporate governance models remain different from the institutional model of American corporations and their pursuit of return on investment and shareholder value at all costs, research (notably in France) shows that the economic

Nevertheless, it may be generally stated that the logic driving capital investors in today's economy can be summarized by O'Sullivan's conclusion in her study of struggles for corporate control in the United States and Germany: "the sole measure of corporate performance became the enhanced market capitalization of the company" (2000: 7–8). This is another way of describing what we call the *instrumental rationality* of capital investors: investment in capital is not an end in itself; it is a means to the highest potential return on investment, whatever the form this return may take (increased value of shares, dividends, etc.). As we have seen, it is precisely for this reason that capital investors are perceived as the optimal representatives and guarantors of instrumental rationality within a firm. In the words of the agency theory, they are its "principal," and ultimate master. To conclude, we will identify capital investors as the most faithful representatives of instrumental rationality in the firm.

Expressive Rationality: Moving Labor Investors in the Service-Based Economy

Non-instrumental rationality underpins the existence of the firm to at least the same extent as instrumental rationality. We will be developing an understanding of the firm as a *political entity* that combines the instrumental and expressive rationalities that drive, respectively, capital and labor investors. Here, the term *expressive* used to describe workers' relationship with work, and with the firm in general, refers to the register of meaning and values, as opposed to the register of instrumentality; it refers to the realm in which signification is built through lived experience, values, and ultimately, conceptions about justice, and should be contrasted with the realm of pure technique or of means. In other words, this understanding of the firm is rooted in the observation that beyond instrumental considerations, one's relationship to, and investment in, work, and the firm more generally, is nourished by meaning. Centrally, this relationship itself is substantively a vehicle for meaning. The experience of work

elites, including political elites and high-ranking public servants, have already been converted to the values this model espouses. François and Lemercier (2016)' s fascinating study of the French economic elites has shown that even in cases where the laws of the financial market are not technically predominant, for example, in large firms in which the French government holds the majority stake, instrumental rationality is all-powerful and dominates expectations about investments. Even in these cases, a strict return on investment, measured in financial terms, is the highest goal, rather than the broader priorities one might expect of a government-held firm.

contributes directly to the construction of meaning in human life, and in this sense its analysis cannot be reduced to any form of instrumentality, in this case, acting to make profit or wages. Although it will seem contradictory to those who read Marx only superficially, this approach shares with Marx the idea that work is the central component of the *essence of man* (Méda 1998), which underlies his critique of capitalism. As it was for Marx, Hegel's assertion that human life is a creative deployment of the (human) mind is the wellspring of our understanding of the firm as a political entity.

This conception of the firm as constituted by two types of rationality makes use of a central distinction in sociology that originated in Max Weber's seminal work on the logic of actions (1971). Weber identified major types of rationality that motivated people's everyday actions. The first was "value-rational action," defined by Weber as the "subordination of realities to values." We shall refer to this as "expressive rationality" in order to underline the importance of attributing meaning to action, a process to which values are central.[2] The second type of rationality Weber described in terms of "means-end calculation," and is generally known as "instrumental rationality" (Kalberg, 1980: 1161). Contrary to prevailing interpretations of Weber's account of the homogeneous and inevitable rationalization (more often known as the process of bureaucratization) in the Western world, Weber did not "reduce the multidimensionality of rationalization processes to a single dimension" (Kalberg 1980: 1157). Our view of the firm, in keeping with the observations of the founder of economic sociology, acknowledges the constant interplay between two types of rationality – and processes of rationalization. Through this dynamic, their struggle to cohabit with and to influence each other, the *political theory of the firm* acknowledges that instrumental and expressive rationalities come together to bring the firm to life.

There is something more than money in daily employment.
    Morris R. Cohen (1927: 28)

Do employees sit at work only for the wage they receive? The reasons for working are manifold, and not merely instrumental. The contribution of the entire field of the sociology of work goes "well beyond conceptions of work as exchange of labor for money to show the need of people to

---

[2] We rely on Jeremy Bentham's use of the term "meaning": a dynamic conception that "refers to the intention to relay a desire, a sentiment, an interest; that is, elements of the active faculty of the mind" (Bentham 1997: 249).

interpret what they do," and "how people attribute meaning to their work" (Bandelj 2009: 12) It is only fitting, then, to approach the firm with a more substantive theory of work, adapted to the contemporary service-based economy in which we live. To do so requires a clearer understanding of what work is to those who perform and experience it. Defining what work is requires us to report and interpret workers' *work experience*. Research into this question is vast, and cannot be exhaustively discussed in the present text. We shall then refer to our previous work on the topic (Ferreras 2007, 2012c) in order to provide an overview of the meaning of the work experience from the perspective of workers, to whom it is *expressive, public*, and, fundamentally, *political.*[3]

Expressive Relationship to Work

Most often, labor economics summarizes the individual's attitude to work in a simple equation: pain (at work) versus pleasure (outside of work). The utility of a salary through the access it provides to self-sustenance and leisure activities compensates directly for the disutility of work (Lane 1992: 49). The classical economic opposition of work and leisure (Juster 1986, Lane 1992) assumes an entirely instrumental attitude to work, and ignores a more comprehensive view of the "work experience" (Ferreras, 2007), as a fundamentally social relationship. As my own research has shown, the instrumental dimension of work ("making a living") is only one of five dimensions that characterize an individual's attitude to work. Work takes on its full meaning only when these five dimensions are considered together. The other four expressive dimensions that participate directly in defining work's meaning are "feeling autonomous" in one's capability to lead one's own life; "being included" in the social fabric; "feeling useful," be it to someone specifically, to the firm, or to society

---

[3] I analyzed the work experience more fully in a book devoted to the case of supermarket checkout employees, which is critically unique in the methodological sense (Ferreras 2007). My study was built from an exploration of the reality of contemporary work, and there is not room enough here to account for the inductive nature of the theoretical process. Recently, the Wage Indicator online survey collected responses from 100,000 workers from nine countries in Europe and the Americas about the three fundamental dimensions of the work experience – the expressive, the public, and the political. This data was collected with support from the Harvard Labor and Worklife Program and the Wage Indicator Foundation, based in Amsterdam. The preliminary analysis strongly confirms this understanding of work as driven by expressive rationality. On the broad array of expressive, non-instrumental dimensions comprised in individuals' attitudes toward work, see (Meda and Vendramin 2017) and their discussion of the most comprehensive survey data available in Europe.

in general; and, finally, what is known as the intrinsic value of the job, "doing interesting work." These expressive dimensions are dominant in the meaning ascribed to work by employees, even in those critical cases[4] where the tasks discharged are not considered by most to constitute an "interesting job."[5]

In short, an individual's relationship to work is as much a relationship of meaning (working is "being included, being useful, being independent, doing interesting work") as it is instrumental (working is "earning money to be able to meet your needs outside of work"). More precisely, even in jobs that are unfulfilling and draining, with no opportunity for career advancement, as is the case for supermarket cashiers described in note 6, the individual's relationship to work is, ultimately, an expressive one. Because work always has expressive connotations, even if they are minimal, it cannot be reduced to its instrumental dimension, no matter

---

[4] The example of supermarket cashiers is a critical case – that is, a case so restrictive that if it can confirm an initial hypothesis this thesis may be logically extended to less restrictive cases. The intrinsic value of work is largely absent for supermarket cashiers, who could therefore be assumed to be particularly likely to have a relationship to work in which the instrumental dimension is dominant. But in their accounts of their relationship to work, the three expressive dimensions (all, that is, except the intrinsic value of work) are even more present than the instrumental one. Such a relationship to work may be described as autonomously expressive – that is, independent of the interest inherent in the work itself. By extension, it may be concluded that an individual's expressive relationship is still more intense in cases where the work being done is perceived as more interesting than the work of the cashier. It is only reasonable to assume that a member of any professional category who finds any aspect of her work even a little bit more interesting than a cashier's would relate to that work in a manner even more marked by the expressive dimensions. Examining the other end of the salary spectrum, Massaro (2003: 14) cites a similar relationship to work: once one has achieved a level of pay that enables them to decently sustain their own life, an individual's relationship to their work is more affected by how interesting they find it than by the remuneration that comes with it. To illustrate this, Massaro quotes a partner in a major New York law firm: "the novocaine of your paycheck wears off quickly if you don't enjoy what you do." Coutant's recent case study (2016) offers a unique longitudinal view of an entire organizational hierarchy during a merger between two firms in the aeronautic industry, and is an excellent example of how investment "of person" (of labor, in other words) in a firm has expressive dimensions all the way up a firm's hierarchy, from the way its very smallest work teams coordinate to decisions made by its board.

[5] Management research essentially identifies the same reality when, using scientifically controlled studies, it looks for sources of people's motivation in the context of work. Pink (2009) assembled research available in behavioral economics and psychology to demonstrate that motivation – and therefore productivity – in the workplace are dependent on three factors that precisely mirror the three expressive dimensions described earlier. He identifies them as *autonomy* ("the desire to be self-directed," i.e. the capacity to determine the way one's work function is organized), *mastery* ("our urge to get better at stuff," i.e. self-improvement, gaining expertise in a particular field), and *purpose* ("serving an end recognizably greater than oneself and the actual task being done").

how significant that dimension is: work is always more than just a way to earn a living.[6] Therefore, theories that posit that the instrumental relationship to work is the most important are unhelpful if we are to continue to reflect productively on the broader context of work, the workplace, and the firm, as they do not address the complex ways in which individuals relate to their work.

Public Character of Work

Western economies shifted from industry to service in the last thirty years of the twentieth century. This sea change, though its consequences have not yet been fully understood and accounted for by the social sciences, has had a transformative effect on the way the experience of work is experienced by workers, one that cannot be ignored in an analysis of the contemporary firm. In the 1980s, after the continuous "shared growth" that marked the period following the Second World War, which was driven by manufacturing, the service sector became the central motor of Western economies. This sector includes a number of heterogeneous activities, including transportation, commerce, telecommunications, health, education, research and development, financial and legal services, insurance, real estate, hospitality, utilities, etc. Today, the service sector accounts for more than 75% of jobs in Europe and North America. Forecasts all agree that this industry will only gain importance in the coming years.

The goals of the primary industry (agricultural production and the extraction industry), as well as those of the secondary industry (the transformation of raw materials, the production of goods, and construction) are clear and easy to define; this is not the case for the service industry. Very broadly, the latter may be said to be engaged in the economic production of services, most commonly in the following way:

organization A, which possesses or controls a technical or human capability..., sells (or offers free of charge...) to economic agent B the right to use this capability and/or skills for a set amount of time, to produce useful effects on agent B, or upon C goods which agent B possesses or is responsible for (Gadrey 2003: 20).

As is the case in the primary and secondary sectors, service work takes place in the presence of a worker's colleagues (equal, superior, or inferior); unlike the first two sectors, however, tertiary work is also

---

[6] For a strong statement on the "right to meaningful work," grounded in a capability approach and the right to lead one's own life, see the research by Yeoman (2014), which connects a moral imperative to integrate workers' expectations of meaning in the structuring of global supply chains.

characterized by the presence of a third party, that of the client. This may take place either in person, at points of direct service, or indirectly, via various forms of communication or intermediary mediations. From a sociological perspective, as well as from the perspective of those actually living it, this characteristic is a cornerstone in the redefinition of the contemporary work experience.[7]

From the perspective of the worker's lived experience, the client's presence in the workplace has caused a fundamental shift in the actual fabric – and conceptual location – of the workplace, pushing it away from the familiar space it once occupied at the margins of the private sphere. The best way to characterize this space is as *public*. In Ferreras's (2007) study of cashiers' subjective experiences of their work, workers referred most often to the regime of *civic* interaction[8] typical of the public sphere, rooted in the equal dignity of all, which involves (sometimes forced) respect for others, equal consideration, and the right to maintain a private life without letting its specificities affect the impartiality with which others are considered. Beneath the customer's unceasing gaze, employees expect that interactions will take place within the regime typical of the public space of democratic societies – that they will be organized, in other words, through its principle of equal dignity. However, the relationship established between employee and customer is, in reality, determined by another regime of interaction, one that is actively promoted by management, which expects a service relationship, modeled on the regime of *domestic* subordination. This situation causes serious tensions, and even open conflict in the contemporary workplace.

Historically, the regime of *domestic* subordination dates back to predemocratic regimes of interaction (which Martuccelli called "hierarchical regimes"). In this regime, "the esteem due a person is clearly accessory to his rank" (Martuccelli 2002: 246). Those of superior rank are indisputably entitled to greater respect. Here, the qualifier "domestic" is used to accentuate the often arbitrary dynamic of subordination and fixed status-related discrimination that plays out in the workplace. It makes deliberate reference to the domestic servants of the ruling classes in past

---

[7] My study of supermarket cashiers is highly germane to the sociology of service work. The work of its subjects is typical of the service economy: cashiers work constantly in the presence of customers while at the same time remaining in the presence of their coworkers and under the surveillance of their hierarchical superiors.

[8] The concept of the regime of interaction, based on the "political regime of interaction" described by Martuccelli (2002, 246), seeks to describe the "conventional backdrop against which interactions take place and from which they derive meaning."

centuries, who were required to cater to their masters' whims, and generally lived under their roofs. This regime of interaction is described as "domestic" because, in the contemporary context of advanced democracies, it has remained rooted in the private sphere.

"Even when they're wrong, the customer is always right," as 1 cashier put it. "The customer is king," stated another. The experience of service work is thus characterized by subordination, focused on satisfying customers' wishes and not defying their injunctions. "Never talk back," a cashier is told, whether a customer insults an employee or is merely impolite; "never argue," "never disagree," "never contradict," "accept contempt without reacting." It is clear from those statements that their work is carried out in a non-civic regime of interaction, one that harkens back to pre-democratic regimes of interaction. But today, cashiers are citizens too, whose status is "equal in dignity and rights" in every way to those they serve, which implies that they expect to be treated by customers in a manner consistent with and respectful of this fundamental norm of the civic regime of interaction. These two regimes – the one expected by the employee, the other demanded by the employer – fall neatly on either side of the dividing line between the public and private spheres, a dividing line that has marked the history of social relations in Western society in general, and labor and industrial relations in particular.

Sociological analysis shows that in the era of the service economy, working to serve others within the context of a commercial economic transaction that is regulated by a work contract does not necessarily imply, from the point of view of the person rendering the service, assuming the status of a domestic servant. To the contrary, in their eyes, their work is perfectly compatible with their status as citizens and equal participants in the public sphere. In any case, that is the employee's expectation. Today, the prevailing models of work organization and "customer relations," however, promote domestic-style relations between the customer and the employee. Like the "labor input" in the capitalist firm's production equation, the domestic regime of interaction in the service context is the material manifestation of the dystopian ideal that drives capitalism as described by Marx. It leads to a specific form of alienation: the worker is potentially transformed into a commodity, 1 tool of production among many, in the service of a project decided upon by a corporation's capital investors, to whom he or she is nothing but an instrument[9].

---

[9] For a seminal account on the major consequences of this situation on the worker at the subjective and emotional level, see Hochschild (1983).

Political Logic of Work

Just as the customer's presence in the workplace gives rise to a new understanding of that place as a space employees experience as located in the *public* sphere, so, too, does it incite us to pursue the analysis of contemporary work in the specific context of evermore prevalent policies of flexibility. To this end, two dimensions of work must be taken into consideration, expectations of justice and expectations of flexibility, and we will explore both of them here.

The experience of work in the era of flexible labor implies continuous and increased confrontation with others. From the worker's point of view, this means being confronted with multiple sources of normativity – customers, colleagues, members of the firm hierarchy. Employees' assessments of their work and the multitude of situations it entails have one feature in common: the principles of justice are used to understand, analyze, and judge work situations. Whatever is at stake, be it scheduling issues (who takes on what shift? evenings? weekends? etc.), access to training, the announcement of a major restructuring plan, or the decision to invest in a given department or product – each decision, each interaction that constitutes the work experience offers employees an opportunity to compare and contrast, dispute, or revise – implicitly or explicitly – their values and ideas of what is just. What might initially be understood as employees' expressions of discomfort, frustration, anger, or suffering – which may at times be expressed as workplace-related illnesses – are fundamentally experiences of *injustice*, of which these expressions are merely a symptom. For example, when describing altercations such as the one in the interview in the following text, they all use similar terms to describe work-related suffering, which, in some cases, ends in burnout and exhaustion so severe that they must take sick leave:[10]

G1/M: Because I remember one day an old guy came through with his grandson, and he said to him: "See why you have to work hard in school? So you don't end up like this lady!" [laughs] We just take it. Ring it up, shove it in your cash drawer, move on, you know? But the thing is . . . it's all stuff like that!

I: He just said that straight out, right in front of you?

G1/M: Of course! [. . .]

I: Without looking at you?

---

[10] Interview conducted by the author (identified as I in the text) with two cashiers employed by the M supermarket (Ferreras 2007).

G1/M: Yes! Of course! He said, "See why you have to work hard in school, and all the rest ... " the kid was maybe five, six years old?

I: And what are you supposed to do? Smile?

G1/M: Well, I looked at him – I didn't say anything because you can't, because the customer is always right, just like in any store, and ... [...] you just take it.

C2/M: People even insult you, huh? They even insult you!

G1/M: People call you a stupid cunt because a price doesn't go through [when the product is being scanned]! [...] Oh yes. I've already been told straight out. "You're a stupid cunt." [...] But people, because you're a "checkout girl" – well, you're just a checkout girl. No one has to respect you, because you're a "checkout girl!"

Experiencing expressions of contempt from customers is common for service workers, and they react to them with a profound feeling of injustice, which is intensified by the fact that they are not allowed to respond. The customer truly is "always right": the cashier cannot contradict them. Some cashiers "toughen up" after years of coping with this reality; others cannot and suffer from psychological or physical breakdowns (one may be substituted for the other). They may fall victim to long-term illness, or, with better luck, be transferred to a part of the store that requires less interaction with customers. The idea of justice informs an employee's apprehension of all events playing out in the workplace, be they connected to a standard for organizing the work itself or the way in which that standard is applied. Justice (and injustice) orders the normative grammar of work and the workplace[11].

At the same time, the forms of *flexibility* that shape the work experience in the era of the service economy are all experienced as instances of *insertion and positioning within collectives*. By personalizing schedules, responsibilities, tasks, etc., flexibility as it is concretely experienced by workers requires those who work to position themselves with regard to the individuals and groups of individuals who make up the workplace,

---

[11] Many scholars have identified justice as the central normative reference of the work experience, perhaps most importantly in the field of the economy of conventions, starting with the pathbreaking contributions of Boltanski and Thévenot (1989, 1991). See also Muirhead (2004), François Dubet et alii (2006), de Nanteuil (2016). Here, French and English differ, as separate words do not exist for "just" and "fair" in French; they are both translated as "*juste*." Whereas a cashier reviewing their schedule might complain in English that it was unfair, they would not likely describe it as "unjust." For their French counterpart, on the other hand, getting short shrift in the week's schedule or being the victim of discrimination in the workplace would both be "*injuste*." Here, I use the word "justice" as a broad regulative ideal comprising instances judged by workers to be just or unjust as well as fair or unfair.

or with whom they are expected to coordinate, no matter their status or affilation to the same organization. This aspect of contemporary life is indisputable: work today has been entirely redefined by strategies of both qualitative and quantitative flexibility[12] (Guélaud, 1991). With quantitative flexibility, this translates into part-time work and variable working hours, while for qualitative flexibility it means multidisciplinary tasks and work team mobility. If it has traditionally been supposed that flexibility "individualizes" employees (in terms of schedules, tasks, and even salaries), I develop a sociological understanding that reveals a different reality: flexibility is lived, from the perspective of the individual, as an unceasing experience of inscription in the collective, or, at least, of reference to and positioning with regard to the others. It is therefore only logical to note that the working individual would apprehend their work experience using the ideas of justice and injustice they mobilize in any other – public – context in which they relate to a collective.

An analysis of contemporary work could not show any more clearly that work is a continuous lesson in how to situate oneself with regard to others in the context of a reference to the collective. Individuals at work learn, by choice or by necessity, to respect the place of others and situate themselves with regard to a hierarchy; they learn about compliance with authority and the conditions for its legitimacy; they learn that their own claims may not necessarily be recognized or justified; they learn to compromise and reposition themselves when their expectations and ideas of justice have been frustrated. For these two reasons – because workers mobilize an understanding of the work-related situation through the lenses of justice *and* because they mobilize it in the context of the continuous experience of placing themselves within a collective – we must conclude that the core of the work experience is *political*. To summarize, working means engaging in the following experiment: mobilizing the conceptions of the just (or the unjust) within the frame of reference of the collective. It is for this reason that I speak of *political* logic, since mobilizing conceptions of justice in (the context of a) reference to the collective is what many traditions of political philosophy consider as central to the experience of "the political."

---

[12] Qualitative flexibility – "flexible work" – aims to maximize workers' investment in tasks in order to avoid dead time (it may take the form of expanded functions, multiple disciplines, teamwork, training, etc.), while quantitative flexibility – "flexible employment" – aims to adapt the "work factor" – that is, the workforce (the number of employees or hours worked) – as closely as possible to the needs of the production process (it takes the form of new types of work, irregular working hours, part-time contracts, fixed-term contracts, subcontracting, the use of temp agencies, etc.) (Barbier and Nadel 2000).

Intuition of Democratic Justice

Each person in a work environment possesses their own individual ideas about justice. Justice might be measured through performance (merit-based) or it might require family situation to be taken into account; then again it might use seniority as an ordering principle, or merely value formal equality (in the determination of work schedules, for instance). Different substantive conceptions about what is just are present in any work environment. Yet, beyond this diversity, those who work are aware that their co-workers do not necessarily share their vision of how any given aspect of work life should be decided. All of them, however, share the same intuition that their individual vision should matter. Put another way, they do not see why that vision is not taken into account when decisions are made. In this we may distinguish the outline of a meta-conception of justice that transects individual ones: workers share an intuition that all coworkers have a legitimate claim to participate in forming the specific conception of justice that will in the end regulate their life in the workplace. They aspire to, or they intuit that a decision about how to organize life in the workplace can only be felt as just once each worker's voice has been taken into account (Ferreras 2007). This procedural norm, intuitively identified as the standard that should govern the organization of a collective and the substantive choices of the criteria of justice that structure it, is none other than the principle of *democratic justice*.[13] This principle emerges as the one that should order debate and decision-making in the workplace. This intuition, shared among employees, that decisions over how life should be organized in the firm should be governed by a deliberation in which all employees are represented shall therefore henceforth be referred to as the meta-norm of democratic justice.

Vaguely as it may be felt among employees, the notion exists among employees that it would be fair and just to be considered as "equals" – responsible partners, *citizens in the workplace*, on equal footing with the firm's other actors, the managers, the capital investors. I call this the critical intuition of democratic justice, and when it goes unrecognized, a fundamental conflict slowly ferments, one that touches all work contexts, at

---

[13] I use the term "democratic justice" (Shapiro 1999) based on a classic understanding of the following principle of justice: each member of the *polity* (or *demos* i.e., the concerned community) must participate on an equal footing in deliberation about norms that will be applied to them or with which they will have to comply (direct participation) or, at the very least, have equal weight in determining the procedure by which the norm will be established (representative systems).

times unstated, but clearly felt. In everyday work life, it may be glimpsed in words of anger or of resignation,[14] in ordinary indignation, in gestures of discouragement or exasperation; worse, it sometimes takes the form of "workplace suffering" and physical and psychological problems of all sorts.[15] All these phenomena are symptomatic of the conflict emerging from the gap between workers' expectations as to the regime of interaction in which their work should take place – which, in their minds, is felt as, and should be, civic and democratic – and the regime of interaction that is actually promoted in the corporate firm, which remains domestic.

As the history of labor has shown time and again, workers have always been affected by the injustice of various situations they experience at, and around work (Green 2000, 2007, Zinn 2001, Renault 2004, Faure and Rancière 2007). But until recently, until the rise of the service economy, workers were not constantly reminded in their day-to-day work of the norm of equal dignity and expectation to collective autonomy[16] upheld by the ideal of democratic justice in the public sphere experience, via the regular and repeated appearance of third parties. In the domestic atmosphere of a factory, as a foreman treated a worker poorly, it could feel unjust, but that was more easily considered a common fact of the closed, private sphere of the economy.[17] In the service economy, on the other hand, workers are confronted daily with the third-party figure of the customer, who introduces, willingly or not, the conventions typical of the democratic public sphere into the world of work. The term *expressive* rationality is

---

[14] Two figures matter here: in the case of the United States, which is traditionally considered to be rather hostile to unions, unionization has dipped below 7 percent in the private sector, but 90 percent of American workers say they are in favor of a form of independent organization for employees in their companies, whose purpose would be to represent workers and communicate their viewpoints to management. See the most complete study carried out in the United States on American workers' expectations regarding representation and participation in work (Freeman and Rogers 2006). See also Bryson and Freeman (2006), Freeman and Hilbrich (2013).

[15] Studies of the "psychodynamics of work" have illustrated these phenomena in abundant detail. In particular, see the pioneering work of Dejours (1993). From the French service sector to Chinese computer and microprocessor production facilities, cases of work-related suicide, which have received increasing media attention in the past few years, are their logical and most dramatic outcome.

[16] "Collective autonomy among equals" is one simple and powerful way to give a substantive definition to democracy, according to the French political philosopher Castoriadis (1999).

[17] As mentioned earlier, an appropriate name in Greek: *oikos-nomos*, the law of the household, under the ruling of the *despotes*. Today, as I explain, the economy has lost all resemblance to the private *oikos*, and has fully entered the public sphere.

used here to describe what drives those who invest their person and work in the firm, because they relate to their own work experience in expressive terms in the context of a redefined, broader, and more inclusive public sphere, in which they expect democratic justice to organize their shared existence. Behind the concept of expressive rationality lies the broader idea that the employees' investment in the firm is an expressive, public, and political experience that mobilizes their intuition of democratic justice. This book contrasts expressive rationality with *instrumental* rationality, which is defined by means-ends calculation, and informs capital investors' relationships to the firm as an instrument whose purpose is to bring return on investment.

Conclusion: The Firm as the Conjoining of Instrumental and Expressive Rationalities

Acknowledging this cohabitation of instrumental and expressive rationalities in the firm has two major consequences. First, on the analytical level, it requires that the firm be understood as, more than a mere economic vehicle, a *political entity* in which power is exercised by the two categories of investors in the firm, investors in capital and investors "in person," or *labor investors*, and deployed via their two types of rationality. Each firm generates an active combination, a particular equilibrium of these two. When the firm, defined in this way, is held up to other political institutions active in democratic society, the exceptional status previously accorded to firms as a mere vehicle for instrumental rationality – and therefore expected, required, and designed to uphold the primacy of capital investors' interests – can no longer be considered legitimate.

Practically, to acknowledge this definition is to recast the firm as a place in which these two rationalities compete for influence. This competition may currently be better defined as a struggle, in that the firm does not yet possess a set of institutions that would allow this competition to create productive outcomes. And on a normative level, looking to the future, this definition implies that the firm's current exemptions from the demands and obligations of the democratic norm will be difficult to maintain: democratic justice is the *political* standard in the culture of contemporary democratic societies – why should it not be applied to the firm? The challenges raised by this redefinition will be addressed in Part III of this book. First though, we will delve deeper in identifying the constitutive parts of the *political theory of the firm*.

A DESCRIPTIVE ACCOUNT OF THE FIRM: FUNDAMENTAL DIMENSIONS

As explained in Chapter 5, presupposing the domination of instrumental rationality in the economic life of the firm leads to one of two views of the firm, which, although located on opposite ends of the ideological spectrum, are built on the same core assumption, which is that the firm is a vehicle – an instrument. The first sees the firm as a set of contracts and nothing more – a *nexus of contracts*, it is sometimes called. The second identifies the firm as a structure through which the strong exploit the weak. Neither view is broad enough to identify the firm's relevant features for a comprehensive descriptive account. The substantive account of the firm previously given has begun this task: it observes that the firm is the locus of two intertwined rationalities, the instrumental and the expressive, deployed by two groups of actors. This broader definition allows us to mobilize a battery of intellectual resources not available to us from within the confines of the corporate, reductionist liberal and Marxist frameworks we have previously described. In this section, we will draw together these resources, from fields as diverse as law, sociology, economics, philosophy, psychology, history, and industrial relations, in order to lay the foundations for an understanding of the inner life of the *firm as a political entity*. This makes it possible for us to broaden our focus from the reductionist lens of the economic theory of the firm, which reveals only the *corporation*, and apprehend a more rigorous, more comprehensive alternative, which I propose be called the *political theory of the firm*.

The *political theory of the firm* spans at least eight fundamental dimensions, which we will sketch out in this section. It offers a conception of the firm as an entity powered by different categories of investors, labor and capital, and moved by distinct rationalities – we have identified two major ones, instrumental and expressive. It is a conception that is not only empirically relevant, but also evaluative and critical in a manner comparable to that of the *economic theory of the firm*.[18] This last dimension will be laid out in Part III of this book, which addresses the normative dimension of

[18] Inspired by the tradition of the critical social sciences, we wish to develop a concept that is not only factually grounded, but which helps assess reality by enabling us to measure the distance between that reality and the democratic aspiration to collective autonomy that drives human agency. Although it claims to be scientifically objective, it is crucial to recognize that the particular concept of the firm developed by the economic theory of the firm also serves an evaluative purpose, as it advances the interests of a specific category of investors in the firm – the shareholders of the corporation. See Jung and Dobbin (2016).

the *political theory of the firm*. These evaluative and critical aspects will flow straightforwardly from the substantive and descriptive dimensions of the firm for which are mobilized the analytical categories coming from political analysis and political theory. This exploratory book is not the appropriate venue for a full literature review of each dimension, each of which must be informed by numerous existing works, which have yet to be organized into the field of the *political theory of the firm*. The goal of the paragraphs that follow is merely to demonstrate that these sources exist, and to establish that founding such an interdisciplinary academic field is now possible. Many more works remain to be explored and integrated, drawn together, and developed by relevant specialists in order to foster scientific debate fertile enough to sustain the field. This cannot be an individual endeavor and will require the work and expertise of scholars grounded in a wide variety of disciplines.

Corporate Law and the *Reductio ad Corporationem:* Distinguishing the Firm from the Corporation

As the legal scholar Jean-Philippe Robé puts it, "firms are structured *using* corporations; they are *not* corporations" (2011: 7); as it is evident that discussion of firms should be legally sound, let us begin by explaining the meaning of the terms we shall use:

A *corporation* (or company, its frequent synonym) is a legal entity founded by a group of capital owners who organize themselves using a certificate of incorporation, which is a legal instrument recognized and administered by a state, and which has legal standing in its courts.[19] These owners set capital apart from their other, personal assets in order to jointly pursue the development of a business activity, which is granted the status of a *legal, "moral persona"* by the court. The creation of this fictional "person" protects investors from risk by ensuring that, should the venture fail, they will lose only the capital they invested in it, not their personal assets, and will not be held personally responsible for the actions of the legal entity. The corporation is usually run by a board of directors (or simply a director), which is empowered to mobilize it as a *legal entity*

---

[19] The oldest such company was established in 1600: "the Company of merchants of London trading into The East Indies is granted a royal charter by Queen Elizabeth I, established with 125 shareholders under the name 'The East India Company,' with £72,000 of capital. Sir Thomas Smythe is The Company's first Governor. Elizabeth also limited the liability of the EIC's investors as well as her liabilities in granting a Royal Charter. This made The Company the world's first limited liability corporation." Source: http://theeastindiacompany.com

to enter and honor contracts (with employees, other businesses, suppliers, etc.). The directors (also known as associates) use the assets that the corporation controls to develop the *firm*.

As a firm grows,[20] its board of directors is forced to delegate managerial responsibility to a group of officers hired for their specialized knowledge in management and organization. The present text will consider corporations that are sufficiently large and complex to be run by professional managers rather than directors or proprietors. Firms of this size necessarily display a significant degree of separation between the *ownership* of shares and the *control* of the firm performed by these professional managers, in the classic sense used by Berle and Means (1932). The present text uses the word *firm* to mean an organization mature enough to be run by a group of officers composed of professional managers hired and overseen by the board and given the authority to mobilize that corporation's assets in order to fund the profit-making activities of the firm. Both public and privately held corporations – those with shares that are widely held and tradable on a stock market as well as those with private ownership shares restricted from public trading – are included in this definition.[21]

The goal a corporation pursues is specified in its incorporation charter. This goal may change over time; for example, a corporation may be incorporated in the seventeenth century with the narrow goal of importing luxury goods from India, then add a bank in the eighteenth century, branch out to building railroads in the nineteenth century, and then renew its charter in the twentieth century with a stated goal so broad as to pose no limitations at all on the scope of its activity.[22] To pursue its stated goal,

[20] For a full account of the organic and ideal-typical development of the corporate story of a firm, from the venture of a single entrepreneur all the way to its incorporation, transnationalization, and public offering, read Robé's detailed (and entertaining) account (2011).

[21] Privately held corporations sacrifice access to the large, highly liquid public equity markets in order to evade oversight and disclosure requirements imposed by securities regulators. The closed nature of these corporations renders the possibility of exit more difficult for capital investors – generally large, sophisticated investment funds or wealthy individuals – and increases the incentive for such investors to exercise close oversight over managers to protect their investments, often demanding representation on the corporate board or certain voting rights for their shares that protect their investment.

[22] Just one example of the breadth of ends for which corporations may be granted the status of *legal personality* is the transnational firm Pfizer. On its website, its stated goal is to "apply science and our global resources to bring therapies to people that extend and significantly improve their lives" (See http://www.pfizer.com/about). However, under its Certificate of Incorporation, the latest restatement of which was filed in 2006, Pfizer Incorporated, which is headquartered in and established according to laws of the State

the corporation must organize a firm; that is, a wide array of coordinated actions, mobilizing resources within the legal infrastructure provided by the corporation. Robé describes this process as "building the firm *around* the corporation" (2011: 36). We use the term "firm" to describe this field of coordinated activities. When used in this sense, the *firm* (or business enterprise, as it is sometimes called) is not confined or defined by the legal existence of the corporation alone, and indeed has no clear definition under the law. It is a deliberately broad term, used here to refer to the many actions that are required to pursue the profit-making activities of the corporation. As Fama has aptly recalled, highlighting Berle and Means

of Delaware, USA, this same corporation states its goal in such a loose way that it could be applied to many different industries beyond healthcare: "the nature of the business, or objects or purposes to be transacted, promoted or carried on are as follows:

To carry on the business of chemists, druggists, chemical manufacturers, importers, exporters, manufacturers of and dealers in chemical, pharmaceutical, medicinal, and other preparations and chemicals.

To engage in, conduct, perform or participate in every kind of commercial, agricultural, mercantile, manufacturing, mining, transportation, industrial or other enterprise, business, work, contract, undertaking, venture or operation.

To buy, sell, manufacture, refine, import, export and deal in all products, goods, wares, merchandise, substances, apparatus, and property of every kind, nature and description, and to construct, maintain, and alter any buildings, works or mines.

To enter into, make and perform contracts of every kind with any person, firm or corporation.

To take out patents, trade-marks, trade names and copyrights, acquire those taken out by others, acquire or grant licenses in respect of any of the foregoing, or work, transfer, or do whatever else with them may be thought fit.

To acquire the good-will, property, rights, franchises, contracts and assets of every kind and undertake the liabilities of any person, firm, association or corporation, either wholly or in part, and pay for the same in the stock, bonds or other obligations of the Corporation or otherwise.

To purchase, hold, own, sell, assign, transfer, mortgage, pledge or otherwise dispose of shares of the capital stock of any other corporation or corporations, association or associations, of any state, territory or country, and while owner of such stock, to exercise all the rights, powers and privileges of ownership including the right to vote thereon.

To issue bonds, debentures or obligations of the Corporation, at the options of the Corporation, secure the same by mortgage, pledge, deed of trust or otherwise, and dispose of and market the same.

To purchase, hold and re-issue the shares of its capital stock and its bonds and other obligations.

To do all and everything necessary, suitable, convenient or proper for the accomplishment of any of the purposes or the attainment of one or more of the objects herein enumerated, or of the powers herein named, or which shall at any time appear conducive to or expedient for the protection, or benefit of the Corporation, either as holder of, or interested in, any property or otherwise, to the same extent as natural persons might or could do, in any part of the world." Source: http://www.pfizer.com/sites/default/files/investors/corporate/certification_inc.pdf

(1932)'s distinction between ownership and control, and the importance of managers, and contrary to the prevalent definition employed by the *economic theory of the firm,* which reduces the firm to its corporate form: "ownership of the firm is an irrelevant concept. Dispelling the tenacious notion that a firm is owned by its security holders is important because it is a first step toward understanding that control over a firm's decisions is not necessarily the province of security holders" (1980).

As we have suggested, the economic theory of the firm is flawed in that it treats the firm as nothing more than a discrete legal entity at the center of a nexus of contracts, in particular trade and labor contracts. In this sense, it practices a *Reductio ad Corporationem,* folding the firm into the corporation by pretending that the fundamental qualities of a firm are identical to those of the corporation. This occludes an immense and incommensurable portion of the firm's reality. In doing so, the economic theory of *the firm,* while claiming scientific neutrality, has in fact upheld and validated a very narrow understanding of the conflicts and motives of firms, casting the shareholders, board of directors, and the executive officers in the simplistic framework of the principal-agent model. Counter to law and jurisprudence,[23] it has transformed them into mere agents of their principals, the shareholders and the board, respectively.

The *political theory of the firm* offers an alternative to this *Reductio ad Corporationem* by shedding light on the actual and very dense relationship *between* the corporation and the firm, rather than ignoring or obscuring that relationship. To this end it will examine all the relationships that make a firm, identifying the different power relationships that play out within it. Whereas the power relationships of capital investors are organized through the legal vehicle of the corporation, the network of labor investors lacks structure, and is not organized in any way within the institution of the firm. Currently, capital investors are the only recognized organized constituency of the firm. The corporation is the institutional structure through which they exercise power over the internal life of the firm and its fate. If we define political rights in the firm as the right to participate in the government of the entity that exercises power over a constituent, or participant (for example, through representation in

---

[23] Robé, writing on corporate law and jurisprudence, insists on the fact that "in the decisions they make, the directors must make their own judgment based on the best interest of the *corporation* (...). The widespread belief that directors are the "agents-of-the-shareholders-who-own-the-corporation" does not correspond at all to the reality" (Robé 2011 32–33). The whole debate in corporate law around independent vs shareholder-dependent boards revolves around that disputed issue. See Olson (2008).

the general assembly and participation in the nomination of board members), then shareholders are the only investors who currently have any such rights. If we look at this situation from a democratic perspective, the fact that all other constituents or non-capital investors in the firm are disenfranchised becomes striking: they have indeed no binding influence over the future of the collective endeavor in which they are participating.[24]

Labor Law and Sociology: Recognizing the Institution in the Firm

The nature of the firm has been hotly debated in the field of labor law, and the great French labor lawyer Alain Supiot identifies two opposing approaches within the field. The first, which he calls the individualist approach, follows the reductionist views of the firm discussed at the beginning of Part II: "The individualist approach sees the firm as the combined deployment of ownership of means of production and contractual freedom. Capital owners control the legal status through which it is put into operation.[25] The network of contracts through which the firm is established is not intended to organize any sort of community, but, rather, to provide a framework for its owners' relationship with other economic operators, including its employees. This approach is rooted both in economic liberalism (as a sort of consecration of the abstraction *homo economicus*) and in Marxism (it fits with the idea that Capital and Labor have opposing interests).[26]" (Supiot 2002: 177) The second approach he identifies as the communitarian approach, "rooted both in the social doctrine of the Catholic Church and in German legal doctrine" (Supiot 2002: 178). Here, he makes an observation crucial to the advancement of the *political theory of the firm*: "the communitarian approach analyzes the firm as an institution that includes capital holders and employees in the same community – as well as, more recently, what J. K. Galbraith has called 'technostructure,'[27] ... Not a mesh of legal and economic operators set up by and for capital owners, but, to the contrary, an institution that brings together Capital and Labor around a common goal: the interest of the firm" (Supiot 2002: 177).

The observation that the firm is an institution is one of the building blocks of the *political theory of the firm*. But whereas the communitarian approach to the institution of the firm narrows it down to a corporatist perspective, from which the firm appears as a "community" driven by a

---

[24] This is a general statement which holds even in contexts where unions are present, or when employees' views are solicited through dynamic HR policies.

[25] This approach is precisely the *Reductio ad Corporationem* perspective.

[26] See G. Et A. Lyon-Caen (1978: 599).   [27] See Galbraith (1973).

"common interest," the *political theory of the firm* asserts that the firm is
an institution that should be understood in political, and thus in potentially agonistic terms.

Of course, the very question of how exactly to define an institution
is a thorny one: indeed, Boltanski has called it "the disembodied spirit
haunting sociology" (2008: 26). His definition is simple and descriptively
powerful: institutions take up "the task of confirming what is; of describing and prioritizing" (2008: 26). Seen in this light, they are the ultimate
seat of symbolic violence and domination: to confirm, describe, and prioritize reality is to exert power over others' realities. Boltanski cautions
that institutions must be distinguished from "*organizations*, on the one
hand, which hold functions of *coordination*," and "*administrations*, on
the other, which hold *policing* functions." For Boltanski, this makes organizations and administrations "the means institutions must be given in
order to act in the embodied world" (2008: 27). The paradox of the institution, as Boltanski sees it, "which is at the core of sociology's ambivalence toward it, may be summed up as follows. Yes, institutions really are,
as has so often been repeated in the theoretical discourses of the 1960s
and 1970s, instruments that risk being put to the service of *domination*,
and in this sense, they constrain action and bind it within more or less
confining limits. And yet, as those working in the tradition of Durkheim
have repeated time and again, within another set of relations, they are
necessary in that they reduce uncertainty about what is – and that is a necessary condition for action to take place" (2008: 34).[28] A firm is clearly
an institution in the fullest sense of the sociological use of that term. It is
a space in which power relations are expressed and deployed, and, as a
result, in which conflict and potential patterns of domination are a constant. It confirms what is, describes and prioritizes, is the ultimate seat of
symbolic violence and domination, and harbors functions of organization
and administration.[29]

---

[28] "From there, a deep ambivalence toward institutions, which is inherent in all social life.
On the one hand, institutions are trusted, one 'believes' in them. What alternative is
there, since without their intervention, anxiety over what is could only grow, with the
attendant risks of discord, violence, or, at least, dissipation into private languages that
would suppose. But, on the other hand, these institutions are suspected of being mere
fictions, in which the only reality is the human beings that make them up, who speak in
their name, and who, endowed with desires, impulses, etc., possess no particular quality
that would make one inclined to trust them." Boltanski proposes that "in this tension
there is an insurmountable contradiction, which is, in some ways, at the bedrock of shared
social life," which he calls "*hermeneutic contradiction*" (Boltanski 2008: 28–29).

[29] Segrestin (1992) concluded his pioneering work on the firm, the first of its kind in French
sociology, *Sociologie de l'entreprise* (The Sociology of the Firm), published in 1992, with

Organization of the Firm: Networked and Fissured

Organizational sociology has observed dramatic changes in the nature of the firm over time. Sabel's contribution to the organizational perspective bolsters our observation that the nature of work in firms has shifted as the economy has. As he explains it, "the canonical form of [firm] organization in the period from the late nineteenth century to roughly 1980" was typically "hierarchical and closed." According to Chandler (1977), the classic firm in this period was "a vast machine for generating 1 set of rules for decomposing a broad goal into countless small, easily mastered steps, and another set of rules for checking compliance with the first. Subordinates are rewarded for following the rules" (Sabel 2006: 107). This generated massive economies of scale, which led to economic success.

Starting in the 1980s, firms made innovation a top priority, and the dominant form of organization in the rapidly globalizing economy in search of flexibility became and still is "federated and open" (Sabel 2006: 107). Sabel calls these new firms *network firms*, observing that they "manifestly outperform hierarchies in volatile environments, where goals change so quickly that reducing them to a seamless set of task specifications is highly risky, if it is possible at all" (Sabel 2006: 108). In volatile economic environments, characterized by rapidly changing market conditions, the network firm is defined by "the centrality of search routines" for innovation,[30] as these represent an efficient "alternative to the decomposition of tasks as a solution to the problem of bounded rationality" (Sabel 2006: 124). The networked organization makes "a kind of permanent uprising against habit the key to survival in an otherwise unmanageably turbulent world" (Sabel 2006: 107). It is characterized by "organizational routines [that] define methods for choosing provisional, initial designs and production set-ups, and revising them in the light of further review and operating experience. Collaborators are rewarded for achieving broad goals according to standards defined as part of the process by which the goals themselves are set. Rule following entails ... the obligation to propose a new rule when the current one arguably defeats its purpose" (Sabel 2006: 108). According to Sabel, the organization in search of innovation manifests these features because of a "deep sociological truth – long obscured by classic organizational theory – that innovation can only

a chapter titled "Trends: the Firm as Institution." The term referred to the firm's significance, claims, aspirations, and "civic responsibilities" (Segrestin 1992: 213) in the society of the future.
30 To highlight the centrality of this "search" attitude to a new way of organizing the firm he identifies, Sabel (2006) uses "search network" as a synonym for "network firm."

become routine when the innovators are 'loosely coupled' (Weick 1976) – intimate enough to learn from nuance, but detached enough to break with the convention and the habits of the group" (Sabel 2006: 116).

Sabel's contribution is central to the development of the *political theory of the firm* because the consequences of prioritizing innovation over economies of scale have been just as enormous for labor investors as they have been for organizations. Transformations of organizational conditions in order to foster efficiency have produced a range of new ways to deal with human capital. Seeking to maximize their capability to innovate, firms have sought maximal flexibility externally and internally. Externally, through strategies of outsourcing, subcontracting, and offshoring, this transformation led to the emergence of the transnational firm as a so-called supply chain of distinct legal entities driven by a "hub firm" (Chassagnon 2014) or a "lead firm" (Weil 2014) that sustains, organizes, and governs the network (Sabel 2006: 132–139).

Internally, this shift has had an equally dramatic impact: the workplace has become *"fissured,"* according to the metaphor used by Weil (2014), who offers a powerfully evocative description of the contemporary workplace:

twenty years ago, workers in the distribution center of a major manufacturer or retailer would be hired, supervised, evaluated, and paid by that company. Today, workers might receive a paycheck from a labor supplier or be managed by the personnel of a logistics company, while their work is governed by the detailed operating standards of the nationally known retailer or consumer brand serviced by the facility. And whereas IBM in its ascendency directly employed workers from designers and engineers to the people on the factory floor producing its computers, Apple can be our economy's most highly valued company while directly employing only 63,000 of the more than 750,000 workers globally responsible for designing, selling, manufacturing, and assembling its products (2014: 7–8)

Firms employ these fissuring strategies to cut costs. They allow firms to escape their responsibilities to their workers, while maintaining the capability to command them. Weil calls this "having it both ways." Firms "can embrace and institute standards and exert enormous control over the activities of subsidiary bodies"; at the same time, "they can also eschew any responsibility for the consequences of that control" (2014: 12–14). Or, as Robé writes, "by oversimplifying the issues of corporate governance in a globalizing world, the proponents of shareholder value contribute to the sustenance of corporate governance systems which systematically *convert externalities* – costs imposed upon others and the environment, social and natural, via biased governance systems – *into profits."* (Robé 2011: 65) The transformation identified by Sabel, Weil, and others highlights the necessity of a thorough understanding of power relationships in contemporary firms to building an adequate *political theory of the firm*. Rethinking the government of firms is not feasible so long as their current de facto government remains largely invisible, as it is today. The firm as it exists today has been obscured by the corporation, which has been given the limelight while all other aspects of the firm's reality are relegated to the shadows.

Power: Authority, De Jure and De Facto Powers, Intra-Firm and Inter-Firm Relationships

Even if the firm is considered from the (supposedly) narrow lens of private property, the issue of how power is deployed within it, and whether and how that power should be regulated, is a crucial one: as the great legal scholar Morris R. Cohen pointed out long ago, the line separating the principles of sovereignty that apply to politics and those that apply to property is difficult to draw. Arguing that "a property right is a relation not between an owner and a thing, but between the owner and other individuals in reference to things" (1927: 12), Cohen proposed not just an understanding of property but a means to identify its limits. He showed how, in practical terms, property law confronts the same issues at stake in political sovereignty; 1 important example he gave was employer-employee relations. He pled for a non-absolutist understanding of property law, pointing out that it emerged as a field during the political struggles against absolute monarchy that marked the seventeenth and eighteenth centuries. In an equally seminal article published in 1978, Miller extended Cohen's analysis, arguing that because firms had what he called "governing power" over individual lives, they should not be exempted from constitutional rights and responsibilities; in particular, he believed they should guarantee due process (Miller 1978: 189). Miller believed that the time had come to treat firms as private[31] political powers, and that it was legitimate to impose constitutional demands on them.[32]

However, as the preceding subsections have shown, a firm is not just a nexus of contracts or the private property of its shareholders. This is an institution in its own right. As Chassagnon argues, if an institution is a

---

[31] Miller meant that they had internal political power that was distinct from "public" administrative agencies.

[32] Robé's work on the constitutionalization of the firm in the context of the world-system sustains and extends this line of thinking (2011, 2012b) (Robé, Lyon-Caen, Vernac 2016).

place in which power relationships[33] pervasively play at all levels, then it is all the more necessary to the establishment of a *political theory of the firm* to identify concepts and terms that will help to account for the way power is exercised in the firm. The fact that firms have become increasingly networked and fissured makes it more necessary than ever to consider them in terms of the power they deploy and exert: such considerations help to re-inject the issue of responsibility into public conversation about them. In this context, Chassagnon underscores the arguments deployed in the preceding sections, writing (2014: 263), "the boundaries of the firm are no longer defined by property rights and formal contracts, but instead by power relationships (Caniëls and Roeleveld, 2009; Chassagnon 2011a; Chassagnon 2011b)." Chassagnon (2010, 2014) suggests two further distinctions which are helpful in establishing an accurate description the contemporary firm. First, he calls attention to the difference between *intra-* and *inter-firm relationships*, and second, between *de jure* and *de facto powers*. De jure powers are the formal powers conferred by the corporation to agents so that they can sign contracts, or to its officers so that they can exercise authority over workers. De jure powers are always exercised in the context of intra-firm relationships. Chassagnon asserts that

the origins of power are different within and between firms. Intra-firm governance rests on formal and informal mechanisms that are linked with authority and *de jure* power. However, at the inter-firm level, there are no employment contracts that regulate the subordinate relationship between order taker and order maker. Power no longer coexists with authority. In an employment relationship, the transfer of power is understood by its legal definition, whereas in an inter-firm relationship, it is economic dependence that is at the origin of this power. Similarly, *de jure* power that results from the ownership of assets is not a characteristic of inter-firm governance. Power does not work in the same way within and between firms. Only *de facto* power is a source of coordination in the network-firm (Chassagnon 2011b) (Chassagnon 2014: 263).

De facto power mechanisms, as Chassagnon calls them, have been described by Weil as "sophisticated systems [that] establish standards, monitor performance, and reward or punish compliance or noncompliance. It is clear that lead organizations do not lack the capacity to monitor and oversee behavior or creativity to find different organizational forms to implement improved standards, nor do they lack the technologies and systems to make monitoring of the tiers of businesses surrounding them

---

[33] We follow Chassagnon's definition of power (2011b: 39): "power is an individual or collective entity's ability (that will be exerted or not) to structure and restrain choices and actions of another individual or collective entity by some particular mechanism intrinsic to the given social relationship that may be formal, as well as informal."

cost-effective" (Weil 2014: 287–288). As Chassagnon, Weil, and Cohen all show, it is impossible not to observe power relationships within and between firms.

Incompleteness and Goal Setting: The Reconstructive Identification of the Firm, Its Investors, and Their Specific Interests

In his critical study of the economic theory of the firm, Rebérioux points out that, in spite of its initial normative assumptions that a firm exists exclusively to serve its shareholders, this school of thought is fated to evolve from a contractual and shareholder-based understanding of the firm to what he calls a "partner-based" (*partenariale*, in French) understanding of the firm as "an association to pursue a common goal" (2003: 98). Exposing what might be called the substrate of the cooperative nature of production, without which no firm may hope to be productive, Rebérioux describes the firm as a *process* of learning and knowledge building. In so doing he aligns himself with the work of institutionalist economists such as Favereau (1994, 1996, 1998) and Lester and Piore (2004), who see the firm as a context for cognition and situated action, in which defining a common goal is a central problem that is never definitively resolved. Rebérioux concludes his analysis of the limits of transactional cost theory with the observation that "the political structure of the firm is less a response to a contractual problem than it is a response to a problem of defining collective identity" (2003: 100). Building on previous work by Sabel and Rebérioux, we suggest that the firm be understood as a learning process that deploys itself in the context of contested power relations, partially organized through the legal vehicle of one or more corporations, which must constantly work to define and redefine its own common goals. We suggest taking this as the descriptive definition for the *firm as a political entity*.

This returns us to James March's pathbreaking 1962 article, in which he described the firm as a "political coalition." The firm, to him, was a conflict (or conflict resolution) system whose executive was a "political broker." March claimed that "the composition of the firm is not given; it is negotiated. The goals of the firm are not given; they are bargained" (March 1962: 672). March built on the pioneering work of Commons, which showed that the economy is defined by the tensions created by the collective actions and conflicts of its actors, and by the "transactions" these generate. In line with this, institutionalist economists have continued to point to the incompleteness of labor contracts. As a result, some have argued that the firm, as is the industry in which it operates, is a site of political conflict, and must therefore be regulated to some degree by an industrial relations system (Dunlop 1993).

The different actors that make up the firm constantly redefine the purpose of its existence. By investing in the firm, in other words, these actors basically bring the firm to life. Here again, we identify two broad categories of *investor* who make the firm, those who invest their capital and those who invest their labor or their person. Acknowledging that these two investments are fundamentally different brings us back to the observations made in the substantive account of the firm developed earlier in this book. As institutionalist economists have observed, those who invest capital are not involved on a daily basis in the firm, fostering an instrumental attitude toward their investment. By this logic, those who invest their personal presence in the firm will develop an attitude to the firm that is much more shaped by expressive rationality. Since, as has been observed, it is these groups of actors' definition of the firm's goals that makes the firm, both of their specific interests must be taken into consideration for the firm to grow.[34] This view of the firm as a process whose goals are defined by its actors has been broadened by "stakeholders'" approaches to the firm, which has inspired the literature on Corporate Social Responsibility. Whether a broad version of inclusion is retained to define the firm, or whether it is one of the narrower ones discussed earlier, it is clear that a rigorous and comprehensive understanding of a firm's actors – its *polity* – cannot be accurately limited to the shareholders bound by the corporation.

We suggest that the firm's *polity*[35] should be defined as those who are both actively concerned with goal setting, and those who are "affected" by those goals (Gosseries 2012). Building upon Sabel's (2006) analysis, labor investors in the contemporary workplace are involved in search

---

[34] Obviously, this requires further investigation into what is meant by the term "growth." See (Cassiers 2015). Research into alternatives to GDP as a wealth indicator would be useful in considering the firm; for example, see in this light the idea of a "triple bottom line" for a *sustainable* firm according to developments in the Corporate Social Responsibility literature.

[35] This term, originally used as the title for Plato's *Republic*, has no direct equivalent in English. It refers to the city-state as well as to the body of citizens who have an active role in it. In the *Leviathan*, Hobbes uses the term to refer to the state or to the subordinate civil authorities such as provinces, cities, or municipalities as well as to the people living under these jurisdictions. Historically, then, the term connotes a deep connection to a geographic area, and therefore requires rethinking in the context of the *political theory of the firm*, since contemporary firms challenge this connection. This is an additional reason why substituting political entity for polity is justified.

actions in order to innovate, and therefore play a de facto role in goal setting. Only capital investors, however, are officially empowered, via the corporation, to do so. This imbalance affects both categories of actor. As a category, capital investors are more easily identifiable than the labor investors. Indeed, as the firm becomes increasingly networked and fissured upstream and downstream in the supply chain, suppliers, subcontractors, and increasingly, users (such as consumers, and patients), as well as neighbors, might potentially be considered as investing their person in the firm. All of these actors, in other words, are potentially affected by a firm's goals, and therefore have the potential right to participate in goal setting (think, for example, of a user-developer adding a new application to the Apple App Store). In the rest of the text we will consider the most obvious case in this constituency, which is the case of those who invest their person through intensely contributing their labor in the firm –its workers.

The Firm as a Governed Polity, a Political Entity

Building on the foundations of the *political theory of the firm* previously described helps us to avoid the aporia created by the vast body of literature on corporate social responsibility, which has not yet perceived that the firm has yet to be satisfactorily defined as something different from the corporation, both substantively and descriptively. As Robé has written, "the stakeholder proponents, working on the same false assumption that firms and corporations are the same thing and that firms are owned by shareholders, have a hard time advocating alternative governance mechanisms. Since they do not challenge the shareholders' ownership of the firm, they are placed in the position of asking shareholders to give up some of their ownership rights, or to exercise these rights in 'socially responsible' ways, either by arguing that it will be in their own long-term interests to do so or by appealing to their altruism" (Robé 2011: 58).

The descriptive task of the *political theory of the firm* is to identify, in a manner adapted and adaptable to the various stages of development of every firm, how the firm as polity is organized, who is concerned with goal setting, and how its power relationships are institutionally structured. Here we will substitute the term *polity* for *political entity*. We make this choice because the term "entity" has a long history in corporate law, where it is used to identify the incorporated *legal* entity of the corporation. In a seminal paper, Berle (1945) pointed out a potential distinction between the idea of the firm and the idea of the corporation. But the distinction and the link between the two have never been precisely articulated, which is one of the goals this book has set for itself by suggesting that a *political theory of the firm* is needed to account for the stark difference between the structuring of capital into a corporation and the "underlying enterprise," to use Berle's own imprecise terms (1947: 345). Berle's "theory of enterprise entity" rested on the notion – that we share- that there were more parties involved in the enterprise than just shareholders, but did not describe clearly how it was distinct from the *corporation*.[36]

Furthermore, a few economists, including but not limited to Chassagnon (Gindis 2007), (Biondi, Canziani and Kirat 2007), have advanced the notion of the firm as a "real entity," an idea already present in debates at the turn of the twentieth century (Philipps 1994). Chassagnon posited that "the firm as a single, real *entity* is perpetuated by institutional and organizational structures that unify certain particular individual entities into a singular collective entity.... The integration of the entire network cannot be reduced to contract and ownership but must be extended to power arising wherever the effective economic dependence of 1 party upon the other is significant. Power[37] is not exclusively provided by ownership but also by control and access to critical resources" (2011: 114–115). In this same perspective, our suggestion that firms be defined as *political entities* is intended to highlight the crucial distinction that should be made between the corporation and the firm. A larger, real *entity*, deeply connected to the corporation but extending well beyond it, is what makes the firm exist, and the corporation effective. And those relationships, between the particular *corporation* and the larger *firm*, are precisely what we have to clarify. We have suggested that this reality is best understood as *political*, meaning involving ongoing decisions about the goals of the coordinated actions pursued in this framework, which are bound up in issues of efficiency and justice, and which affect the lives of all those involved. The *corporation* should be placed where it belongs, within the larger power structure of the relationships that define the *firm*.

---

[36] This statement is typical in its ambiguity: "the corporation is emerging as an enterprise bounded by economics, rather than as an artificial mystic personality bounded by forms of words in a charter, minute books, and books of account" (Berle 1945: 345).

[37] Chassagnon (2011b: 39) defines power as follows: "in a whole system power is an individual or collective entity's ability (that will be exerted or not) to structure and restrain choices and actions of another individual or collective entity by some particular mechanism intrinsic to the given social relationship that may be formal, as well as informal. By definition, power is the ability to act on and change human behaviors and actions" (see Dahl 1957).

The reconstructive work necessary to identify the contours and content of *firms as political entities* will provide an evaluative tool capable of asking critical questions about firm government and accountability. The institutional design for capital investors in firms is highly developed; for this reason, the *political theory of the firm* will take the bodies established by corporate law seriously; as the vehicle of representation of capital investors. The government of the firm must, however, necessarily include the firm's other constituency, its labor investors, in the goal-setting process, and serve their interests, as well.

A study of the function of the *corporation* as established by law speaks to a reality political philosopher Bernard Manin (1995) has described in vivid terms. He highlights the "distance" that does and ought to exist between a representative government and the citizens. Robé clarifies with regard to the corporation that "the board's governance powers are determined by law and corporate charters and are neither delegated by, nor derived from, the shareholders.... The directors of the corporation have to make their decisions *in the best interests of the corporation*, with a duty of loyalty and a duty of care.... the board of directors is a decision-making body of the corporation, as a *separate* juridical person.... in the management of the corporation, both officers and directors have fiduciary duties towards both the corporation and the shareholders because the shareholders' interests are affected by the power they exercise" (Robé 2011: 30–32). The existing literature on the director's primacy debate, as well as the literature on shareholder democracy might take on new meaning in the context of the *political theory of the firm*. Read in this light, it should help to anticipate the institutional structure of a government of the firm as a *polity* and help to describe the contours of a firm in which labor investors were also granted the right to a say in their government.

The Firm as a Political Actor, Externally

As a first step in the development of the *political theory of the firm*, we have chosen to focus our attention on the inner life of the firm because extensive work remains to be done on the internal life of the firm as a political entity. Yet, its external life is just as important: externally, the firm is a critical political actor (George 2015). It has a strong presence in the traditional political arena, intervening with and at times diminishing the sovereignty of democratic states. Law and globalization studies have followed the development of the transnational firm in the era of global capital mobility, showing the extent to which firms have the potential to extend their reach across territories and resemble sovereign entities in their own right (Sassen 2006, 2014). Consequently, Robé, studying the activities of transnational firms and the conditions under which they conduct them argues that constitutionalizing the power of firms[38] is just as necessary to the well-being of our societies as the constitutionalization of the power of nations (Robé 2011, 2012; Robé, Lyon-Caen, Vernac 2015). The next part of this book will examine precisely this challenge.

The problem of business interests' influence over the state has long been identified and explored extensively by scholars working from the classical Marxist perspective (Miliband 1969). It has received renewed attention as globalization spreads. Fligstein describes how corporations manage to "co-opt political actors" with the goal of "controlling a given market or capturing Congress or regulatory agencies" (Fligstein 2001 12). In recent years, the concept of *regulatory capture* has been given renewed attention, as it highlights how corporate actors manage "to stunt competition and innovation, as firms able to capture their regulators effectively wield the regulatory power of the state and can use it as a weapon to block the entry or success of other firms. Some critics even blame regulatory capture for the outbreak of financial crises and other manmade disasters" (Carpenter and Moss 2013: 1). Distinguishing between an internal dimension and an external one is no easy task, however, particularly in analytical terms – nor should it be. Fannion has examined "the behavior of firms [which] have a political dimension" (Fannion 2006: 38), showing how, because firms are entirely embedded in their environment, their internal challenges have external consequences, and vice versa. Fannion argues that the "governance mechanisms" on which firms rely to function are shaped by state actors, and influence them in return, in a never-ending exchange.

The study of this interplay, and of the external impact of the firm as a political actor, requires as much effort as that of its internal life. Important research on the issue already exists (Kirsch 2014, Urban 2014) and it is beyond the scope of this book, which focuses on the internal life of the firm. Only when both dimensions, internal and external, have been explored will it be possible to build a fully functional *political theory of the firm*, making it possible to better explain and understand our

---

[38] Already in 1990, Collins (1990: 744) advanced the idea that, whatever its specific form, the network firm should be seen as a "united group for the purpose of the ascription of legal responsibility." By the same token, Weil writes that we must find ways to "reestablish that lead companies have some shared responsibility for the condition arising in the network of workplaces they influence through their other activities" (2014: 288).

contemporary reality, and the challenges faced by the projet of a democratic society in the global age.

* *

The previous sections have offered a descriptive account of the firm in an attempt to show the tremendous advantage of moving from a simplistic *economic theory of the firm*, which equates the firm and *corporation* – the view we identify as practicing *Reductio ad Corporationem* – to an account of the *firm* that seeks to comprehend its complex reality. This book discusses firms mature enough and large enough to be run by an executive committee composed of a group of professional officers hired by the corporation and given the authority to mobilize that *corporation*'s assets to fund the endeavor pursued by the *firm*. The corporation is the legal entity created to structure the input of capital investors. Yet, the firm is a much larger reality, a fundamentally *political entity*, one that has not yet been properly understood and has yet to be addressed as such by the law. This is the task we assign to the *political theory of the firm*. This perspective understands the firm substantively, not as the *locus* of expansion of pure instrumental rationality, but as a governed polity, institutionally structured, combining instrumental with expressive rationality, and animated by its main carriers, labor and capital investors who both engage in goal setting and are affected in return. These two bodies of investors both take multiple kinds of risks and have specific interests in the endeavor that they pursue together through the firm. The descriptive challenge we face is to fully apprehend the *political entity* that is the firm, to look past the thick shadows cast by the corporation over the progress of the firm itself, and over the success and prosperity of democracy as a whole. Having laid the foundations of a substantive and a descriptive account of the firm, we may now turn to the third, normative challenge this *political theory of the firm* raises in describing the firm for what it is when considered using the analytical categories of political analysis and theory: a *political entity* in a specific historical context, our capitalist democracies, in a global age still committed to the democratic ideal.

I shall not be surprised if the experts on corporation law should at first regard my suggestions as wildly impracticable...

This, however, is no reason for not seriously examining these possibilities, even if it were only in order to free ourselves from the belief that the developments which have taken place were inevitable.

It is probable that on the [idea] I want to consider the existing arrangements were adopted, not by deliberate choice and in awareness of the consequences, but because the alternatives *were never seriously considered.*

Friedrich A. Hayek (1960: 110)

PART III

LOOKING TO THE FUTURE

From Political Bicameralism to Economic Bicameralism

P art III of this book will address the normative challenge raised by
Parts I and II. The critical history of capitalist democracies given in
Part I showed that the government of the firm is to be considered in light of
the steady emancipation of work from the domestic regime of the private
sphere, and its expansion into the public sphere of our democratic societies, and, within this, its transition from being governed despotically to
being governed democratically. This process of transition continues today,
as described in Part II, which showed that, as the economy has become
network- and service-based, the firm, behind the legal shadow of the corporation now obscuring it, is more accurately accounted for as *a political
entity, moved by specific actors, capital investors and labor investors, and
driven by two distinct rationalities, the instrumental and the expressive.*
Part III will look to the future, and specifically, to the issue of how the
capitalist firm might continue to evolve in the public sphere with a form
and structure that reflect our society's commitment to democracy. To this
end we will examine the idea of bicameral government, an institutional
design mechanism that has played a key role in transitional moments of
history on the long road to free and democratic societies, this process of
transition being still underway.

We have seen how the institutional design that governs capitalist firms
mistaken as corporations rests on a single, basic misconception – that
firms are driven by instrumental rationality alone. Over the past two
centuries, the labor movement has helped to make fundamental changes
to work and to firms, through concessions to the expressive rationality
of workers (think of policies that address basic integrity, employee
health, decent wages and working time, recognition and appreciation,

motivation, etc.). All the same, and despite in some more privileged settings and countries the establishment of works councils and other representative bodies responsible for informing employees and negotiating on their behalf, there has been no change to *the basic understanding of the firm as serving the corporation* – nor were these bodies intended for that purpose. Labor is still seen by most as a production factor among others, and the relationship between labor investors and their labor continues to be thought of in instrumental terms: employees work for pay. Even the labor movement all too often functions from this point of view, framing investment in firms in instrumentalist terms. Actions are pursued for ends other than themselves, in other words: capital is invested in order to earn dividends; labor is invested in order to earn wages.

All contemporary capitalist firms are governed nondemocratically[1]. Their government might be described as "capitalo-cratic," in that capital investors hold power over the firm via the corporation. Still, since firms are perceived as operating on the basis of instrumental rationality alone, it appears logical and legitimate that they be governed by their capital investors, as the latter will best represent and guarantee that instrumental rationality. From this perspective, it is only reasonable that the *polity* include the shareholders of the corporation alone: they alone are the legitimate bearers of instrumental rationality. The firm is their tool for earning profit; its governance is there to ensure the tool serves that purpose as efficiently as possible – what could there be to debate?

---

[1] Except for some efforts worth mentioning through which a CEO or principle shareholders behave as enlightened despots and decide to "free" their employees, a "liberation process" that hands decision-making power to employees. While power over managerial decisions (those regarding the means of production) may become democratized, this does not mean that these powers extend to issues of government (those regarding ends). For a crucial analytical distinction between participating in management and participating in government, see Part I. For detailed existing examples, see Semler, Carney and Getz, and Laloux. Typically, in these experiments, enlightened despots see an increase in workers' satisfaction and productivity. But these corporate despots do not go on to fully share the government and decision-making power over issues such as profit-sharing, which remain the prerogatives of the board of the corporation. These cases prove the ultimate power of "the spirit of capitalism," which is able to absorb criticism and turn it to its advantage (see Max Weber' seminal work, or more recently Boltanski and Chiapello 2006). In this current phase, it would seem that employees' political critiques (Ferreras 2007) – that is, their intuition of democratic justice, which leads them to expect to participate in decisions that concern them – has been taken into consideration, but rarely to the point of including them in goal-setting, or sharing power over the firm as a whole with them.

Seen in this light, capital investors bear more than a passing resemblance to absolute monarchs,[2] and while the *legitimacy* of their rule has sometimes been questioned in these terms, its *logic* has gone largely unnoticed. But it is the logic of this perspective to which I wish to call attention now: the power structure of the firm is debatable because it is founded on a questionable assumption. Moreover, I would argue that it is founded on a kind of intellectual sleight of hand, one that opened the way to a political incursion that has never been questioned. For it is an assumption that firms are (and ought to be) governed by capital investors – it is hypothesis, not certainty; an axiom but not a law. Firms are called "capitalist" in recognition of capital investors' supposed *ownership* of the firm, while we now know(see Part II) that what they actually own are shares in the corporation. The time has come to take note of this essential distinction. The capitalist *firm* is not driven or definable by a single rationality. It is not, by law of nature, the vehicle of the corporation.

The intellectual leap to be made here is as simple analytically as it is radical in terms of its practical consequences: the capitalist *firm* is driven by both instrumental and expressive rationalities, and its government must no longer privilege one over the other. By the same token, it must cease to give 1 portion of its investors a say while leaving the other in near silence. It must, in other words, cease to favor capital investors over labor investors. But how to right this imbalance? How to create an institution that recognizes this duality? History offers the foundations of an answer to this question, in the development of bicameral politics. Liberal, representative democracies grew from widespread recognition of the duality of interests in the societies they were designed to represent. Indeed, recognizing this duality was the linchpin of Western society's emancipation from absolute monarchy. The parallel between absolute monarchy and *capital investor*–controlled firms is a fertile one. It allows us to move past considering the degree of enlightenment of those in power, and on into questions about how their power might efficiently and effectively be shared. Just as government was redesigned as society shifted away from absolute monarchy, so must the government of the firm be redesigned so it is responsible to both of its constituent bodies: not just to capital investors, but to labor

---

[2] As monarchs claim to rule for the good of all. In *Politics* (III.7), Aristotle articulated this difference between monarchy and tyranny: he defined monarchy as the reign of a single person for the good of the collective, and tyranny as a corrupt form of monarchy, in which a single person reigns for his good alone. A classic justification for capital owners' monopoly over the government of the firm is indeed the utility of monarchy in its just form. See Aristotle (350BC), Turchetti (2008).

investors, as well. Just as most modern democratic governments possess governing bodies that check and balance the different interests at work in society, so must firm governments be endowed with a form of legislature that represents its different constitutive interests in decisions concerning the life of the firm, so that each body is forced to cooperate with the other to form a single legislative power, the firm's "parliament," composed of two "chambers."

The History of Rome. The Sacred Mount Secession or *Secessio Plebis* (BC 494) Book II. Chapter 32

Thereupon the senators became alarmed, fearing that if the army should be disbanded there would again be secret gatherings and conspiracies....This brought the revolt to a head....without orders from the consuls [the legions] withdrew to the Sacred Mount, which is situated across the river Anio, three miles from the City. – This version of the story is more general than that given by Piso, namely that the Aventine was the place of their secession. – There, without any leader, they fortified their camp with stockade and trench, and continued quietly, taking nothing but what they required for their subsistence, for several days, neither receiving provocation nor giving any.

...There was a great panic in the City, and mutual apprehension caused the suspension of all activities. The plebeians, having been abandoned by their friends, feared violence at the hands of the senators; the senators feared the plebeians who were left behind in Rome, being uncertain whether they had rather they stayed or went. Besides, how long would the seceding multitude continue peaceable? What would happen next if some foreign war should break out in the interim? Assuredly no hope was left save in harmony amongst the citizens, and this they concluded they must restore to the state by fair means or foul. They therefore decided to send as an ambassador to the commons Agrippa Menenius, an eloquent man and dear to the plebeians as being one of themselves by birth.

...On being admitted to the camp he is said merely to have related the following apologue, in the quaint and uncouth style of that age: In the days when man's members⁴ did not all agree amongst themselves, as is now the case, but had each its own ideas and a voice of its own, the other parts thought it unfair that they should have the worry and the trouble and the labour of providing everything for the belly, while the belly remained quietly in their midst with nothing to do but to enjoy the good things which they bestowed upon it; they therefore conspired together that the hands should carry no food to the mouth, nor the mouth accept anything that was given it, nor the teeth grind up what they received. While they sought in this angry spirit to starve the belly into submission, the members themselves and the whole body were reduced to the utmost weakness. Hence it had become clear that even the belly had no idle task to perform, and was no more nourished than it nourished the rest, by giving out to all parts of the body that by which we live and thrive, when it has been divided equally amongst the veins and is enriched with digested food – that is, the blood. Drawing a parallel from this to show how like was the internal dissension of the bodily members to the anger of the plebs against the Fathers [the Senators], he prevailed upon the minds of his hearers.

The Right to Name Two Tribunes of the Plebs (BC 493) Book II.
Chapter 33

Steps were then taken towards harmony, and a compromise was effected on these terms: the plebeians were to have magistrates of their own, who should be inviolable, and in them should lie the right to aid the people against the consuls, nor should any senator be permitted to take this magistracy. And so they chose two "tribunes of the people [the plebs]."

The Sharing of the Conquered Territory among the Plebs (BC 479) Book II. Chapter 48

On taking office his first concern was neither war nor the raising of troops nor anything else, save that the prospect of harmony which had been already partly realized should ripen at the earliest possible moment into a good understanding between the patricians and the plebs. He therefore proposed at the outset of his term that before one of the tribunes should rise up and advocate a land-law, the Fathers [the Senators] themselves should anticipate him by making it their own affair and bestowing the conquered territory upon the plebs with the utmost impartiality; for it was right that they should possess it by whose blood and toil it had been won.

Livy

7

Bicameral Moments

A Pivotal Institutional Innovation for Governments in Democratic Transition

The history of the transition from despotism to democracy, and particularly the history of the bicameral legislative design that has emerged at revolutionary moments, offers a rich anchor point for thinking about how the institutional structure of firms might evolve. Because the duality visible in modern bicameralism can be seen as a constant in Western political history, it is helpful to discuss the invention of modern bicameralism from the perspective of its origins. Indeed, I posit that this duality has been driving the advance of political freedom in the West since Roman times.

In Ancient Rome, citizens were divided into two categories: patricians and plebeians (Ellul 1961). Patricians owned the vast majority of land and slaves and spent their time pursuing noble occupations (*otium*, or leisure) such as politics and the art of war. The plebeians comprised the inferior social strata (excluding slaves), who worked as manual laborers or tradesmen, or lived marginal lives of delinquency and poverty. They did not participate in political life. The Senate, Rome's consultative body, was elected by patricians alone, and legislative and executive functions were exercised by two "magistrates," or *consuls*, chosen from among the patrician class. This continued until the beginning of the fifth century BCE, when the people rebelled in an event known as the *Secessio Plebis*. Livy's account describes how members of the plebeian class came together in a body to confront the patricians. The outcome of this conflict was an historic political compromise, through which the equal rights of plebeians were slowly recognized. One immediate result of this confrontation was the creation of a Tribune of the Plebs, to which plebeians had the right to name two magistrates. These magistrates were given what was known as "negative sovereignty" (Ellul 1961: 272), meaning that while they exercised no active power, they had both preventive (*prohibitio*) and a posteriori (*intercessio*) veto rights, as Michel Humbert explains (2007: 303). As Jacques Ellul explains, Rome's two consuls thenceforth needed the approval of the plebeian magistrates to govern, since the latter could block any of their decisions. Consuls maintained exclusive legislative and executive power, but their "negative sovereignty" gave the Tribunes *auxilium plebis*, a voice of opposition that allowed them to block consular decisions they considered "harmful to the plebs" (Ellul id.).

The episode Livy describes bears testament to how old this political duality really is. Since his time, it has become a constant in political relations. Marx identified and described it as "class conflict." Seen positively or negatively, it undeniably is embedded in the social structure generated by capitalism: from slaveholding to feudalism to capitalism, the history of the Western world has turned on the profits earned by the few exploiting the many, with each era characterized by the dominance of a given social group or class over another. Whatever the utility of the concept of class "conflict," may be, it masks a simpler and more fundamental aspect of political structures and their evolution. Leaving the notion of conflict aside, society is always structured around fundamental cleavages (Lipset and Rokkan, 1967), meaning that it is always composed of at least two encompassing interest groups. It is their recognition of one another, whatever the differences in their status, that makes social cooperation possible. This recognition may occur through conflict, but conflict is not necessary for it to occur. The organicist analogy used by Menenius Agrippa in Livy's account demonstrates the social solidarity that can emerge from recognizing this cleavage. Ancient Roman society's intuition that its two constituent parts were interdependent both necessitated and justified the compromise they ultimately reached:[1] each group fulfilled a different role; each one was necessary to the other. The human body has been used as an analogy, as well: the stomach requires hands, hands require teeth, and so on. This primitive functionalism, which grew from the idea of reciprocity, gave rise to an impressively powerful strategy, which expanded through the Middle Ages (Gierke 1900, Coker 1910,

---

[1] Nachi and de Nanteuil (2005) study compromise as particularly well adapted to the government of complex societies. They refer to this quote from Aristotle's *Politics*: "in the realm of measurement, compromise lies at the middle. In the realm of virtue, it is the summit."

Lewis 1938, Archambault 1967, Hale 1971) and is visible in Talcott Parsons's conception of modernity, which drew on Emile Durkheim's concept of organic solidarity (Durkheim 1893). At last, tracing the bicameral impulse back to the *Secessio Plebis*[2] is relevant because of the tremendous impact it had on Roman society: the fruits of the conflict between plebians and patricians, because together they found a way to transform structural exploitation into productive cooperation, made social cooperation possible again. Soldiers returned to their camps and merchants to their stalls; Rome breathed anew. The dawn of the fifth century marked the beginning of an era of unprecedented prosperity.

---

[2] It is Michel Serres, a great reader of Livy, who pointed out to me the roots of bicameralism in this formative moment in Rome's history.

The consideration which tells most, in my judgment, in favour of two Chambers ... is the evil effect produced upon the mind of any holder of power, whether an individual or an assembly, by the consciousness of having only themselves to consult. It is important that no set of persons should, in great affairs, be able, even temporarily, to make their sic volo prevail, without asking any one else for his consent. A majority in a single assembly, when it has assumed a permanent character – when composed of the same persons habitually acting together, and always assured of victory in their own House – easily becomes despotic and overweening, if released from the necessity of considering whether its acts will be concurred in by another constituted authority. The same reason which induced the Romans to have two Consuls, makes it desirable there should be two Chambers: that neither of them may be exposed to the corrupting influence of undivided power, even for the space of a single year."

John Stuart Mill (1861: 385)

MODERN REASONS FOR BICAMERAL LEGISLATURE

The Great Modern Example: The British Compromise

Although the roots of bicameralism stretch back to ancient Rome, it was not until the thirteenth century CE that the ancestor of the modern-day bicameral legislature was developed in Britain. As British historians remind us in their account of the origins of political bicameralism in England[3], this innovation came about when the King of England decided it would be prudent to consult the land-owning aristocracy and the heads of the Church when making major decisions; eventually, these consultations came to include representatives of towns and counties. Rather than risk losing power, the king chose to share it.

The House of Commons met for the first time in 1377, independently of what would become the House of Lords. England's two-house parliament expresses a dualist ontology of society with landowners on 1 side and the people (or at least their representatives) on the other. In its early years, the parliament's power was extremely limited and subordinate to the king's, but the Magna Carta, signed in 1215, established the rule of taxation by consent, a prerogative that parliament would later use as leverage to strengthen its position with regard to the king.[4] When the Stuarts attempted to raise taxes without parliament's consent in the seventeenth century, revolution broke out and Cromwell took power.

---

[3] We rely on Derek Hirst (1975), Donald Shell (2001).

[4] Article 12 of the Magna Carta, signed on June 15, 1215, by John Lackland, King of England. "No scutage or aid shall be imposed in our kingdom except by the common council of our kingdom" (Magna Carta, 1215).

Although the monarchy was restored with James II, the political crisis was not fully resolved until William of Orange acceded to the throne in 1689, following the Glorious Revolution. The bicameral legislature only became an established in the eighteenth century, after years of unrest, civil war, regicide, and the temporary abolition of both the monarchy and the House of Lords. The case of England, reminds us that, as in the Rome of antiquity, the establishment of a bicameral legislature represents a compromise struck to ensure and maintain social cohesion. In 1 way or another, such compromise is always reached from a context of civil unrest, deep social tensions, violence, and even war, for it helps transition societies toward more democratized forms of government.

Modern legal scholars and political theorists have justified the expedience of the bicameral legislature in different ways, which may be divided into three main categories. All three of these types of justification have been produced at various points in history to support the establishment of a government based on bicameral legislative power.

Condition of Legitimate Government

William of Orange, at the turn of the eighteenth century, instituted the principle of separation of powers when he acceded to the throne, taking the English Revolution's principle of democratic power to its logical conclusion and placing legislative power in the hands of parliament, and retaining executive powers for the throne. That the English Revolution enshrined the fundamental distinction between its House of Commons, which was recognized as representing the people, and the House of Lords, which "represented property" (Shell 2001: 9) is the lynchpin of our historical argument: *both together* were considered to be the legitimate source of legislative power, and both were considered necessary to the proper functioning of British society. Britain resolved its social conflict by recognizing that it was composed of two social groups with differing interests; it resolved its democratic revolution with class compromise. Britain accepted the existence of classes with conflicting constituencies as reality, and rather than trying to suppress or efface the conflict, obliged the two conflicting classes to cooperate with each other.

This solution laid the foundations for the balance of powers, a doctrine that would gather influence as time went on.[5] At the time of the

---

[5] The United Kingdom and the United States use different terms to describe the same idea: in general, the English refer to the theory of mixed government and Americans to checks and balances.

Great Reform Act of 1832, there was no interest in doing away with the House of Lords in the name of advancing democracy; rather "of greater concern than any desire to democratize the system was the perceived need to prevent the House of Lords from losing the independence essential for it to fulfill the balancing role demanded of it by the classical theory of the constitution" (Shell 2001: 9).

Condition of Reasonable Government

The theory of the separation and balance of power attracted America's founding fathers to bicameral politics, though they did not at first justify bicameralism in those terms; it was adopted in the first instance as a means of federating the states. The fledgling United States implemented bicameralism for reasons different from those in Britain, however: the former colony employed it as a path to compromise between state and federal interests. The Senate was given the role of federating the states in an American union: each state, no matter its population, elected two senators to this "chamber." The House of Representatives was organized based on the principle of proportional representation. The number of state representatives elected to this chamber was determined by a state's population. The two together composed the Congress, a bicameral representative body with a Senate that recognizes states as individual entities with equal rights and powers, and a House of Representatives that federates the population as a whole, across those states.[6]

As Gordon Wood points out, the separation and balance of powers was only given as a justification for bicameralism after the Philadelphia Constitutional Convention, in response to criticism from anti-federalists, who were opposed to the idea of a House of Representatives (Wood 1969: 552). In the case of the United States, the true justification for bicameralism was in large part an issue of the balance of powers (Dehousse 1990), "and, more specifically... the Madisonian idea of the necessity of a protection against the risk of factionalism" (Doria 2006: 20). Swift (1996) describes a Senate designed to be an "American House

---

[6] The *Federalist Paper* #39 by James Madison: "the House of Representatives will derive its powers from the people of America; and the people will be represented in the same proportion and on the same principle as they are in the legislature of a particular State. So far, the government is national, not federal. The Senate, on the other hand, will derive its powers from the States as political and coequal societies; and these will be represented on the principle of equality in the Senate, as they are now in the existing Congress. So far, the government is federal, not national" (in Doria 2006: 13).

of Lords" made up of a smaller number of members who, instead of a title, could boast "high social and economic status, substantial political autonomy, and sweeping legislative and executive power" (Swift 1996: 47). This, as Giancarlo Doria explains, because the Senate was supposed to be "a bulwark against the excesses of democracy, and particularly of popular transient impressions – as part of that system of check and balances which they were beginning to consider the true essence[7] of the new, republican government" (Doria 2006: 24)[8].

This sort of pacifying virtue also comes through in the second chamber's function as a bridge, a buffer, or a facilitator in relation to its counterpart or the executive power in the form of president or king, depending on the situation (Shell 2001: 10).

Condition of Intelligent Government

Doria, citing Madison, identifies two ways in which the existence of a senate is crucial to the pursuit of reasonable government: first, senators are independent from the people, thanks to longer terms of office; second, they possess greater wisdom than other elected officials, because they know they are "the true depository of the state's highest interest" (Doria 2006: 26). Intelligent government is the ultimate justification for bicameral politics: two chambers, working together, exercise power more wisely and make more intelligent decisions than they would working alone. In Mill's words, it counters "the evil effect produced upon the mind of any holder of power, whether an individual or an assembly, by the consciousness of having only themselves to consult." (Mill 1861: 385). A second chamber ensures there is a place for mature and reasoned argument in the legislative process; as Shell puts it, it "allow[s] for second thoughts" (2001: 10). This is, in other words, a very basic argument for the epistemic superiority of democratic government (Landemore 2012, 2014; Landemore and Elster 2012).

---

[7] Montesquieu is widely cited as the main inspiration for the American federalists' theory of the balance of powers, but it would seem that the Greek philosopher Polybius deserves at least as much of the credit (Lloyd 1998). See also James Madison, the *Federalist Papers*, Nos. 51 and 63.

[8] Doria also points out that bicameralism was a ready solution for the American founding fathers, since the federated states were already organized into bicameral parliaments. For him, this is further proof that America's founders were not motivated by the goal of a federal union, but by their desire to achieve a balance of power; indeed, at the state level this was the principle used to justify bicameralism (Doria 2006: 24).

Legislative power exercised by equal chambers that complement, confront, and balance one another is one of political history's most important inventions. Over the centuries, the institution of the bicameral parliament has been instrumental in shifting power from the hands of a single person (tyranny or monarchy) to a small number of people (oligarchy) to the majority (democracy). Broadly speaking, every state's transition to democratic (or at least more democratic) government has at least passed through a bicameral phase. It remains highly relevant in political democracy. Certain contemporary commentators have claimed bicameralism is losing its meaning and influence, but the fact remains that more than half of nations today, including all federal countries, are governed by bicameral assemblies. Indeed, constitutional scholar Francis Delpérée described a "fervor for bicameralism in the four corners of the world. Today, sixty-eight countries (in other words, half again as many as in 1970) possess a senate" (Delpérée 2004: 5).

Bicameral moments that created two-chamber legislatures have taken place under many different historical circumstances. Yet, they have always been justified based on the three ideas previously reviewed: legislative representation through bicameral politics is identified as a necessary condition for a *legitimate* government (class compromise or concord among heterogeneous subnational entities), for a *reasonable* or limited government (balance of power theory) and for *intelligent* government (rational representation). The latter two justifications are complementary. Their effects are collateral, but also desirable in and of themselves: our common wish to be governed reasonably and intelligently, through legitimate, viable compromises between society's two constituent bodies, drives bicameral innovation.

The *political theory of the firm* can serve as an evaluative theory, as well. As we have reviewed, the *firm is a political entity* central to our global capitalist era *and* to the future of capitalist democracies. If we do not treat it as such, as discussed in the Introduction with the help of Polanyi, we put the future of the democratic project itself at risk. The section that follows continues this line of argument, and shows why and how the bicameral approach should be extended to firms.

8

Analogy

The Executive of the Firm Answering to a Two-Chamber Parliament

JUSTIFICATION

Pre-democratic politics were criticized using exactly the same arguments that can now be made against the current manner in which corporate firms are governed: the way power is deployed in firms today is *not legitimate, not reasonable, and not intelligent.* As Part II explains, the firm should be understood as a *political entity* whose existence relies on the combining of instrumental and expressive rationality – and on the continued collaboration of its *capital investors* and its *labor investors.* We have suggested that these be acknowledged as the firm's two constituent bodies. As the history of capitalism shows, capital investors have from the beginning held political rights in the form of the power to decide upon the future of their joint enterprise, organized through the corporation, which then becomes a legal cloth covering up the firm. The rights of labor investors have not been so broadly recognized, nor so well organized. Part I of this book reviewed the critical history of power in the firm, and showed how labor has shifted from a form of managed subordination toward a position of knowledge contribution that would justify a claim to a role in the government of the firm. As yet, labor investors have not been recognized as full partners in the firm's government: the system of power relations governing capitalist firms currently in place recognizes only the need to represent the *instrumental rationality* of capital investors, and their interests, via the *corporation.* The *expressive rationality* that workers invest in the workplace has not yet been acknowledged as an equally important factor in the life and success of firms. As a result, the right of a firm's employees to a voice in its government in order to ensure that their rationality is accounted for has not been recognized either, despite the fact that the expressive logic of the worker is just as necessary to the life of the firm as the instrumental logic of the capital investor.

In light of this state of affairs, it seems appropriate to qualify contemporary capitalist firms' government as *illegitimate*, given that only one of their two constituent bodies is represented in their government. By the same token it may be deemed *unreasonable*, in that it places the government of the firm in the hands of the corporation, i.e. the vehicle organizing its capital investors, and is thus specifically designed to serve their interests. As a consequence, we have now reached an historic peak in the distortion of the interests served by boards, with intra-firm pay inequality – between the compensation of entry-level jobs and the CEO – reaching historic levels (Gabaix and Landier 2008, Barth, Bryson, Davis, Freeman, 2014). There is also every reason to doubt that this kind of governance features any excess of *intelligence*. The Western economy is a service economy – also known as a "knowledge economy": it is based on innovation and efficiency. In such an economy, the strategic and operational management of firms serves no purpose without their employees' knowledge. To achieve the innovative and competitive edge necessary to keep pace with the demands of their customers and their markets, firms must maintain a kind of flexibility foreign to the Taylorist model, in which design and execution were kept separate. In such a flexible age, Sabel (1994) argued that the design of a product or service can no longer be thought of as separate from its execution. In the context of the contemporary service economy, this extends to the moment of sale, which should be generally thought of as an integral part of the production process. The financial industry before the 2008 crisis is one example: front desk employees at banks have testified that they were pressured to sell as many loans as possible even though they were aware that they were not appropriate to recommend to all the clients they were expected to sell to. Many, too, have now spoken out about their inability to explain the derivatives they had been instructed to sell, or about their discomfort over granting loans to clients whose profiles made them ineligible according to classic prudential criteria (Honegger, Neckel, and Magnin, 2010). But of course these banks' employees had no voice in the determination of company strategy: return on capital investment was the sole principle guiding commercial policies. Can such government be qualified as *legitimate, reasonable,* and *intelligent*? If the firms that drive our economy are governed in a manner that is arguably illegitimate, unreasonable, and unintelligent, it seems only rational to call that system of government it into question, and to dig deeper to find better solutions.

As we saw in Part II of this book, if we are to fully apprehend the firm as it actually is, we must acknowledge that it is an entity upon which an ideological misconception has been projected: the firm, as we have seen, is not actually driven by instrumental rationality alone. To restrict our understanding of the firm to its economic aspects, defined by its balance sheet and bottom line, would be as limited as seeing the state as a mere economic structure designed to balance budgets, collect taxes, and pay benefits. While we all recognize that conceptions of justice are embodied in the decisions taken by the state – how do we want to recognize and reward each other? What do we owe each other as fellow citizens? What do we want to secure collectively? – we are still living in the shadow of both liberal and Marxist theories that do not recognize the questions of justice that inform the firm as an entity[1]. Yet, when considered less from an abstract or ideological perspective, and more from a more empirically grounded one, it must be acknowledged that the firm is founded on – and its success made possible by – the encounter between two rationalities, the one *instrumental*, the other *expressive* and containing conceptions of justice; in an era of global capitalism, the one primarily held by capital investors, the other by labor investors. This is all the more true if we choose to measure success and efficiency not only in terms of financial productivity, but also in terms of "social performance" – significantly, employees' well-being, labor relations that foster collaboration and innovation, or respect for the environment. In a service economy with high human added-value, in our innovation- and knowledge-based economy, where even manual labor requires more training and commitment than ever before, continuing to ignore the *expressive* rationality driving labor

---

[1] Examining the issue of the extension of democracy into the economic sphere, Cohen (1989) identified the "parallel case argument" as the most convincing: "since enterprises comprise forms of cooperation for common benefit, and workers have the capacity to assess the rules that regulate workplace cooperation, they have a right to determine those rules through their own deliberation. The deliberative ideal of justification carries over from the state to firms" (Cohen 1989: 46). This analogy has been fiercely fought, however. Landemore and Ferreras (2016) tested its robustness by considering 6 major objections to it: (1) the objection from a difference in ends, (2) the objection from shareholders' property rights, (3) the objection from workers' consent, (4) the objection from workers' exit opportunities, (5) the objection from workers' (lack of) expertise, and (6) the objection from the fragility of firms. All of these objections were found invalid, and the authors concluded from this that there is a crucial need for further descriptive work accounting for what a firm is – one of the goals behind the present book.

investors in firms risks damaging not only our democracies, but the productivity of firms, and the economy as a whole. If this damage is to be avoided, it must be acknowledged that the existence and the success of a capitalist firm relies on two rationalities, held by the firm's two constituent bodies, and that these two rationalities are incommensurable, cannot replace one another, and must collaborate, cooperate, and compromise.

Extending the tradition of bicameral innovation to the economic realm would inscribe the firm as an institution in its own right in the history of democratization, and complete the historic shift that is the emancipation of work from the private sphere (see Part I). It is fruitful, to this end, to examine what it might mean in concrete terms to grant labor investors the same right to representation in the government of a firm's affairs as that which has long been accorded to capital investors via the corporation. Bearing in mind the political compromises of historic bicameral moments, from Rome in the fifth century BCE to the English monarchy in the fourteenth century to the American founding fathers in the eighteenth century, as well as myriad European and non-European nations in the nineteenth and twentieth centuries, this section will consider the proposal of an appropriate government for the firm, which means, in practical terms, that labor investors name representatives to a chamber of their own. These representatives would sit in a *Labor Investors' Chamber of Representatives*, alongside the Chamber of Capital Owners (currently known as the board of directors, supervisory board, etc.), which would be renamed to reflect its constituents: the *Capital Investors' Chamber of Representatives*. Such a structure, we argue, would allow us to say that power in the capitalist firm is exercised *legitimately, reasonably*, and *intelligently*, as it would hold its directors, or executive board members, responsible before a single parliament composed of two chambers, rather than before a "chamber" of capital investors alone, as is currently the case in the corporate firm.

RELATIONS BETWEEN THE TWO CHAMBERS

As we have seen earlier, a bicameral legislature is characterized by "the idea of mutual and reciprocal surveillance that...itself is built on the famous dialectical combination of the powers of action and restraint, or, to paraphrase Montesquieu, the faculties of deciding and preventing" (Pierre-Caps 2004: 358–359). This equilibrium informs the way the two chambers relate to one another, as well as their relationship as a parliament[2] to the executive branch, which constitutes the government in the strictest sense of that word.

Bicameralism offers a number of different alternatives in the determination of the role assigned to any given parliament. To use Philip Norton's terminology (1984), parliamentary models all fall somewhere along a spectrum, which ranges from "policy-influencing" on one end to "policy-making" on the other. Here, Norton is elaborating on Nelson Polsby's classic analysis (1975), which contrasted parliaments that functioned as "arenas" with those functioning as "policy transformers." According to Norton (1984: 20), the weak legislature of the British Parliament falls on one end of this spectrum – parliament as arena. At the other end is the U.S. Congress, whose broad parliamentary mandate allows it to draft and propose laws – parliament as policy transformer. Most countries, including most in Continental Europe, lie somewhere between the two extremes. Norton further nuanced his idea (2010) with reference to Jean Blondel's concept of "legislative viscosity" (1970), which measures a legislature's influence on the legislation process. Legislative viscosity describes the extent to which a legislature is able to resist the advance of a law drafted by a government, by slowing it or even blocking it (through veto power), and to force the government to negotiate, change the text of the draft law, and accept proposed amendments. This viscosity may go so far as to allow the legislature to propose its own laws. If a legislature holds all these powers it is considered to be highly "viscous." Depending on how bicameralism is applied in the construction of a parliament, the executive branch may have the upper hand in government, or it may find itself in competition with the legislature.

Let us imagine a classic structure modeled on parliamentary democracy applied to a firm: in a bicameral firm, its top management, or executive committee, would constitute the executive branch of government. Members of the executive branch would be appointed by and held accountable to the firm's two chambers, who would hold seats won through legislative elections. The executive branch would have to be approved by a majority in both chambers – that is, 50% + 1 vote in each. More sophisticated governmental arrangements do exist, in which the legislature is composed

---

[2] In the context of bicameral representation, the term "parliament" is used to designate a two-chamber, legislative branch of government. Practically speaking, different nations have different traditions and different terms. Thus, we speak of the U.S. Senate and House of Representatives as "Congress," while the French Senate and National Assembly are known as "Parlement or Congrès du Parlement," the House of Lords and Commons of the UK known simply as "Parliament," etc.

through uncoordinated election cycles that yield different (asymmetric) majorities in the two chambers, with the executive branch appointed at still other moments in the election cycle. This is notably the case in the United States, where the framers of the Constitution intentionally sought to secure powerful checks and balances of power, which were created using the divided and competing influences of the legislative, the executive, and the judicial branches of government. The theoretical scheme followed here, in which the executive is appointed by the legislature, is simpler, a more classic and less extreme version that does not reflect the internal division of American bicameralism.[3]

As is the case in our bicameral democracies, the first act of the firm government upon taking office would be to issue a policy statement in the form of a management plan. This would indicate its main goals for the firm and the initiatives it proposes to pursue. Based on this, the executive government would (or would not) obtain the approval of the firm's two chambers through a majority vote (50 % + 1) in *both* the Capital Investors' Chamber of Representatives in the Labor Investors' Chamber of Representatives.

Of course, the viscosity of firm parliaments is open for debate and reflection: we might imagine high viscosity on all issues, or a viscosity that varies depending on the issue at hand. From the point of view of the overall efficiency of institutional design, it seems reasonable to choose a structure in which the firm's executive branch had more control over the legislative agenda, leaving its parliament the role of "arena" in which laws are passed or vetoed, without necessarily being proposed.

The essential – and sought-after – effect of Economic Bicameralism is to allow all of the firm's investors, through the representatives they elected to the Capital and Labor Investors' Chambers, to participate in decisions about all issues affecting the life of the firm, without exception. In a bicameral governance structure, the firm's main decisions, particularly all its strategic decisions, would be subject to approval by its two constituent bodies. In concrete terms, what is currently known as the

---

[3] The functioning of the U.S. Congress should not be taken as concrete evidence for the (in)efficiency of the institutional invention of bicameralism. Indeed, the reader should bear in mind that the U.S. case is an extreme one: the oppositional forces of its system of checks and balances are strong enough to block one another entirely. This seems counterproductive in the case of the firm, where an alignment of powers in the appointment of the executive branch by the legislature seems desirable in order to produce an environment respectful of each party's interests, since all share a superior goal, and indeed depend on it: the prosperity of the firm.

supervisory board or board of directors, representing the shareholders, would be obliged to recognize the firm's "other half"; this half, in addition to being at least as dependent on and attached to the firm,[4] is certainly just as vital to the firm's proper function. If we wish corporate governance to be *legitimate, reasonable*, and *intelligent*, therefore, then the interests of this "other half" must be taken into account and included in the firm's core functioning, via its equal participation through the board in all the main decisions that affect the life of the firm.[5] That both chambers must participate in all decisions should be reiterated here: reserving certain issues for 1 chamber alone would create an incomplete form of bicameralism, and reproduce the power imbalances that characterize firms' current unicameral system, which has caused the *illegitimate, unreasonable*, and *unintelligent* governance now all too common in the contemporary business world, with the dire consequences we know today. Such imbalanced structures would not reflect the plan of Economic Bicameralism proposed herein.[6]

CONDITIONS FOR RESPONSIBILITY

The question of conflict necessarily looms large in any discussion of bicameralism. What would happen if the two chambers opposed one another? What if deadlock were to occur? Acknowledging the existence of a specific power dynamic is a necessary precondition for building effective bicameralism in firms – a power dynamic between two different,

---

4 In the context of publicly traded companies, an employee's investment is certainly much less "liquid" than that of shareholders. The sociology of work has identified other forms of investment; for example, educational investments through which employees develop skills that, though sought out by certain firms, are not necessarily transferable, and therefore valuable, in other parts of the labor market. On the other hand, although exceptional cases may exist, there is no grounds for believing that capital investors would have – by nature, culture, or reflex – any greater loyalty to a firm than its employees would, or would desire its continued existence or prosperity more strongly.

5 Incidentally, this idea also offers the beginnings of a response to the critique that began with reactions to the work of Berle and Means (1932) deploring shareholders' limited influence on corporate decision making, since corporate law sets limits on the scope of their intervention in the *corporation* and distances them from the real power held by management, which, in concrete terms actually governs the *firm*. For a contemporary reformulation of this issue, see Bebchuk (2005).

6 To use Lijphart's system for classifying political systems (1999), the Economic Bicameralism proposed here is a form of "strong" bicameralism (as opposed to weak or insignificant systems), in the sense that it is both "incongruent" (different electoral bodies leading to diverging political compositions) and "symmetrical" (identical powers granted to both chambers).

complementary, and incommensurable rationalities that value two different types of interests, the one instrumental, the other expressive. Bicameralism offers an alternative to adversarial or confrontational relations between the two interest groups by providing a structure in which cooperation can take place. The existence of a power structure considered just and legitimate by all, in the form of two chambers, requires each body to recognize the other as a partner, and to take their interests into consideration. Bicameralism, by definition, recognizes the existence of different interests, and creates balance between them by offering the means to ensure they are respected. In a bicameral firm, each party's interests would be harnessed to build compromises beneficial to both, since both have it in their best interests, albeit for different reasons, to ensure that the firm functions optimally. Put more simply, conflict leading to deadlock is unlikely because both parties would suffer so greatly from the diminished productivity that would ensue: capital investors would lose profit in the form of potential earnings and dividends, while labor investors would face lower salaries or job losses. The equilibrium struck by Economic Bicameralism makes it possible to transform the status quo, marked as it is by generally inarticulate, often tense or even conflictual relations, into "quality conflict".[7] It offers a means of avoiding the dead ends and the zero-sum games so common in contemporary firms, where 1 group's losses are another's gains.

There is no reason to think that conflict would be as common or more common under Economic Bicameralism than it is today – if nothing else because, it need hardly be recalled, the situation is already so dire: the discontent of employees in the contemporary work world is growing and cannot be forgotten or ignored. Already, between 2005 and 2009, in a European economy composed entirely of unicameral, corporate firms, the number of workdays lost to labor conflicts was considerable, and has not improved since. Denmark topped the list in this period, with a yearly average of 159.4 days of work lost for every thousand employees. France came

---

[7] With regard to labor conflict, the issue might be redefined around the capability of employees and their labor unions to create what we have called "quality conflict" (Ferreras 2006) – that is, conflict whose outcome makes possible the structural transformation of the situation that gave rise to the conflict in the first place. A poor-quality conflict is typically one whose outcome does not fundamentally change the situation that created it. In such conflicts, whatever issue caused the conflict will reemerge shortly in one form or another. Quality conflicts lead to outcomes that help surmount the problems that caused the conflict. This echoes an idea found in medicine, that *crisis* must lead to a solution that guarantees a new equilibrium; otherwise the patient remains in the state that caused the initial crisis, which will inevitably recur. See Serres (2009).

in second, with 132 days lost, followed by Belgium, with 78.8 days lost (Carley 2010: 12). In France, this means that more than one employee in ten ceased work for one day a year due to a labor conflict; subsequent attempts to reform labor laws, culminating in the "loi El Khomri" in 2016, have only added tension. Since work stoppage is the final step in the escalation of a labor conflict, these figures should be taken as the tip of an iceberg of labor tensions caused by *illegitimate, unreasonable*, and *unintelligent* governance in today's firms.

This is not to say that labor tensions would disappear if firms were governed bicamerally by two chambers – only that they would change. Working together within the firm, representatives of both chambers would be obliged to clarify and negotiate tensions face-to-face, with the goal of finding a constructive solution for both parties. In cases of total deadlock between the two chambers, we need only return to the history of bicameral democracy, in which examples of conflict resolution abound. Deadlock, it may be observed, is relatively rare,[8] as the problems that cause it are generally dealt with through internal mediation and negotiation procedures via ad hoc conciliation committees made up of members from both chambers. Furthermore – in ways that vary depending on their specific structure –provide for the executive branch to intervene in such cases. As Jean-François Flauss recalls (1997: 147), "more generally speaking, conflict resolution between the two Chambers … is hardly carried out according to a single method." In case of prolonged deadlock, in which all other recourses to conciliation have been exhausted, the entire electoral body may be consulted to resolve a conflict, by electing new representatives or by referendum.[9]

This is, in fact, a crucial advantage of the bicameral balance of power: it makes possible, even requires, quality conflict, along with responsibility, which is a necessary precondition for quality conflict to occur. It should be recalled that the word "responsible" comes from the Latin *respondere*, "to pledge," or "to guarantee." Seen in this light, it is not in fact realistic

---

[8] For the "extreme" – in terms of checks and balances – case of the United States, see earlier discussion.

[9] Belgium, a country deeply divided between the Flemish and the French-speaking communities, has long experience in this matter and probably offers a good idea of a worst-case scenario. Despite grave deadlock of a type that seems difficult to "replicate" in the context of a firm, the country has continued to function thanks to what is known as its *gouvernement en affaires courantes* (executive branch for ongoing affairs), an arrangement by which the outgoing administration continued to make necessary decisions during the year and a half it took to form a new federal government following elections in June 2010.

to expect that executive managers in today's unicameral, capital-managed firms will actually behave responsibly with regard to labor investors; indeed, why would they? They do not answer to labor investors; they have pledged nothing to them. Their responsibility lies with their *principal*, the corporate shareholders: it is to them they must answer. And of course, this same logic may be applied in the other direction: there is little reason to believe that labor investors would behave responsibly with regard to the current unicameral, corporate firm. They have nothing pledged to it; they do not guarantee anything on its behalf. They are simply there to do a job, to fulfill a labor contract within a power structure to which they are subordinate. Under institutional conditions that strip them of their sense of responsibility, what reason do they have to behave responsibly?

Seen in these terms, the incidence of labor conflict might actually be judged as rather low. The absence of strife may largely be attributed to labor investors' responsibilities *in other areas of their lives*, which condition their commitment to their firms. With families to feed and homes to pay for, labor investors have strong responsibilities that should not be misinterpreted as loyalty to firms or their capital investors. Furthermore, as we have seen, they draw meaning from the work they do, which lies outside the domestic subordination that conditions their relationships to firm management.[10] Karl Marx was among the first to identify this tidy system of constraints, in which the property-owning class relies on the fact that the proletariat has no other means of survival other than working for pay. In a nutshell, this was Marx's definition of the proletariat, and the constraints his definition identified have not lessened over time. Despite a power structure in which the worker is at a total disadvantage, despite the injustice of the institutions governing their work lives, labor investors continue to shoulder their responsibilities. Now, as we move deeper into the twenty-first century, it is time to examine the conditions that would be required to create a legitimate framework in which labor investors and capital investors might ground their responsibilities together, something other than an exploitative relationship.[11] As the liberties and

---

[10] The alarming figures related to employee stress in the workplace should be considered as an indicator as well, a shadow image of strike-day figures, which reflect on an individual level the impasse in which today's workforce finds itself. Clinical psychology and sociology of work are full of examples of how, with no hope of truly exercising their responsibilities, workers turn the violence and pressure they feel inward on themselves (see Dejours).

[11] De Munck and Ferreras (2012) have advanced the concept of "democratic exchange" as a basis for exchanges in the context of economic life that would respect the principles of

responsibilities of capital investors have long been established, this implies laying the foundations for the emancipation of labor investors from a system in which their liberties and responsibilities have long been ignored or denied.

THE CLASSIC CAPITALIST FIRM: THE UNICAMERAL, CAPITAL-MANAGED INSTITUTION MISTAKEN FOR THE CORPORATION

The practical question of how the bicameral principle could be applied in a firm must be addressed in light of the government structure currently predominant in capital-managed firms. The political structure that governs today's corporate firms may be usefully considered as analogous to a representative government organized through a unicameral legislature. Firms today resemble what Great Britain might look like if it were governed by the property owners – that is, the House of Lords, alone. The sovereign *demos* of these firms is identified as the general meeting of the shareholders – in other words, those who own shares in the corporation,[12] which appoints representatives to sit on a board of directors (or supervisory board). This body exercises legislative power, and oversees the exercise of executive power by the executive committee, which includes the chief executive officer and the firm's top management, the chief operating officer, the chief financial officer, etc.

As Part II explains, the rationality behind this political structure is instrumental, and it is considered to be the only logic necessary to guide the firm. This view of firms as dedicated exclusively to the deployment of instrumental rationality – return on investment for shareholders, wages for workers – justifies the existing chain of command. It is designed to further the interests of shareholders, upon whose successes workers' interests are pinned – and upon whose earnings workers' wages are

a democratic society. There are three dimensions to this type of exchange: deliberation about ends, bargaining about means, and experimentation over possible futures. True democratic exchange is born of the consolidation of these three components. When one of them is missing, the exchange can no longer be considered democratic, as is the case with capitalist economic exchanges. The bicameral firm, on the other hand, would provide an institutional structure capable of fostering democratic exchange.

[12] For the sake of clarity of the example, let us assume that all shares are voting shares. In reality, corporations issue special categories of shares, including non-voting shares (which come without the right to vote in the general assembly, but guarantee the same right to dividends as voting shares), or with multiple votes, as in a plural voting system.

indexed.[13] Because the corporation's shareholders are understood to be the best representatives of this rationality, it follows logically that the entire institution of the firm be organized to ensure the satisfaction of their interests by placing power in their hands.

The institutional shape of the classic capitalist firm is a unicameral, capital-controlled corporate structure where only capital investors' instrumental rationality is represented, via the board of directors. It would be more apt to call this board the Capital Investors' Chamber of Representatives, as it is appointed by the shareholders, and thus, quite logically, is expected to pursue their interests. Ownership of shares in a corporation is considered sufficient to grant capital investors legitimate sovereignty over the firm. Reduced to its simplest terms, the unicameral, capital-controlled firm is a particular form of oligarchy. It is a *plutocracy*,[14] a political system in which power is exercised by those in possession of material wealth, the property owners.

Let us now return to a crucial point made in Part II. The perception that this form of government is appropriate government for the *firm* arises from the confusion of two realities, the corporation and the firm. A *corporation* is a legal entity that pulls together capital investors' assets, structured as shares. Notwithstanding this frequent misconception, these shareholders do not legally *own* the firm – legally speaking, they do not even own the *corporation*. What they own is one (or many) share(s) *issued* by the corporation, a legal entity that serves as the organizing vehicle for capital investors. Corporations are defined by a specific institutional design: its shareholders appoint a board of directors, which oversees an executive committee, which acts in the interest of the shareholders. That capital investors have succeeded in claiming the government of the *firm* merely because they are organized as a *corporation* is a formidable coup. By perpetuating and encouraging the confusion of the corporation with the firm, by behaving *as if* these were the same entity, capital investors have erected a kind of despotism. Some of these despots are more enlightened than others; some more paternalistic, more moral, more visionary, or more selfless – but all disenfranchise the political rights of the firm's other investors, those who invest their labor and their persons.

---

[13] If shareholder earnings are a necessary condition to the very existence of the salary, they are not a sufficient one. Instrumental rationality is upheld by capital investors, whose official goal is to "add value" to a firm (defined exclusively as increasing share value), not to ensure that any growth in productivity is shared between capital investors, through dividends or earnings, or for labor investors, through salary increases.

[14] From the Greek roots: power = *kratos* and *plutos* = wealth.

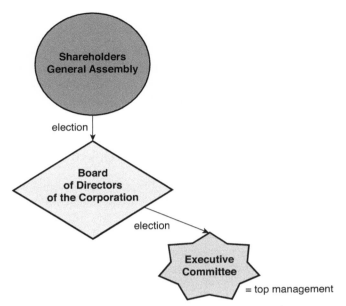

FIGURE 5. The Corporate Firm, a Capital Monocameral Government

In the unicameral, corporate firm, the executive committee of the *corporation* serves as the executive committee of the firm. The confusion could not be more serious: if the firm were in fact the same as the corporation – that is, defined by the interests of its shareholders – this design would be ideal. Yet, as we have argued, it is a mistake to understand the *firm* (as opposed to the corporation) so narrowly, and an injustice to leave its executive power in the hands of a – quite logically – very partial and biased legislature.

As this book has explained, the firm is driven by not one, but two rationalities, grounded in the values, goals, and interests that motivate its two main constituent bodies, its capital and labor investors. And if this is the case, then we must consider that the *expressive* rationality of those who invest their work and person in the firm ought to be represented and to have a say in the executive body of the *firm* – not of the corporation, which is, in its own right, the vehicle by which capital investors are organized.

For now, corporate firms are governed by a capital-managed, unicameral system that has succeeded thanks to the mistaking of the firm for the corporation. This is not to say that *expressive* rationality is entirely invisible in the contemporary firm: it is perceptible in workers' motivations and expectations, as well as in employee representative bodies such as works councils, work safety committees – when these exist – or in obligatory consultations of personnel representatives or union delegations. While such institutional arrangements have been necessary to ensure that workers' rights were (more or less) minimally respected, they cannot seriously be said to constitute a genuine voice in the government of the firm by labor investors.

GOVERNMENT STRUCTURE OF THE BICAMERAL FIRM

Economic Bicameralism acknowledges the legitimacy of the instrumental logic behind the economic pursuits of *capital investors*, and would maintain their representation within its governance structure via the structure of the corporation (general assembly and board) which is maintained, considering it is a fitting vehicule to organize and represent the interests of capital investors. What it does not accept is the confusion of the firm with the legal entity that serves as vehicle for organizing capital investors. Economic Bicameralism adds a second channel of representation to the existing government structure in order to guarantee equal representation to *labor investors*. Its goal is to shift from a *corporate governance* structure that serves capital investors alone by imposing the board of the corporation as the legislature of the firm, to a structure of government that serves the constituents of the firm, i.e. including those who invest their person, rather than their capital alone. A *Labor Investors' General Assembly*, composed of all those who invest their labor in the firm, would be held in parallel to the General Assembly of Shareholders, which would be known as the *Capital Investors' General Assembly*. The latter would retain the right currently held by the General Assembly of Shareholders to elect members to the Board of Directors. In a bicameral firm, however, this body would be called by a more descriptively accurate name: the *Capital Investors' Chamber of Representatives*. The *Labor Investors' General Assembly*, given equal standing within the firm's governance structure, would have the same right to elect the members of the *Labor Investors' Chamber of Representatives*.

Under this system, the firm's executive committee would become the true executive branch of the firm government, one that answered to a parliament composed of two chambers, and not just one, as is the case with contemporary unicameral corporate governance. In other words, as is true of bicameral political systems, the firm's two constituent bodies would assemble for the *Labor Investors' General Assembly* and the

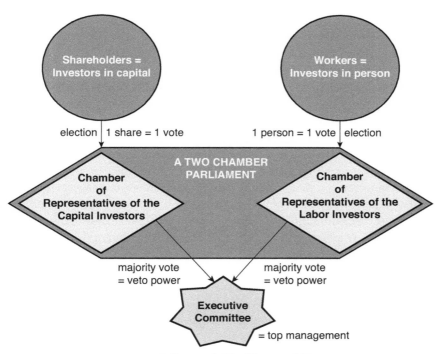

FIGURE 6. Proposal: The Bicameral Firm

Capital Investors' General Assembly, during which they would elect representatives to their respective chambers, who would jointly hold legislative power within the firm. An executive branch would then be chosen to sit before these two chambers, which would act as the firm's government per se (what is currently known as the supervisory committee, the executive committee, or other body composed of members of upper management). In practical terms, any policy that the executive branch wished to pursue would have to obtain a majority of votes (50% + 1 vote) in *both* chambers, not just from the board of directors, as is currently the case in contemporary unicameral firms. Following is a diagram of the institutional structure of the bicameral firm:

Composition of Chambers

This institutional design would at last establish a legitimate, reasonable, and intelligent government for the firm. Its design would finally meet the requirements of a "representative government."[15] Its parliament would be made up of a *Labor Investors' Chamber of Representatives*, which would be elected following the democratic principle of "one person, one vote"– that is, each labor investor would have one vote.[16] Of course, in the contemporary firm, labor investors are not the only stakeholders who invest their person in the firm or develop a relationship to the firm through expressive rationality. Depending on the industry and the firm in question, users might be just as personally invested as workers. Users' health (patients, neighbors), their social network (members of social media platforms), their mobility (users of transportation means), or their education (students) are all examples of expressive interests in firms. This is noted here to make the point that bicameral firm government necessitates careful examination on a firm-by-firm basis. In all cases, however, it is certain that labor investors must be central in the composition of the Labor Investors' Chamber of Representatives. It is possible, nevertheless, to imagine a quorum of seats reserved for other types of investors "of person", depending on the specific nature of the activity of a given firm in a given industry. Here, in our discussion of a theoretical bicameral firm, we explore a minimalist version of the *Labor Investors' Chamber of Representatives*, composed only by employees. The *Capital Investors' Chamber of Representatives* would continue to be constituted following the current principle of "shareholder democracy" (Bebchuk 2005), which grants one vote per share.[17]

---

[15] By "representative government" (Manin 1995) we mean the entire institutional arrangement that allows for and produces a political community's expression of sovereignty. Representative government institutions are created by the election of representatives to one or two legislative chambers and the nomination of an executive body, generally known as the *executive branch*. The overall structure of a representative government, which is the modern institutional form taken by liberal democracy, should not be confused with one of its constituent parts – the government, as it is referred to in some countries, in the strict sense of that term, in other words the executive government or branch, as opposed to the parliament.

[16] If the logic of investment in a firm justifies representation, a part-time worker has just as much right to an entire vote as a full-time worker, particularly as working part time is often not a choice, and since all workers are equally affected by a firm's decisions, no matter how many actual hours they work. In situations where employees have chosen to work part time, one might imagine representation proportional to the percentage of a full-time position worked by the employee; a half-time worker would thus be granted half a vote. Such decisions are constitutional in nature and rest in the hands of a firm's parliament.

[17] Currently, voting rights for shares or stocks held in a corporation take many forms. Depending on a corporation's history, and, for example, the continued involvement of its founders, some shares grant more than one vote to their holders in the general assembly,

In a bicameral firm, both chambers would be composed of people elected to represent their peers. Since both are *representative chambers*, one's eligibility would be determined by one's status as a capital or labor investor in a given firm. It is possible to imagine, as previously mentioned, that capital and labor investors in a firm might wish to ask people from outside the firm who share their sensibilities and who care for the firm's future to run for election to the chambers. This would be justified as long as both chambers agreed to it and both were allowed to do so. Indeed, the position of "outside director" in boards of directors today is considered good practice in corporate governance. For a Capital Investors' Chamber of Representatives, it should be made clear that the strategy of Economic Bicameralism includes the idea of reconnecting capital owners to their investments in the perspective of sustainable firms. The main difficulty that globalization has raised for democratic nation-states is that capital cannot be contained by national borders. Compelling capital investors to elect representatives from their ranks and to learn to dialogue with Labor Investors' Chambers of Representatives seems a good way to provoke an increase in pertinent knowledge among capital investors of the reality lived by labor investors, and, by the same token, to nourish in them the possibility of developing a rationality that is not solely instrumental. The history of great corporations is filled with examples of the ties that bind familial or historical shareholders to their investments; their history with and their knowledge of the contexts in which their behavior is rooted means that they cannot justify their actions with instrumental reasoning alone. Until the 1960s, this was the case of the majority of Western Europe's great industrial families, who saw themselves as tied to a place, a nation, and its people, and believed they had a higher responsibility toward them, as well. Since that time, capital mobility has made it possible for instrumental logic to become the only motive considered germane to investment strategies. From this perspective, the bicameral plan for the firm, and for the global firm in particular, is an answer to the current state of economic globalization without global democratic sovereignty. This speaks to 1 of the effects Economic Bicameralism would have: to push capital investors to (re)connect with their own expressive rationality and responsability beyond a strict definition of return on investment.

while others simply grant ownership of a share in a corporation's capital with no right to representation. From this perspective, even true shareholder democracy does not yet exist. Infamously, Elisabeth Holmes, the founder of Theranos, had golden shares with 100 votes attached to each one of them.

Size of Chambers

For each chamber, the total number of labor investors or the total number of stocks (or shares) would be divided by the total number of representatives sought for each chamber, in order to arrive at the number of votes required to elect a representative.[18] The chambers would deliberately be kept to a reasonable size; this constraint seems necessary if we wish to avoid the disadvantages of political bicameralism raised by Jeremy Bentham.[19] The optimal size of these chambers should fall somewhere on the spectrum between the committee system (referred to in the EU as "comitology") and full assembly (or direct democracy). The current size of corporate boards makes them too small to function as effective parliaments, given the deliberative dimension they are supposed to have; at the same time, they also risk the disadvantages inherent to committee systems. Since the role of each chamber is a representative one, in the interests of effective debate, each chamber must necessarily limit the number of its participants. This is the inherent challenge to building a parliament capable of functioning as a "policy transformer" (Polsby 1975, Norton 2010), in which elected officials have a collective "viscosity" with regard to the law.[20] Here, a difference between the unicameral, capital-managed firm and the bicameral model should be highlighted: broadly speaking, the General Assembly of Shareholders in a unicameral firm has limited legislative competences (it names members to the board of directors and votes on major strategic orientations); the board of directors wields the actual legislative and executive power. In the bicameral model, which is inspired by the political theory of the balance of powers, authority would be distributed in a more clear-cut fashion: legislative authority would

---

[18] We will not venture into the question of the electoral process here. Proportional representation ensures a richer deliberation: representation of different rationalities, mobilization of knowledge held by investors from both sides with their different experiences of, and perspectives on, the life of the firm. As an alternative to preferential voting and its attendant disadvantages, contemporary scholars are reexamining random selection, which was used in antiquity to select representatives. See (Landemore 2013). Here again, Economic Bicameralism is flexible, and may be adapted to any number of preferences. But these questions are not negligible: as the great architect Mies van der Rohe said, "the devil is in the details."

[19] The main drawbacks cited by Bentham are delay and complication (Bentham, cited in Elster, 2012). Bentham was in favor of political bicameralism, whose advantages outweighed its shortcomings, he felt. He called for assemblies of reduced size to limit these potential drawbacks.

[20] See earlier for the exposé of the concept. A significant body of work exists on the optimal size of governing boards. No exhaustive or universally applicable conclusions have yet been drawn (Wang, Young and Chaplin 2009).

be exercised by the two-chamber parliament and executive authority by the top management, the executive committee. Evidently, as we pointed out earlier on, and as is the case in most bicameral political systems, the government would also be empowered to introduce draft laws.

In order to maintain the bilateral logic by which the mutual recognition of instrumental and expressive rationalities form the basis of the firm, it seems ideal, symbolically speaking, that the size of the two chambers be numerically identical. The number of representatives elected to each chamber would be equal, which would, among other things, make calculating majority thresholds simpler. It is possible to envision chambers of different sizes, given that the overarching goal of any bicameral structure is simply to ensure that each chamber, collectively, has an equal weight in the life of the firm, be they composed of 3, 30, or 50 representatives. But the existence of asymmetrical chambers would imply that representatives had different symbolic weight in the firm's government system. For example, if the Capital Investors' Chamber of Representatives were composed of six people and the Labor Investors' Chamber of Representatives were composed of 30 people, it would be difficult not to come away with the idea that the representatives elected to the Labor Investors' Chamber of Representatives were "worth" less, in that each individual representative would have less say in a chamber whose influence was equal to the other. Bicameral political systems have indeed often chosen to restrict the size of one of their two chambers, in order to give the elected officials in the "upper" chamber greater symbolic weight than those in the "lower" chamber. Emblematic is the case of the American senate (Swift 1996). Since the goal of the bicameral firm is to give equal footing to two incommensurable rationalities, it is only reasonable and logical to bear symbolic witness to this mutual recognition by ensuring that representatives of labor and capital have equal weight in equal numbers.

Convocation and Prerogatives of the Chambers

All matters regarding the life of a firm fall into the purview of the firm's bicameral government, for what decision regarding the life of a firm could realistically be seen to affect 1 rationality and not the other? The compensation of a firm's CEO, lowest-ranked worker, or capital investor; the distribution of work among different business units; the nomination of directors; investments in research and development, the development of a new product, or training and continuing education policies; issues of outsourcing and international development – any decision regarding the life of a firm mobilizes both instrumental *and* expressive rationalities. All such decisions have an impact on the firm in terms of efficiency *and* justice. It is therefore only logical that all main issues affecting the firm fall under the joint authority of the two-chamber parliament, with a particular focus on the strategy of the firm; that is, in the ends it pursues.

As they exercise legislative power within the firm, the chambers should meet on a regular basis. Monthly or bimonthly meetings of the two chambers would seem efficient and reasonable, given that the elected officials seated in both chambers would presumably be well informed about the firm, since they are directly implicated in it by dint of their labor or their capital. By default, it is important that both chambers meet jointly as a parliament or congress. Why? Because, as Bernard Manin (1995: 241) explains, the "specific function" of discussion within the two chambers is to "produce agreement and consent." Asymmetrical circulation of messages and information between the two chambers would be a danger to the well-being of the firm. The idea behind Economic Bicameralism is well and truly to *compel* representatives of a firm's two constituent bodies to govern *together*, counterbalancing each other in situations of excess in either direction. The very existence of the two chambers acknowledges that the interests represented within them process, interpret, and apply information regarding the life of the firm from different perspectives, using different logics (instrumental versus expressive). So if concessions are to be made by both parties, if productive compromises are to be made in view of the "common good" of the firm – to echo the vocabulary of political philosophy – representatives in both chambers must have access to the same information, and, more importantly, must learn to understand one another. In particular, situations in which the firm's executive committee might make selective reports to one chamber or another should be avoided at all costs. This cannot be stressed enough: if need be, the two chambers should be allowed to meet separately, but under ordinary circumstances they should meet jointly, and the firm's executive branch should report to them as a single body, its parliament.

Role of the Executive Committee

A firm's executive committee should be named by majorities in both chambers, and should therefore report to the parliament. The committee should be a veritable *executive branch*, in that it should exercise executive power in the broadest sense of that term, steering the firm based on decisions and directives issued by the two chambers. It should also have the power to propose legislation on any matter it wishes to the two chambers. When implementing firm policy, the firm's executive branch ensures that the interests of both rationalities are respected. In all aspects of the life of the firm, this means taking both political and expressive rationality into account. As in any bicameral system, the executive branch must have the trust and respect of both chambers in order to exercise power.

The exercise of executive power in the firm is collegial. As in contemporary unicameral firms, the executive committee should include different operational positions (chief executive officer, chief financial officer, chief operations officer, etc.). To echo the language of Principal-Agent theory, the goal of bicameral reform in the government of firms is to fundamentally change its system of incentives by making it *responsive* to the needs of *both* the firm's constituent bodies. The constraint of having to obtain a majority in both chambers guarantees that the need for democratic justice among employees be respected to the same degree as the imperatives imposed by instrumental rationality, and obliges the firm's government to come up with productive, equitable compromises between these two rationalities. Any decision proposed by the executive branch must be the object of a compromise that obtains a majority in both chambers.

The scope of action of a firm's executive committee would be radically different from its current role in today's unicameral context: here, the executive government's job would be to seek compromises that are both instrumentally and politically effective. The model of the firm manager acting on behalf of the shareholder, *agent of its principal*, would be obsolete. The firm's executive branch becomes the driving force behind its "representative government," a central idea in political theory (Manin 1995). Management studies regularly raise the alarm that managers lack the leeway necessary to foster creativity and innovation, pressured as they are to conform to shareholders' interests. Indeed, stock options and other incentives for executive managers were created to this end, to ensure that agents' interests were aligned with the corporate principal, the shareholders.

This situation has, increasingly, raised concern. "As soon as directors are supposed to represent the – shareholders," write Segrestin and Hatchuel (2011: 18), "the legitimacy of their power depends on the extent to which it is exercised with respect to the wills of the people they represent. Managers have no latitude to propose innovative projects." Blanche Segrestin and Armand Hatchuel argue that top management should be "empowered" with established autonomy *(pouvoir habilité)*, which they see as the condition for managers to become true "creators" (Segrestin and Hatchuel 2011). Economic Bicameralism represents a solution to this problem, too. In his study of the principles of representative government in political history, Manin shows that 1 of the organizing principles of representative government is precisely the extent to which "the decision-making of those who govern retains a degree of independence from the wishes of the electorate" (Manin 1995: 252). Here, indeed, we should highlight a strength of representative government: representation makes it possible to seek the general interest precisely *because* it places a certain distance between the direct interests of voters and the functions of elected representatives or members of the executive government.[21] This is precisely the position that the bicameral structure of government would offer to the executive committee's top managers: equidistance from both capital and labor. This is an ideal position for managers to gain the leeway necessary to generate innovative and productive compromise.

Organization of Work, Hierarchy, and Delegation of Powers

Bicameralism rests on the principle of representation. Its government follows the principles of representative democracy, as opposed to purely direct democracy or consensus assemblies. Chambers in a bicameral firm would not hold session every day. As mentioned earlier, the executive committee would be given broad initiative in the bicameral system, and should be considered as the actual driving force in a firm's everyday life. The chambers would have the power of legislative review; they constitute a "viscous" parliament (Norton 2010), while the firm's executive branch fills the role of leader in the firm's executive and legislative life. As in a bicameral nation, the two chambers must approve the executive committee's policies: its overall policy plan must be submitted to the two chambers, and must be ratified by a majority in both chambers before it is implemented.

Beyond that, however, specific hierarchical structures and the delegation of powers would be determined by the internal organization of each bicameral firm on its own. The goal of Economic Bicameralism is not to make participation in common deliberations the sole means to action in a firm: the chambers need not meet for each and every decision made on the firm's behalf. Quite to the contrary, Economic Bicameralism allows for the same degree of hierarchization and power delegation as exists in

---

[21] It is precisely this gap that Manin describes through the concept of "representative link" (1995: 249).

a unicameral firm. The salient difference is a simple one: decisions in a bicameral firm would be made from a legitimate foundational structure. The two chambers might choose to designate division or department heads, committees, or commissions to deal with specific questions. In short, the two chambers could approve whatever chain of command was needed for a given firm to function efficiently, however complicated it might be – so long as the firm hierarchy acted under the chambers' leadership and respected the guidelines they had established, which would generally have been proposed by the executive committee. This is not to gloss over the real limitations of representative democracy, which have been documented by the deliberative, associative, and participatory democracy literature. Indeed, with this literature in mind, it should be explicitly noted that the idea of Economic Bicameralism ought not to be considered applied as an added layer of formality in a firm; rather, it should be seen as an institutional roadmap for mobilizing a firm's investors and democratizing its decision-making process from top to bottom.

Ideally, in large, transnational firms, Economic Bicameralism would be implemented at several levels within a firm. It should of course be put in place at a firm's highest level, be that national, multinational, or transnational. But the bicameral structure may also be reproduced at a more local level (national, regional, sitewide) to manage matters delegated from further up in the hierarchy, in accordance with the subsidiarity principle and with the specific legislation of a given country. This is, of course, how things work in large federalized nations, for which bicameral government is seen as a particularly well-adapted system (Flauss 1997, Doria 2006) as is often the case with large federal states. Germany and the United States are the best-known examples; there, federated sub-entities may also be organized along the bicameral model. In these highly globalized times, global firms, with their highly diverse internal organizations, have come to resemble large federalized nations.[22] Reproducing the bicameral system at lower levels in a multinational firm's hierarchy would certainly be a powerful means to induce its capital investors to become involved in the life of the firm. This is a further argument in favor of bicameral firms, since the absence of this involvement is often cited as 1 of the major causes of harmful short-term investment strategies (Roundtable Institute for Corporate Ethics Report 2006).

---

[22] See Kristensen and Zeitlin's qualitative study of a major British multinational and its subsidiaries (2005).

On a more local level, the point of the bicameral firm is not to promote structures for the sake of structures: the bicameral model has a logical affinity with existing methods for increasing participation by labor investors in the life of the firm. Numerous forms of cooperation and participation exist to grant employees more collective autonomy, as well as to ensure they are more satisfied, productive, and responsible in the workplace.[23] Institutional structures can only be effective in their roles if people participate in them. Hence, methods must be found to encourage the involvement of the firm's two constituent bodies in bicameral government. The firm should motivate labor investors to express differing opinions while providing the tools to build consent and generate creativity, innovation, and commitment in the workplace (Pink 2009). Endenburg (2002)'s sociocratic circular organizing method might be used as a starting point: the sociocratic model would seem to fit logically with a bicameral structure, particularly because 1 of the key principles of sociocracy is double linking (Charest 2007). Just as it did with paired Roman consuls, double linking helps limit the abuse of power while involving more employees, who are, after all, the firm's major source of innovation and efficiency.

Role of Unions and Labor Organizations

Labor unions have a dual role to play in the bicameral firm. They must be taken as the collective representatives of workers and as conduits for solidarity across firms. Where they exist, labor unions are the logical vehicle for worker representation, with a history and a set of skills that can help them to organize employees' voices (Freeman and Medoff 1984) while also helping to train elected officials. It is only logical to assume that union culture would change as union representatives participated in the government of bicameral firms through the Labor Investors' Chamber of Representatives.[24] Participating in the government of the bicameral firm should help labor unions to develop a truly responsible relationship with

---

[23] For specific examples of innovative, high-performing firms in which employees enjoy a high degree of autonomy and are satisfied with their work, see Carney and Getz (2009), Laloux (2014).

[24] We at this point recall Rogers's evaluation of the impact of union members' participation in the election of works councils: "In countries with multiunionism, works council elections force unions to match their policies to the preferences of large numbers of workers, unionized or not, and to measure regularly and publicly their support against that of their competitors. In these ways, a council system promotes a certain accountability of unions to those they purport to serve" (Rogers 1995b: 383).

the economic endeavor, on a healthy basis of legitimate compromise, where the *expressive* rationality driving work is finally understood and respected on equal footing with instrumental rationality.

At the same time, it makes sense to extend (or to maintain, if this right is already in place) exclusivity of worker representation to recognized labor unions by making affiliation with an existing and legally recognized organization a condition for candidacy in elections to the Labor Investors' Chamber of Representatives. The goal of Economic Bicameralism is not to encourage "corporate patriotism," at the expense of solidarity among the working class, and it should not contribute to that. On the contrary, it should foster the human infrastructure of a broad labor movement. A chamber of representatives composed of labor investors who have no connections to any officially recognized labor organization present in more than 1 firm would lead to the disappearance of critical principles of solidarity extending beyond the firm.[25] Nor should Economic Bicameralism be used to intensify competition among firms; indeed, given that chains of production worldwide are becoming more and more complex and interdependent (Berger 2005, Weil 2014), Economic Bicameralism seeks to reconnect capital investors to their investments *and* consolidate employees' implication in their firms by linking them to their peers in other firms, thereby creating the opportunity to build denser non-competitive relationships in the global economic fabric.[26] In this way, Economic Bicameralism would advance the place of the economy as an integral part of the democratic society, and at the same time contribute to the project of democratization of society, both at the national and global level.

Firms Concerned

Wherever capital and labor investors are present, their specific rationalities are present, with their respective concerns, all of which are tied to issues of efficiency and justice. The success of any firm depends on what

---

[25] Georges Friedmann identified the double stakes of solidarity in work life through the distinction between "the firm's solidarity, which binds together all the personnel of a business or a factory, a department store, a workshop, or a mine, and so causes group-solidarity within the firm," and "the solidarity of the workers as wage earners, linking them to other wage-earners *outside* the firm, to the employees, etc. of other firms" (which he called "class solidarity" or "worker solidarity") (Friedmann 1956: 144). It is not the goal of Economic Bicameralism to disrupt the conditions that make possible these two forms of solidarity.

[26] For a description of the challenge that "divisive capitalism" raises for labor unions, see Pech (2007).

happens when they encounter one another. At the same time, as the pioneering work of Joseph Schumpeter (1943) suggested, it seems necessary to distinguish among firms based on maturity and legal status, which indicates the specific state of the relationship between capital and labor investors, and the particular way in which their instrumental and expressive rationalities intertwine[27]. As written earlier, the present text uses the word *firm* to mean an organization mature enough to be run by an executive committee composed of a group of professionals hired by the corporation that gives them the authority to mobilize that corporation's assets in order to fund the endeavor pursued by the firm. Both public or privately held corporations with shares that are tradable on the stock market or held privately are included in this definition.

Economic Bicameralism is particularly adapted to firms that have completed their initial phase of development and become limited liability corporations.[28] And it is even more adapted to any legal structure in which shareholders, by means of the unilateral overvaluation of instrumental rationality through the financial market, are able to exert significant pressure on the boards and executive committees in order to have them managing the firm "in their name," as if it were a mere corporation.

It is to be expected that firms would approach the idea of such a vast change with a wary eye to the costs and risk it might entail. It therefore seems appropriate for nations or regional entities interested in promoting Economic Bicameralism to encourage firms to make the change by offering tax incentives to finance starting costs and smooth the way until the transition is made and firms begin reaping its benefits. Corporate taxes are, after all, regularly lowered for less legitimate reasons than this. For the challenges it would help meet, the bicameral model is ideal for transnational firms, which are run as corporations even as the reality of the networked and fissured firm urgently awaits recognition and consideration for what it is: a political entity embedded in no state, with a

---

[27] Here, we have in mind entrepreneur-led firms in their initial phases of development, whose leaders have a strong vision or project, are personally implicated, and have undertaken personal financial risk. Since entrepreneurs usually risk their own personal money in addition to investing their personal labor in the fledgling endeavor, they are unlikely to risk irresponsible behavior in the same way that a limited liability corporation is. This type of entrepreneur is situated at the point where the capital and labor investor's rationalities intersect, and their acts are fairly equally driven by both.

[28] For a detailed account of the evolution of capitalist firms' legal structures, see Robé (2011). A firm's legal status evolves throughout its life cycle, and data show that the longer ago a firm was founded, the less likely it is to be an unlisted family-owned company (see Franks, Mayer, Volpin and Wagner 2010).

massive impact on the lives of many, including, but not limited to, its labor investors, and, increasingly, with more powerful than individual states[29].

[29] As they count hundreds of thousands of employees and contractors, such transnational firms, in fact, are richer and stronger than many states around the globe. To mention a few examples from 2011, while the trend has only been growing, Bank of America's revenue was bigger than Vietnam's GDP, Walmart's than Norway's, Ford's than Morocco's, Microsoft's than Croatia's, General Motors's than Bangladesh's, General Electric's than New Zealand's, Fannie Mae's than Peru's, Chevron's than the Czech Republic's, Exxon Mobil's than Thailand's. From: http://www.businessinsider.com/25-corporations-bigger-tan-countries-2011–6?op=1

The complete separation of management from ownership, the lack of real power of the stockholders, and the tendency of corporations to develop into self-willed and possibly irresponsible empires, aggregates of enormous and largely uncontrollable power, are not facts which we must accept as inevitable but are largely the result of special conditions the law has created and the law can change.

We have it in our power to halt and reverse this process if we want to.

Friedrich A. Hayek (1948: 115)

Citizens cannot spend eight or more hours a day obeying orders and accepting that they have no rights, legal or otherwise, to participate in important decisions that affect them, and then be expected to engage in robust, critical dialogue about the structure of our society. Eventually the strain of being deferential servants from nine to five diminishes our after-hours liberty and sense of civic entitlement and responsibility.

Elaine Bernard (1996: 2)

The subordination of everything to the single aim of monetary profit leads industrial government to take the form of absolute monarchy.

Monarchy has a certain simplicity and convenience; but in the long run it is seldom the best for all concerned.

Sooner or later it leads to insurrections.

Morris R. Cohen (1927: 28)

Conclusions

One of the questions propelling this book is: What justifies the existence of the institutions that govern our social activities? Broadly speaking, answers to this question may be divided into two categories: a realist approach, which sees institutions as a necessary locus of order, and a *progressive* approach, which sees institutions as playing a role in fostering human emancipation.[1]

The realist approach sees institutions as vehicles for maintaining social order, or "control," in the Habermasian sense of that term. In practical terms, this means maintaining, thus reinforcing, existing structures of domination. The state's main role is maintaining social order in the public sphere and market order in the economy, while assuring that individuals enjoy a basic set of rights. These rights are "negative" individual liberties (Berlin 1969) granted to rational individuals who consent to be governed through elected representatives. This is a highly restrictive understanding of the democratic project, in which liberal democracy is a process of individualization limited to the political domain in the very narrowest sense of that term, whose only real political institution is parliamentary representation. The realist perspective on institutions conceives of society as a space in which individual forces – or coalitions of individual

---

[1] This choice refers to the epistemological alternatives identified by Habermas (Habermas 1971: 301–317). The particular affinity found between the idea of emancipation and critical social theory implies that the latter has devoted itself to contesting the idea that issues generally categorized as "private" should be located beyond the reach of democratic debate and negotiation (Fraser 1992, Ferreras 2007).

agents – interact. Once individual liberties have been guaranteed, there is no need to democratize institutions in other social domains; market forces take care of allocating all categories of goods (from wages to education to healthcare to pollution rights). As we have seen in Part I, collective labor rights as the right to collective bargaining become problematic from this standpoint, and must be fought against.

The progressive approach, on the other hand, sets *emancipation* as the defining goal of the individual and the collective, and sees the two as inextricably intertwined under the democratic horizon. Democracy, according to the progressive approach, is an ongoing project, something that is always in the process of becoming. This is evident in its very name: something progressive is, by nature, engaged in progress. The progressive approach and the realist approach accord individuals the same basic set of rights – which make up the core of political liberalism – but in addition to this the progressive approach undertakes to answer the question of how society can live up to the democratic ideal. Its goal is to bring the democratic ideal to life, in practice, both on the individual level (in terms of the liberty and equality of citizens) and on the collective level (in terms of collective self-determination or autonomy).[2] The progressive viewpoint thus pushes beyond the framework of political liberalism, taking it as a foundational structure, not an end. The progressive approach is an active one, and is manifest in collective mobilizations such as those for the emancipation of slaves, the right to associate, unionization rights, women's rights, civil rights, or for the liberation of colonized peoples or those living under dictatorship.

This progressive philosophy of democracy sees the institutions governing various areas of social life as offering opportunities to nurture the democratic ideal. It offers a maximalist understanding of democracy as an ideal standard for living together, one that can expand infinitely alongside individual and collective self-determination[3]. This means that contemporary arrangements may always be viewed as steps along a path of experimentation towards something else, including something more

---

[2] For a clarification of this point, the reader is referred to the idea of "collective capability," which builds on Amartya Sen's concept of capability. I suggested this notion in order to account for the specifically collective dimension of individual liberty. See Ferreras (2012b).

[3] As a result, scholars in this tradition have sought not to reason in an abstract way about the human nature but to connect the conditions of political equality to the specific material, economic conditions people face. See Cohen (1989, 1997), Cohen and Rogers (1983), for a general overview of the institutions of a deepened, "productive" democracy across the different fields of life (except the firm) in a global era. Also see Rogers (2012).

thoroughly democratic (Sabel 2012). According to this perspective, this ideal of self-determination – both individual and collective – seeks to ultimately shape all areas of society. This of course includes the domain of what we currently consider to be politics: in a maximalist view of democracy, parliamentary representation is just a building block for individual and collective sovereignty, not its unique expression (this viewpoint is evident in contemporary citizens' growing demand for greater involvement in decisions that concern them directly). But it also extends to all domains of life, including culture and education, as well as international relations, as the growing demand for global justice finds voice in myriad ways (Pleyers 2010). Most germanely to this book, of course, is its inclusion of the economy: the progressive approach has brought to life many inventions in the economic field, such as works councils, collective bargaining, and social dialogue. Economic Bicameralism for the firm is proposed by this book as another, in line with the progressive standpoint that institutional arrangements governing the capitalist economy, and the firm in particular, should be seen along a possible path of *democratic transition*. The task is to recognize that the institutional mode of government of the firm has the potential to evolve, that it is *in transition*, and can be moved along a political spectrum that goes from despotism to collective autonomy – that is, democracy.

The realist viewpoint takes an opposite, if not an opposing stance: it understands the political realm in the narrowest sense of that term, as the institutions organized around parliamentary representation; indeed, according to the realist approach, parliamentary representation is the only field to which democracy may be applied. From this perspective, the idea that the democratic ideal might in any way apply to the field of economic practice is simply meaningless. Economic Bicameralism cannot fit into such a narrow understanding of the democratic ideal; it is born of the progressive approach to institutions, and undertakes to engage in democracy as an ongoing process. The progressive approach is one that fosters individual and collective autonomy in all areas of society, and Economic Bicameralism engages it to raise the question of autonomy in the realm of work. This book has observed that the people who invest their person, their labor, in firms develop an *expressive* rationality, and that they are moved by the intuition of democratic justice in the work environment while it becomes increasingly part of the public sphere. Its conclusion takes a progressive view of these observations: institutions must, once again, evolve in order to "deepen and expand," as write Olin Wright and Rogers (2015), the democratic promise. If the institutions that currently govern firms continue to ignore what the careful analysis of contemporary work reveals, and continue to refer only to the rationality of capital investors, then the logic and the government of the firm is de facto – and must be called into question.

THE PLACE OF THE FIRM IN DEMOCRACY

Work is undeniably a defining experience in the lives of the active population today. There is an increasingly palpable tension in Western society between the democratic ideal powered by its advanced democratic culture and its economic institutions, which perpetuate a despotic, antidemocratic power structure as outmoded as the domestic regime from which it grew. This tension undermines the credibility and the legitimacy of the democratic project as a whole, as it repeatedly reminds workers that they are not as equal as they were brought up to believe they are.[4] In the era of the service economy, in which workers both serve customers and are customers themselves, the workplace, from the worker's perspective, is experienced as part of the larger public sphere. The fact that the government of firms has yet to acknowledge this reality, and that firms have yet to adapt the ways they exercise power accordingly, makes the need for public debate all the more urgent. It is necessary to think carefully about exactly how firms have become a central institution in democratic society, and to begin considering the obligations that arise from the central role they play.

This book is a response to this tension. Proceeding from the observation that the firm is a political institution driven by two rationalities, instrumental and expressive – not, in other words, a corporation that deploys instrumental rationality alone, as both the economic theory of the firm and the Marxist perspective would have it – this book has proposed the idea of Economic Bicameralism as a legitimate, intelligent, and reasonable means to govern the *firm*. This would represent real progress from the current situation in which the *corporation has usurped the firm*,

---

[4] And yet, every time a far right wing party wins an election, or every time voter participation dips in countries where voting is not compulsory, we hear calls to the people to engage as responsible citizens and to vote accordingly, without ceding to the siren song of populist demagoguery. But in the workplace – that is, in the very place where they are the most highly informed about issues relating to the way their lives are governed, and feel the most concerned – they are denied full participation. How *should* they cope with this? This is the democracy/capital contradiction at the most individual level, and its tremendous repercussions at every level of (public) life are hardly surprising.

a kind of real-life synecdoche. It would give the firm the place it deserves in our society's advancing project of democracy. Economic Bicameralism gives voice to the firms' two constituencies: acknowledging that each is indispensable to the other, it offers a structure in which a firm's *capital investors* and its *labor investors* can hold power together. In addition to the many positive justifications for this government structure, it should be recalled that there are negative ones, as well: if it is true that workers' everyday experience in the workplace is *expressive* and concerned with the intuition of democratic justice, then denying the reality they live in will necessarily have grave consequences. Both for the sake of the credibility of the democratic project, and for the sake of efficiency in the workplace, democratic society owes it to itself to frankly open a space for firms in the democratic public sphere. As scholars and as citizens, we have moved beyond the notion of the "end of history" (Fukuyama 1992): indeed, even a cursory look at the vast field of economic relations reminds us that history is an open book. This book proposes that the next chapter be written in the language of democratic justice.

The expectation of democratic justice in the workplace is, after all, a logical extension of the culture of advanced, deep-rooted democracies that are a core feature of our Western societies. Today, every child born to parents who are citizens of a Western nation will grow up in a family in which both parents and grandparents were born with the right to vote. This is a historic new fact[5]. We cannot yet fully measure the extraordinary cultural change that this historical context has effected. The ideal of democratic autonomy – that is, the ideal of individual and collective self-determination within a community of equals – is a powerful one. As early as 1835, Tocqueville predicted how potent it would be. Little by little, the democratic culture of equality permeates all social relations. It makes no sense, therefore, to confine our idea of democracy to a narrow definition of the political field established in a bygone historical era. And

---

[5] This is a generational phenomenon that marks a major, and underestimated, cultural change currently underway: in a country as liberal as Belgium, the author's own mother was born just barely in time (in 1947) to come of age knowing that she would be able to participate in the electoral process on the day of her majority. She, on the other hand, was raised by a mother whose political emancipation came after she had reached adulthood. Nevertheless, they both had to wait until 1976 to enjoy full autonomy when it came to managing their own money and property; until then, for married women, a husband's consent was required for any significant transaction. The culture that these rights nurture can only deepen individuals' expectations that they ought to have a say in their own lives, including in their work lives. Again, this is what we call the *critical intuition of democratic justice*.

of course, the expectation of democratic justice extends far beyond the bounds of the Western world (Sen 2006) – throughout the 2010s, the scale of democratic uprisings such as the *Indignados*, Occupy Wall Street, the Arab Spring, Black Lives Matter, and many more, is ample evidence of this, even as, as with all progressive movements, it goes through moments of positive progress and regressions, and is met with violent opposition. We may thus speak of a veritable *hunger for democracy* emerging across the globe, across a vast field of social practices, not only in the realm of activities considered to be political in the strictest sense of the term (Ferreras 2007b).

Capitalism is just as an undeniable phenomenon in today's society, and this book does not contest that the stocks and shares of capitalist corporations are held by capital investors. We only assert that this fact alone does not justify the latter's excessive rights and unilateral authority within the *firm*. Employees have every reason to expect recognition as fundamental investors in the firm, on the same terms as capital investors. This is how emancipation has worked throughout history: 1 disenfranchised group at a time, slaves, people from the colonies, people of color, women . . . and now workers. The logic of emancipation informing the democratic project can be summarized in a simple gesture, that of extending equal rights to a group formerly excluded from the term "equal" and therefore from the exercise of those rights. Because work is an experience animated by *expressive* rationality, and because *instrumental* and *expressive* rationalities work together to make possible the existence and guarantee the success of the capitalist firm, it is only right that the firm's "constituent bodies," capital investors and labor investors, hold power together. There is no valid reason why only capital investors should enjoy political rights in the firm, which is, as we have seen, a joint endeavour in which labor investors contribute and are affected in – at least- a symmetrical way. Firms must be governed by representative governments worthy of that title, ruled jointly by their two constituencies. With this in mind, we have searched political history for the moment in which despotism gave way to sovereignty shared with the people, and determined that the advent of bicameralism was the institutional innovation that enabled the democratization of society.

THE CONTRADICTION BETWEEN CAPITALISM AND DEMOCRACY

The tradition of political liberalism has had a defining impact on the democratic model in the Western world. But political liberalism, with the barrier it erected between the realm of political freedoms and the economic domain, was built from an ambiguity. Today, this ambiguity has brought us to an impasse. Freedom of enterprise and contractual freedom have been privileged in the economy, which in concrete terms, translates to an absence of political freedom – that is, the freedom to participate in governing one's own life. The only citizens who have the political right to participate in the government of the circumstances that affect them are those who own capital and exercise power via the corporation; all others are disenfranchised. The invention – the fiction – of the labor *contract*, in which a worker was considered to exercise the full extent of his freedom in consenting to be employed, made it possible to hide the reality of the situation. There is no denying the many advances made since the beginning of the nineteenth century, advances we explored in Part I of this book. Workers' movements have won important victories. Labor rights, including the right to form a union, the invention of collective bargaining, and works councils, all bear witness to the fact that political emancipation in the economy is already underway in some national contexts. But this freedom remains limited, constrained, narrow, and incomplete.[6] We are currently at the very nexus of the *contradiction* between capitalism and democracy – in fact between political and economic liberalism. The unsteady balance once achieved by our capitalist democracies, in which democracy was assigned to the political arena and capitalism to the economy – cannot be sustained much longer. Yet, the contradictions central to capitalism, as understood by Marx – "because of its inner dynamics...capitalism destroys its own conditions of existence" (Olin Wright 2006: 102) – are also excellent opportunities to address these imbalances, and to find a productive way out of this crisis[7]. Work's emancipation from the private sphere must

---

[6] We may here recall the celebrated words of Max Stirner (1845): "*freedom* can only be the whole of freedom; a piece of freedom is *not* freedom."

[7] On the concept of "contradiction of capitalism" central in Marx's analysis of capitalism – i.e. "the body of structural constraints associated with the capitalist dynamic but also of the possibilities for emancipation that it leaves open," Corcuff (2009) continues: "this dual dimension characterizes the Marxist approach to capitalism as a contradictory force. These contradictions in capitalism merely point to possibilities, which require *politicization* to become fully active rationales, to become reality (logically analogous to Aristotle's force/motion dichotomy: a force or potentiality is actualized through motion)." As Corcuff points out, Marx's successors have traditionally focused on the capital/labor contradiction and on the "social question" that arises from it. Corcuff, in contrast, invites us to expand the field of contradictions studied. This book offers one possible means of exploring the democratic question raised by what we can call the "capitalism/democracy contradiction."

lead to its full and total access to the public sphere of our democracies. This book has argued that the way to do this is to recognize firms as political entities in which capital investors already have power, through the institutional representative mechanisms of the corporation, and in which labor investors are still waiting to be recognized in those same terms.

Today, work in the service- and knowledge-based economy, and in particular the interactions with others that take place there (with customers, coworkers, management hierarchies, etc.) has shifted the workplace – or at least the worker's experience of it – into the *public sphere*. This shift has dramatically intensified the tension between instrumental and expressive rationalities in the firm, shedding light on the fact that wage work takes place in a contested field, in which the corporation exercises unilateral power over the interactions of workers, who relate to their work experience *expressively*. Employees' intuition of democratic justice in the workplace, their aspirations to the recognition of their equal dignity, and their conceptions of justice are constantly frustrated by the *domestic regime* under which they continue to work. This contradiction means the continuation of a long history of struggle for power and influence over labor, as old as capitalism itself.

At the individual level, this dissonance reveals the extent to which the impulse for freedom and democracy, which galvanized the battle against political despotism during the Enlightenment, is palpable for those living under economic despotism. Will this impulse be powerful enough to overthrow the barriers erected by liberal theory in the era of political despotism, barriers that opposed the political and the economic, the public and private spheres, political and contractual liberties? Citizens' growing desire to participate in determining the conditions of their own investment in the workplace, and in the firm more generally, is evidence of the subversive power of the democratic ideal upheld by political liberalism itself. Will the democratic impulse gather the force to overcome liberalism's internal contradiction? Will it be powerful enough to bridge the divide that now exists between the political and the economic realms, a divide created in a bygone era to protect its economic interactions from the authoritarian intervention of political despots? Only time will tell.

This book argues that progress is still possible for liberal democracy, that giving core political liberties priority over economic liberalism is the logical and efficient means to advance both our democratic freedoms, and our economies. It is time to push liberalism's taboos into the light, to make it possible for political liberties to take root and flourish in economic life. We must acknowledge that workers are citizens first and foremost – that they are emancipated beings with the inalienable right[8] to participate as equals in determining the standards that guide the institutions in which they live, and which affect their lives. This is indeed the very definition of life in a democracy.

Cited by Friedrich Hayek as expressing the core of his thinking better than he could himself, Milton Friedman penned an impressive threat to those seeking to imagine firms free from capitalist despotism: "if anything is certain to destroy our free society, to destroy its very foundations, it would be a wide-spread acceptance by management of social responsibilities in some sense other than to make as much money as possible. That is a fundamentally subversive doctrine."[9] Let us note that Hayek well understood what was at stake, as he added this comment: "unless we believe that the corporations serve the public interest best by devoting their resources to the single aim of securing the largest return in terms of long-run profits [*to shareholders*], the case for free enterprise [held only by capital investors] breaks down" (Hayek 1960: 116–117).

When despots fear losing their exclusive grip on power, they threaten us with total chaos. This is a classic strategy, and it is nothing less than an intellectual sham. Now that the threat of communism can no longer be brandished against any and all critiques of the liberal economic model, it is time to reopen this critical debate. New perspectives are possible. Friedman has passed on, and with him, an era. It is no longer acceptable to conflate the firm and the corporation, no longer logical to see the firm as a mere instrument over which capital investors must hold absolute power: it is *illegitimate and unreasonable*. Moreover, in an era in which the service and knowledge economy has made human labor the firm's richest source of wealth, it is *no longer intelligent*. Today, we must grant the firm the institutions it so badly needs. This begins with the acknowledgment that the firm is distinct from the corporation, that it is a central, political institution of society, in which a constant balance is sought between the instrumental rationality of capital investors and the expressive rationality of labor investors.

---

[8] For the most powerful and explicit argument in those – liberal – terms, see Ellerman (2010, 2015).

[9] Quote taken from "Three Major Factors in Business Management: Leadership, Decision Making and Social Responsibility," 1958, reproduced in Hayek (1960: 117).

2

64 *Conclusions*

CONSIDERING THE FIRM FOR ITSELF, AT LAST

This book opened by stating its intent to move from analysis to concrete proposal; after all, analysis is hardly pertinent to public debate if it does not at least attempt to present itself in appropriable forms. Today, despite citizens' growing sense that they ought to have the right to participate in governing their own lives, the future of democracy is on shaky ground. The state of U.S. federal politics, climate change, health, and environmental scandals involving major transnational firms around the globe, plummeting voter participation and the rise of the Extreme Right and anti-immigrant sentiment: all of these bear witness to a pervasive – if certainly still hazy – feeling in the world that the future of democracy lies in our ability to regain control of our economy. Our future is too uncertain for academics to abdicate their responsibility to offer constructive contributions to public debate. Economic Bicameralism is one such contribution to this debate, the logical conclusion of an analytical process that examines economic and political relations in light of the history of Western liberal democracy. It offers a response to a great gap in the law: in purely legal terms, the firm as an institution *does not* (yet) *exist* (Robé 1999, 2001, 2011) – only corporate, commercial, and labor law, neither of which addresses the firm as such in its institutional entirety. They are, as a result, unable to account for the firm as it is, a political entity that strikes a balance between the interests of capital investors and labor investors, between instrumental and expressive rationality.

Until now, the strategy of the critical social sciences[10] has been to limit the grip of instrumental rationality typical of capitalism by confining it to the economic sphere.[11] This strategy was doomed to fail, as instrumental

---

[10] Or Critical Theory: these are synonyms.

[11] This study offers a new perspective on the question of social justice, which drives debates in critical theory. It offers a way out of the dilemma of redistribution *versus* recognition, which has so occupied the field since that seminal debate (Fraser and Honneth 2003). The present perspective shows how the quest for social justice will end at an impasse if it cannot include political justice in the economy – even more specifically, if it cannot include democratic justice in the economic field. Consequently, today it is important that the debate over recognition and redistribution be *politicized*. This is a necessary condition for its becoming more incisive in social struggle, and de facto, more pertinent from the perspective of what is at stake in redistribution given that both goals are tightly connected. Indeed, demanding that the equal dignity of all people be acknowledged politically in the economic domain itself, demanding recognition of the fundamental equality of every group that makes up a firm to bear on its government, with labor investors on the same footing as capital investors, would have significant consequences on the way labor and capital share profits. When it comes to economic life, it must be understood

rationality has the potential to become dominant in every domain. As Habermas recognized, life's other "spheres," including the lifeworld, have been at least partially colonized by the demands of instrumental rationality. And yet instrumental rationality, present as it may be in these fields of activity, does not necessarily dominate them.[12] Put another way, in the case of work life, instrumental rationality competes with expressive rationality. The former should therefore be institutionally constrained by the standards of the the latter; that is, by democratic justice. It is urgently necessary to bring economic exchange under the aegis of renewed democratic sovereignty: in other words, it is time to *govern the capitalist firm*, which, so long as effective global public authorities do not exist, constitutes the most straightforward way to *govern capitalism*.

The goal of the *political theory of the firm* we have outlined in this book is to account for the firm as a political entity in and of itself, one that requires more than the analytical and legal tools of the past. This perspective can address the contradiction between capitalism and democracy at the level of the firm, and can help to set the firm on a path toward democratization. This is an original strategy, in an intellectual context where the firm has been largely ignored, mistaken yet again for the corporation. Colin Crouch has expressed worry that we have entered an era of "post-democracy," marked by the growing influence of markets and corporations, and by the weakening of states (2004, 2011). If we are to counter this "post-democratic" trend and reinforce the project of building a democratic society (Unger 1998, Fung and Olin Wright 2003, Rogers 2012, Sabel 2012) through "deepening and extending" democracy (Olin Wright and Rogers 2015: 545–552), in particular at the transnational level (Grewal 2008, McKean 2013), it is urgently important to open the debate over the nature of the firm. Commentators who are pessimistic about the prospects of a democratic future have been looking in the wrong direction. They have systematically ignored the firm, and its dramatic

---

that redistribution demands that workers be included in the government of the workplace. Redistribution requires recognition, understood here as the political emancipation of workers. The debate over the end of wage work will have to be reexamined (Gorz 1964, 1988) in this new context, too. It will be necessary to define precisely how, once wage workers have been politically emancipated within the workplace, the concept of wage work remains (or not) pertinent. Here, there is a crucial connection to be made with the proposal of basic income (Van Parijs and Vanderborght 2017).

[12] Paradoxically, Habermas himself, with his luminous contributions to the field of social theory, worsened this analytic impasse by seeking to fight the pervasive grip of instrumental rationality.

potential for renewed democratic progress, as if spellbound by the corporation too. The social sciences have a central role to play in developing a much-needed *political theory of the firm*, one that provides an alternative to the *economic theory of the firm* (which perpetuates the *Reductio Ad Corporationem*, as we have seen, the confusion of the corporation with the firm). Such an alternative would help in the process of recognizing the firm as a political institution central to our times and engaged with the larger – democratic – goal of society. It would help to develop the conceptual tools needed to begin the process of transitioning the firm toward democratization.

Wolfgang Streeck, an acute observer of the evolution of capitalism, predicts that Western countries will in the future be ruled by market capitalism in ever-deepening crisis as our democracies will slowly be pulled apart by their dependence on financial markets (Streeck 2013). Streeck ends his analysis of this long-term crisis with a call for a renewed project of democratization, urging us to look for the means to nurture institutional mechanisms through which society can control its own markets. Thomas Piketty (2013: 940), in his formidable effort to account for the power of capital in the twenty-first century, also suggested that the increasing levels of inequality he observes alongside the growing power of capitalists could be offset by giving more power to labor unions and granting workers representatives in the boards of corporations. In the face of unsustainable levels of inequality, the great scholar Anthony Atkinson joined in asking for a new "legal framework that allows trade unions to represent workers on level terms" (2016). It is clear that in the current debate over how to regain control over market forces, the firm is the most crucial institution of all. And yet, reduced to and overtaken by the corporation, firms, mistaken for the mere legal clothing that they currently wear, have kept off of our political radar. It is time for them to be constructively identified as the institution that they are. Firms do exist. They are political entities that must be pulled from the shadow of the corporations that currently control them. Firms, reliant as they are on both capital and labor investors, driven by both instrumental and expressive rationalities in a combination that depends on their individual histories, activities, and industries, are the *locus princeps* of the contradiction between capitalism and democracy. Without firms, there are no markets; in particular, there are no financial markets. That the firm has managed to escape the scrutiny of democratic society – and of most of academia – is evidence of the force of the corporation's sway over the firm. Observing this sway – and its extreme convenience to capital investors – is central to the *economic theory of the firm.* If nothing else, we hope that this book has succeeded in pleading for the importance of grasping the firm in its entirety, as well as facing seriously the consequences of this change in perspective.

In a post-1989 world in which private property is enshrined in the Universal Declaration of Human Rights,[13] the corporation and its defenders have managed to obscure the fundamental difference between the vehicle that structures capital investments and the firm. That this vehicle exists as an option to structure capital in a free and democratic society does not give it the exclusive right to analyze, theorize, and govern the firm. The *privately-owned* nature of shares in a corporation cannot cancel out the *political* nature of the firm as an institution central to democratic society, and answerable to its aspirations and expectations. Recognizing this confusion offers renewed hope. Once we begin to consider *firms as political entities* falling within the purview of democratic society, they become vehicles, not of shareholders only, but of all citizens on the path to a prosperous, just, truly democratic and free society.

* * *

This then, was the first goal of this book: to go beyond the reductionist view of the firm as corporation and offer a realistic view of the capitalist firm in its entirety, a *political* entity. Its second goal was to set the firm within the long-term trend of the transition of the economy into the public sphere of our democratic societies. It proposed to do so by expanding the firm's current, monocameral capitalist governance structure so that all its investors, i.e., including its labor investors, are empowered to take part in the firm as responsible citizens capable of participating fully, through representatives, in the collective expression of their sovereignty. As a result, this book suggested that the era of *corporate governance* over the firm be brought to a close, so that we may fully enter the era of the *government of the firm*, via an institutional design aligned with the democratic goals of our societies. The bicameral government of the capitalist firm is 1 way to do so.

Bicameralism stabilizes the firm as an institution by placing it on its true foundations: the encounter between capital investors and labor investors, the combination of *instrumental* and *expressive* rationalities. Power must be justified in a democratic society. Government must be *legitimate, reasonable, and intelligent.* The government of the firm cannot be "outsourced" to the corporation, left in the hands of capital investors

---

[13] Article 17 of the UDHR reads: (1) Everyone has the right to own property alone as well as in association with others. (2) No one shall be arbitrarily deprived of his property.

only. It is time for democracy to set its sights on governing global capitalism, and this should begin by establishing appropriate government of
the firm, global capitalism's central institution. Actors in the workplace
are waiting to experiment. Capital investors have choices to make. Labor
unions and social movements have new strategies to devise. Social scientists have a complete agenda to coordinate. Our democratically elected
officials have a duty to strengthen the institutional equipment of the firm,
so that it can properly contribute as an institution central to our democratic life. The time has come for enfranchised working citizens across
the globe to voice their expectation to play their part in governing their
places of work. There is a way out of corporate despotism, and toward a
renewed and sustainable democracy. History teaches us the path forward.

Philosophers have hitherto only interpreted the world in various ways; the point is to change it.

Karl Marx, *11th thesis on Feuerbach* (*Brussels*, 1845)

That, I believe, is our basic function: to develop alternatives to existing policies, to keep them alive and available until the politically impossible becomes politically inevitable.

Milton Friedman, *Preface* to the 1982 edition (1962: xiv)

A Reader's Guide for Reflection and Debate about Economic Bicameralism

Some have questioned the value of discussing theoretically viable alternatives if they are not strategically achievable. The response to such sceptics would be that there are so many uncertainties and contingencies about what lies ahead that we cannot possibly know now what the limits of achievable alternatives will be in future. Given this uncertainty, there are two reasons why it is important to have clear-headed understandings of the range of viable alternatives.

First, developing such understandings now makes it more likely that, if future conditions expand the boundaries of what is possible, social forces committed to emancipatory change will be in a position to formulate practical strategies for implementing an alternative.

Second, the actual limits of what is achievable depend in part on beliefs about what sorts of alternatives are viable. This is a crucial sociological point: social limits of possibility are not independent of beliefs about limits. When a physicist argues that there is a limit to the maximum speed at which a thing can travel, this is meant as an objective, untransgressable constraint, operating independently of our beliefs about speed. In the social case, however, beliefs about limits systematically affect what is possible. Developing compelling accounts of viable alternatives, therefore, is one component of the process through which these limits can themselves be changed.

Erik Olin Wright (2006: 97–98)

1. *Isn't Economic Bicameralism just German codetermination by another name? It sounds like just another form of labor-management parity.*

No: first, it should be recalled that *Mitbestimmung* is a unicameral system in which a single chamber, the board of overseers or supervisory board, is composed of an equal number of employee and shareholder representatives (hence the "co" in codetermination). In the form of codermination put in place in Germany this single chamber Parliament is chaired by a president appointed by the shareholder representatives and not the employee representatives (see Figure 3) who not only runs the board, but casts the deciding vote in case of deadlock. Thus, in the famous words of the German legal scholar Franz Gamillscheg (1979), German codetermination is a form of "false parity;" in reality, the shareholders enjoy a one-vote majority at all times, because one of their representatives is always able to cast the deciding vote. Economic Bicameralism requires a majority in *both* the Labor Investors' *and* the Capital Investors Chamber of Representatives to approve any decision. This means that each chamber has equal veto power. Second, and contrary to *Mitbestimmung*, Economic Bicameralism is not just another form of labor-management parity in the sense that it is not a technique for *managing* or even *comanaging* firms. It is a form of *government* in which capital and labor investors are represented equally and weigh in on all strategic decisions on the same footing. Hence, in a bicameral firm, decisions must be approved by a majority (50% + 1 vote) in both chambers, by the representatives of *both* labor and capital investors. See Figure 6.

2. *Unions are already stumbling blocks for firms. Giving them more power would intensify conflict and slow the economy.*

Economic Bicameralism is not designed to give unions more or less power. Its goal is to change the way power is held over and in the firm. Contemporary institutions for labor-management dialogue and collective labor rights (bargaining rights, etc.), including unions, were not designed to help firms prosper by involving their forgotten investors – that is, labor investors. This, and not the intensification or attenuation of union influence, is a central goal of Economic Bicameralism. There is no reason to believe that unions, if given a new role in a fundamentally different power system, would not adapt their working methods accordingly. It would certainly seem that given their history, unions would be a fitting vehicle for labor investors' collective representation in the firm, and would be well positioned to help prepare employees to run for election to the Labor Investors' Chamber of Representatives. The history of capitalism shows that labor organizations have, at best, been co-opted into comanaging firms (see Part I). With the exception of a few cases of true-parity *Mitbestimmung*, they have never been asked to participate in the actual government of capitalist firms, and never been placed in a position of direct and practical responsibility over firms' futures. It therefore seems logical enough that they have not, in the past, held themselves responsible for advancing corporations' interests. But if labor investors were placed on equal footing with capital investors and could participate in decisions regarding the firm's future, then it seems just as logical that they would behave responsibly toward their fellow employee-citizens, and hold themselves accountable for decisions affecting the life of the firm. It is not so surprising that unions acting irresponsibly from time to time under current systems of comanagement – indeed, one might even argue that they are provoked by the fact that their cooperation is something of a sham: after all, at the end of the day, all parties know that in a corporation-ruled firm, the capital investors have all the real power. If we hope to see firms thrive – from a standpoint of both economic efficiency and democratic justice – it is necessary to actively acknowledge the complementary roles of their two main constituents by involving them all equally through an appropriate institutional design. This implies guaranteeing equality to labor investors and their representatives and creating an infrastructure that fosters equitable collaboration, which is the goal of the bicameral firm's two-chamber, representative system of government.

3. Isn't Economic Bicameralism just another betrayal of the proletariat, in a long line of betrayals – another attempt to "help the worker" that ends up reinforcing their alienation within the capitalist system?

Economic Bicameralism is a proposal intended to function in the capitalist system as it currently exists. But it is radical departure from all known institutions of comanagement or codetermination in that it is not a structure designed by capital investors to co-opt labor investors in a frame and a set of goals chosen by the former alone. True, it recognizes the existence of capital. If it did not, it would be a form of labor-managed and -governed firms (see Dow 2003). See Figure 4. But – and here is its radical difference – it refuses capital the historic privilege it has enjoyed in the government of the firm. Economic Bicameralism establishes *equality* between capital and labor, providing both of them with equal power and equal political rights through their respective chambers.

Furthermore, Economic Bicameralism may be interpreted as what the Marxist thinker Mandel called a "transitional demand." Such demands, according to Mandel, advanced toward what was "bound to become a struggle which shakes the very foundations of capitalism" (1973: 9). This idea accords with Gorz's (1964) "achievable intermediate goals," which would open up a "practical way forward" to democratic socialism.

Economic Bicameralism may be considered as a "transitional demand" in the sense that it offers an institutional structure that allows firms to shift from unicameral capital ownership and control to unicameral worker ownership and control. It could, in other words, help firms to transition to self-governed, or democratic firms. To achieve self-management, labor investors could purchase a corporation's shares from its capital investors (for discussion of this specific phase, see Dow 2003). If this were their goal, they would be able to achieve it all the more effectively having honed their governance skills during the bicameral phase.

4. *Economic Bicameralism seems like a half-measure. Why not a fully democratic firm that gives no power at all to capitalists?*

A strong case may be made for the full democratization of firms, so that they are run by their real investors; that is, the people who invest not money – which, after all, is a medium – but their person (Ellerman 1992, 2015; Mackin, 2015; Pinto, forthcoming). As mentioned in the answer to the previous question, the bicameral firm may be seen as a bridging institution on the way to a fully democratic firm. In Europe, political bicameralism was implemented in periods of transition from despotism to more democratic forms of government, and has continued to evolve. Lately, for example, the upper chamber of the English Parliament, though initially reserved for the nobility, has been partially reformed so that some of its seats are no longer hereditary. Even a cursory look at the history of political institutions shows that political democracy did not emerge fully formed – it is the product of a long historical process that continues today. No democratic revolution has yet succeeded in producing a perfectly democratic form of government overnight. Indeed, in the political realm, we are still pursuing the democratic ideal, still trying to figure out what it means in the age in which we live. Nor should we forget that the so-called "civilized" nations of the nineteenth century did not allow all their citizens to vote. It took time to extend suffrage to all men (not to mention women), and universal suffrage did not come about in most countries until after the Second World War. Democracy is still being perfected. Today, for example, the suffrage of permanent resident aliens is a highly controversial topic in Europe: in some countries they have voting rights in local elections only; in others, they have none at all.

What is key to recall is that the history of democracies in the West includes what we call a "bicameral moment," in which a compromise is struck between two classes (the aristocratic landholders and the people), or between two sets of interests (subnational entities and the federal state). This "bicameral moment" is just one step on democratization's long and bumpy road to democratization, which has always been marked by compromises. The power structures of firms cannot be transformed overnight from their despotic and corporate reality into democracies. They require representative governments, structured around checks and balances that establish equilibrium among their constituent bodies. Once firms have finally been recognized as political entities, labor and capital investors will at last be acknowledged as their constituent bodies, and the work of democracy can proceed.

5. Bicameralism in firms would weaken union power. It could make unions redundant, and, whether or not this is Economic Bicameralism's intent, ultimately cause them to disappear.

This would only happen if unions themselves refused to participate in bicameralism.

Instead of weakening them, Economic Bicameralism might well have the immediate effect of reinforcing labor organizations, since these organizations have a long tradition of worker representation and of enabling worker voice (Freeman and Medoff 1984), not weakening it. In terms of union' strategy, more than three decades ago Elaine Bernard wrote words more relevant then ever: "rather than relegating workplace democracy to an abstract long-term goal, labor today needs to tap this source of wider appeal for unions by placing the extension of democracy into the workplace front and center in its vision of a new labor movement and its role in the changing workplace." (Bernard 1996: 4) Indeed, candidates might well run for seats in the Labor Investors' Chamber of Representatives on slates assembled by official, state-recognized unions. A bicameral firm would strengthen the role, the ranks, and the raison d'être of unions, since employee representatives would have to be unionized. Unions are central to Economic Bicameralism in a broader sense as well, in that they are responsible for coordinating workers beyond the limits of the firm, working to ensure that solidarity is maintained among workers in different firms, and to coordinate negotiations at the industry or national level, and beyond. It would be up to unions to coordinate the positions and opinions of different firms' Labor Investors' Chambers to promote the ideal of worker solidarity. Economic Bicameralism does not alter the architecture of collective bargaining on the industry level as it exists today in some countries; indeed, at the firm level, it may be seen as the full and final achievement of labor-management dialogue, inspired by its roots in collective bargaining. Making bicameral firms a legal possibility would bolster workers' rights and further their interests, as well as expanding the scope of action of union and personnel delegates in the pursuit of democratizing the government of firms.

6. If it is the only valid form of government, then Economic Bicameralism should be imposed on all firms.

This book does not claim that Economic Bicameralism is the only valid form of firm government; rather, it asserts that the corporation's dominance over the firm is illegitimate and counterproductive. Economic Bicameralism represents one possible institutional design for the legitimate government of the capitalist firm. Tax incentives for companies wishing to implement bicameral government seem an appropriate implementation route, at least at the outset. Classically structured – corporate – firms wishing to make the transition could offset implementation costs through corporate tax reductions or exemptions. Once firms begin adopting Economic Bicameralism, then it could be promoted by taxing bicameral firms at a lower rate than unicameral corporate firms, because of their *added democratic value*.

As is already the case with the reporting of good practices in corporate governance, it would be useful to require corporations that have chosen to retain despotic power over their firms to publicly justify their choice and to explain – particularly with regard to their employees – why a bicameral structure would be inappropriate to their situation.

7. Economic Bicameralism is totally unrealistic in today's globalized world – capital is just too mobile.

No, to the contrary, a multinational Labor Investors' Chamber of Representatives in a multinational firm would help foster the global labor solidarity that is needed to create a serious counterweight to global capital. Contemporary issues such as competition among different plants in the same firm, subcontracting, and union and human rights violations would be dealt with very differently if firms were led by a Labor Investors' Chamber of Representatives, alongside a Capital Investors' Chamber of Representatives, rather than by capital investors alone. Economic Bicameralism is a necessary tool for fighting "divisive capitalism" (Pech 2007) and its devastating effects on workers around the world.

8. Economic Bicameralism is unrealistic because it is impractical; it would make firms less competitive.

It is true that imposing bicameralism on firms in today's competitive environment without changing any of the ground rules of our economy might be a risky proposition. But if governments were serious enough to measure the desirable effects that Economic Bicameralism could produce in our societies – worker well-being, the health of our democracies, mindfulness of environmental impact and concern for neighborhoods, and the increased innovation capabilities and productivity that are known to result when the basis for motivation in the workplace is altered, not to mention lower absenteeism and fewer accidents in the workplace – it seems only legitimate to lower taxes for firms choosing to implement bicameral government structures. After all, in their scramble to attract capital, contemporary governments are all too happy to lower corporate taxes in exchange for smaller results than that. It is nevertheless true that if a country believes that the general interest is best served by maximizing profits for the few (in this case, shareholders), then Economic Bicameralism is not the solution.

9. Firms cannot afford to compensate both a Labor and a Capital Investors' Chamber of Representatives.

This seems extremely unlikely. For one thing, Labor and Capital Investors' Chambers would be limited in size, ideally ranging from 5 to 50 members depending on the size of the firm. Today's corporations seem to have no trouble compensating – often very lavishly – the members of their boards, and there is no reason to believe that this would change were they to be divided into two chambers. Given the amount of money already mobilized to compensate board members – whose utility is relative at best – it seems difficult to imagine that firms would lack the means to compensate – and require more work of in return – the members of two chambers.

10. If firms set up chambers of representatives for capital and labor investors, wouldn't logic demand that they include chambers for suppliers, customers, the environment, etc.?

Bicameral firms could include these parties in their government structure as long as they were counted as "constituent bodies." It should be recalled that the two constitutive logics of the firm are instrumental and expressive. The Labor Investors' Chamber of Representatives might include labor investors not directly employed by the firm through a standard contract of employment, but involved in other ways, such as suppliers (in the case of a tight supply chain), customers, or users (in the case of the platform economy, where such people actually invest their person in the development of the firm). The question of who should be granted membership and voting rights in the Labor Investors' General Assembly is an interesting issue and should remain open to debate. Workers employed by subcontractors who have no say in decisions made by the contracting firm might be included, for example (De Munck and Ferreras 2013). At stake in the question of whether or not to include them is the composition of the chambers, and thus of the way votes are accorded within the Labor Investors' General Assembly. For instance, a bicameral firm might decide that its subcontracted workers ought to be represented alongside other labor investors, on the grounds that these persons invest their person via their labor in the firm's life and growth, and might give them voting rights to elect representatives to the Labor Investors' Chamber.

Beyond these specific investments, which ought to be considered in deciding who counts as a labor investor, it should be recalled that firms exist within the context of contemporary society, and therefore within contemporary society's existing political and legal structures. Issues affecting other stakeholders can and should be dealt with through existing democratic institutions and power structures. National deliberative bodies already decide upon the legal frameworks for environmental or consumer issues, for example. Similarly, environmental and health issues should not be devolved to the decision-making power of individual firms. Rather, regulation should be imposed at the highest possible level in order to ensure a frame within which firms are able to compete, but not over decisions that impact people's health or the environment. Bicameral firms would have limited competence in such matters, just as deliberative bodies on the municipal level of national political structures have limited competence – they are both part of a larger whole. Furthermore, issues relating to a firm's operating environment, its suppliers, its subcontractors, its customers, and the communities affected by its physical presence are likely issues for a Labor Investors' Chamber of Representatives to take into consideration – certainly more likely than they are now to be considered by Capital Investors' Boards, given that people who invest their person in a firm have much more contact with all these different stakeholders, and are more often than not members of the environment in which the firm is located.

11. *Having two chambers in a firm would be totally counterproductive. A firm's efficiency comes from its ability to react quickly to demand. There isn't time for debate in that equation. In a bicameral firm, customer needs would take a back seat to negotiations between the two chambers.*

The goal of Economic Bicameralism is not to cause constant debate and discussion in the workplace – that would be conflating executive and legislative power, and confusing direct democracy with representative democracy. It goes without saying that successfully deployed bicameralism would allow a firm to fulfill its orders in a timely fashion; after all, a firm's success depends on its ability to do so. Of course Economic Bicameralism includes a system of hierarchy and execution, and does not infringe on the managerial authority of the executive committee –this system merely needs to be justified in a legitimate fashion.

12. *The idea that labor representatives would be capable of electing effective leaders (that is, members of the executive committee and a CEO) for a firm is quixotic: how could a leader elected by labor representatives hope to take a firm line and make unpopular decisions if needed, knowing that her job depended on their approbation?*

One has only to look at cooperative businesses with worker-elected executive committees to see that this objection is unfounded: such companies regularly make difficult decisions, including layoff plans or individual dismissals (Erdal 2011). The case of the Semler business evoked earlier in this text (1999) confirms that being appointed and evaluated by employees in no way diminishes a company director's ability to exercise authority. To the contrary, it bolsters a leader's legitimacy. Furthermore, and perhaps even more importantly, if this objection were valid, would it not be applicable to the democratic state?

13. *Self-governed models have been tested and found unsuccessful – if a solution doesn't work, why not let it go and move on?*

This is a false statement. Many cooperatives and self-governed firms are thriving (Pinto, forthcoming). Yet at a macro level, given its relative share in the capitalist economy, no conclusions can be drawn about the success of self-governed firms: the sample size is far too small, and obvious external problems must be accounted for; for example, numerous self-managed businesses have gone under because banks often restrict or refuse financing to nonconventional businesses.[1] In some cases it might be argued that experiments in cooperative businessess have failed because they neglected the drive for efficiency that is the hallmark of instrumental rationality, which is fully represented in the bicameral model, and thus may continue to help foster the firm's success. That said, it bears repeating that Economic Bicameralism is not a form of self-government.

14. *The logic of instrumental rationality lends itself to rapid problem-solving in a way that expressive rationality and democratic account-ability do not. Instrumental rationality is the more efficient one, since democratic logic tends to wait for crisis situations before pro-ceeding to radical measures.*

The most important factor in swift and efficient problem-solving is prox-imity. This means the problem-solver's degree of closeness to the prob-lem, access to information, and the visibility of a problem's impact or potential consequences, as well as that of its solution. So-called problems surface more quickly in small democratic organizations. The more freely and easily information circulates, the more swiftly issues can be articu-lated and dealt with (see Amartya Sen's classic study of the link between drought, freedom of information, and famine in India, which links non-democratic political structures that muzzle freedom of the press to poverty and hunger). Because economic bicameralism guarantees that the voice of *both* instrumental *and* expressive rationalities will be heard, it offers fur-ther assurance that issues of efficiency affecting the future of the firm will be dealt with in a timely fashion.

In further response to this objection, we might look at the origins of the massive economic crisis that began in 2008. The financial firms at the root of the crisis were not, to our knowledge, in any way motivated – or hindered, as the case may be – by the logic of expressive rationality and democratic accountability; to the contrary, they could be considered emblematic of instrumental rationality, ideal-typical of the corporate firm. And yet not 1 of them seems to have been able to prevent or foresee the

---

[1] Indeed, the resounding success of the Basque cooperative group Mondragon is due in part to their access to financing (Whyte and Whyte 1991, Freundlich 2009): when the Group was founded in the middle of the past century, a cooperative bank was founded alongside it to finance its economic growth, meaning that it was not adversely affected by the mistrust of the traditional capitalist lending system.

mistakes that led to this massive recession, and not 1 of them has found a solution in anything approaching a timely fashion.

15. Executive pay is the real problem. When performance pay linked to stock value is a significant part of compensation packages, executives become even more invested in stock prices than shareholders, and even more obsessed with short-term gains. Furthermore, compared to shareholders (to principal shareholders, in any case) executives' positions in firms are relatively temporary, giving them even less reason to care what happens in the long term. Correcting this trend would be enough to guarantee better conditions for firms, allowing them to return their focus to long-term growth, in the interests of shareholders and employees alike.

This is true, in the sense that executive pay packages have been heavily weighted to favor variable compensation (stock options, bonuses, etc.), making high-level managers overly sensitive to stock prices and shortening their perspective on the firm. These practices are the ultimate embodiment of all-instrumental ideology as expressed in "principal-agent theory," a central part of the economic theory of the firm. But lowering the proportion of variable compensation will not clear up the problem of the unjustified heteronomy to which labor investors are currently subject because firms are being run as if they were merely corporations. As long as labor investors do not have equal say in their firms' means and ends, firms will remains structurally biased toward instrumental rationality, and in particular toward shareholder value – and that is not only a problem of efficiency, it is also a problem of democratic justice, and vice versa.

16. The bicameral firm runs counter to the spirit of capitalism.

If capitalism is defined as a monopoly of capital owners over decisions regarding the organization of labor and the allocation of profit, then this is true. It is also true in the sense that bicameral firms might make it possible for the economic fabric of our society to evolve toward a post-capitalist era. Seen in this light, Economic Bicameralism offers a roadmap for transitioning to a post-capitalist society driven by democratic firms, which would progressively evolve from bicameral into unicameral labor-governed firms, for instance, as workers bought back shares in the corporation through an ESOP plan, which would effectively dissolve the Capital Investors' Chamber of Representatives. With support from the states, this transition might well lead to a flourishing economic field composed of an increasing number of self-governed firms, giving true meaning to the idea of economic democracy.

But in the sense that a bicameral firm gives equal weight to capital investors and labor investors, thus fully acknowledging "capitalist reality," then this assertion is false. This point should not be neglected or disregarded and indeed bears repeating if our argument has not yet been clear enough. To return to our analogy with English Parliament – and contrary to the communist approach to government – the English nobility was never overthrown; it retained power through the House of Lords. The nobility was simply checked and balanced by the House of Commons – and was able to check and balance the "commoners" in return. Economic Bicameralism is perfectly compatible with the economy in its current state, which is largely organized along capitalist lines. Furthermore, bicameral firms will be perfectly able to compete within a market environment composed largely of unicameral corporate firms. Furthermore, they should quickly become smarter innovators, and producers of positive externalities at all levels, by improving the satisfaction of their own workers and business partners and by their positive contributions to the common good, particularly to the democratic health of society.

17. *Economic Bicameralism isn't revolutionary enough. What the world needs is unicameral, worker-controlled firms.*

As stated earlier, if this is the goal then bicameral firms would be excellent bridging institutions in the larger transition (Olin Wright 2010) toward a democratic economy (a *demo-nomy*), since they make it possible to transition from 1 unicameral government to another, from capital ownership to employee ownership.

Again, as explained earlier on, a Labor Investors' Chamber of Representatives could take control of a firm by purchasing all its shares, if it wished to (e.g. Dow 2003; see Mackin 2015 on ESOP/employee stock ownership plans). Since the argument for Economic Bicameralism is based in part on the idea that firm government should be *reasonable*, the logic of checks and balances should be respected in those firms too, in particular via ensuring a place for union representation considered as "loyal opposition" (Ellerman 1988). That being said, it might be desirable to carefully maintain the role of instrumental logic in firm government. A firm is defined in large part by its economic ends (the production of a good or service), particularly as it is operating in a market. Even if traditional capital investors are no longer involved in firm government, the firm will still need to take into account the demands of instrumental rationality.

18. Economic Bicameralism denies property rights.

Not at all: bicameral firms are founded on the recognition of shareholders' ownership of capital (via their shares) in the corporation. Economic Bicameralism merely seeks to change the rights attendant on that ownership by creating a new framework in which property rights would be exercised: capital owners would no longer have a monopoly over decisions regarding the firm to which the corporation is attached and in which they hold shares. Instead, they would have the same weight as labor investors in those decisions. And since the two chambers in a bicameral firm are equal, capital investors maintain veto rights over all decisions, just as labor investors do. Economic Bicameralism does not strip capital investors of their rights; it merely grants the (same) rights capital investors (already) enjoy to labor investors. Capital investors merely lose their monopoly in corporate firms. They must share power, in order to guarantee that the government of the firm is *legitimate, reasonable*, and *intelligent*.

19. Economic Bicameralism denies the risks taken by shareholders.

To the contrary, Economic Bicameralism acknowledges the risks taken by *both* the firm's constituent bodies, by labor and capital investors alike. Only when we confuse firms with corporations do we lose sight of the fact that shareholders are not the only risk-takers in a business endeavor. When firms are narrowly understood as the corporation to which they are attached, it might indeed appear that capital investors are the only stakeholders taking any risk. But as soon as the firm is acknowledged in all its complex reality, as soon as it is recognized as an encounter between capital and labor investors, it becomes evident that both groups take risks when they choose to invest in the firm (labor investors through specializing their skill sets, agreeing to a single source of revenue, etc.). If this is so, then shareholders can no longer credibly claim a monopoly over firm government in the name of the risks they take, since they are not the firm's only risk-takers (Landemore and Ferreras 2016).

20. The idea of Economic Bicameralism confuses the state and the firm.

This book does argue that firms are political entities. In Part II, we reviewed the reasons why the firm should be understood as a learning process that deploys itself in the context of contested power relations, partially organized through the legal vehicle of one or more corporations, and which must constantly work to define and redefine its own common goals. We suggested taking this as the descriptive definition for the *firm as a political entity*,which we then confronted with the *critical intuition of democratic justice* that characterizes the expectations of labor investors. This book identifies bicameralism as an escape route from despotism for any political entity on the transition path toward democratization, and concludes that if bicameralism made it possible for societies to transition away from despotism, then this same transition, applied to the corporate firm in order to shift it away from the despotic reign of capital investors, would be just as helpful to the democratic project of our societies.

At no point, however, does it argue that the firm is a state. Rather, it recognizes that both the state and the firm are potential forms a political community might take. Firms are small societies built around the pursuit of a specific goal or set of goals (and yet a firm's goals are never set in stone; indeed, they cannot be in cases of innovation-intensive firms, but the frequent goal redefinition these and other firms require ought ideally to be undertaken by all of their constituent bodies). As we have seen, work is best understood as a fundamentally *expressive* experience, and firms as fundamentally *political entities*, because they are spaces in which power relations must strike a balance between the expressive and instrumental rationalities that bring a firm to life. That is the trait firms share with states: they must be understood, and therefore governed, as fully political entities. This normative argument is sustained by an argument in terms of efficiency: in an era dominated by a service-based and knowledge economy, firms would be able to pursue their goals more efficiently if those goals were subject to the broad – and legitimate – consent of their investors. We have elsewhere given a detailed account of the six main objections to the analogy between firm and state, and rebuttals to these objections: see Landemore and Ferreras (2016).

21. *Economic Bicameralism is not feasible for multinational corporations.*

To the contrary, history shows that bicameralism is particularly well adapted to complex federal entities (see, for example, the cases of the United States, Germany, and Switzerland). Bicameralism, because of its supple institutional form, which is compatible with subsidiarity, is therefore ideal for transnational firms functioning in a globalized economy.

Furthermore, Economic Bicameralism would help to address the challenge these firms pose to state powers, since multinational firms are de facto beyond the control of any individual state. Indeed, Economic Bicameralism offers a way to re-politicize and democratize globalization. Governing transnational firms bicamerally would ensure that their government was grounded in and recognized the transborder interdependence that characterizes them.

22. Economic Bicameralism would only be feasible in large firms.

True, multinational firms are the principal target of Economic Bicameralism, because their massive unicameral corporate structures, disconnected from the local, leave them totally subject to the instrumental logic of capital. Large firms are able to ignore the interests and logic of labor in cases where small, family-owned businesses, which are anchored in their communities, cannot – the latter must be more careful to take expressive rationality into account on a local level if they are to maintain cooperation within their ranks. That being said, smaller businesses would do well to address the tensions that exist between instrumental and expressive logics too, in order to build a healthy collaborative environment, which fosters both innovation and efficiency.

23. Economic Bicameralism was designed for a kind of firm that is going extinct; that is, classic Taylor-model firms whose functions are all performed in-house. Today, firms are built on outsourcing and networking; they have no fixed borders. Economic Bicameralism is outdated in our era of liquid capital.

Much to the contrary! Economic Bicameralism would make it possible to grant voting rights to categories of workers (the outsourced, the subcontracted, etc.) that have been totally forgotten by contemporary institutions for labor-management dialogue (De Munck and Ferreras 2013). It offers a solution tailored to the transformations of traditional borders that firms have encountered in the past forty years, by affirming – and potentially even expanding – today's new borders. Economic Bicameralism is a way for all employees to participate in firm government, including those who have been left on the margins in contemporary firms, due to what Piore and Safford have called a loss of firm "integrity" (2006: 313). Economic Bicameralism seeks to actively reconstruct firms, which today have become fissured and networked to an alarming degree (see Chapter 6). Firms have played with the liquidity of capital since deindustrialization began in the West in the mid-1960s in an attempt to escape their responsibilities toward certain groups of employees: first, toward *peripheral* employees (Piore and Doeringer 1971), and, as the economy has changed, through all sorts of "fissuring" techniques (Weil 2014), such as outsourcing and the transformation of the production network (Withford 2005).

It would be up to labor investors and their representatives to decide which interests they would choose to represent, and how representation would work for part-time employees (for example, half-votes for half-time work, 1 vote per worker, etc.) or for subcontracted employees (for example, representation by special delegates or special-interest groups, full integration into the electoral body, etc.). Certainly, these decisions are open to debate, and that is one of the benefits of Economic Bicameralism: to bring them out in the open. Up until now, corporations have largely worked to keep such questions in the shadows, in order to avoid discussing the issue of precisely who a firm's constituents are, and what responsibilities they hold.

24. *The production regime is not only knowledge- and service-based, it is evolving toward robotization and artificial intelligence. When workers are replaced by robots, the issue you are pondering will disappear.*

In some ways, this may be true. The day corporations can entirely automate their workforce, and thus their production, instrumental rationality will have triumphed. Probably, robots designed for production will not possess any sort of expressive rationality (although, given recent developments in artificial intelligence, that remains to been seen). The only investors in this type of firm will be capital investors, providing that they themselves care for and maintain the robots. Such a case is in fact the ideal type of the (so far nonexistent) firm which is a corporation and nothing more.

More realistically, this trend only highlights the urgent need to address the issue of firm government. Influential studies document that a significant portion of current jobs may be replaced by robots as soon as 2020 (Frey and Osborne 2013, Ford 2015). Setting aside the validity of these results to entertain a vision of such a future, we recall that these trends are shaped by human decisions – more specifically, by decisions usually made by investors in capital. If, as so many have argued, work is indeed a central part of the human experience, then the prospect of robotization makes debating and determining the future of work all the more urgent. The prospect of the elimination of work through robots reminds us that work should not to be mistaken for an instrumental activity, but recognized as an expressive activity that integrates citizens into the public sphere, and intensely mobilizes conceptions about justice. If the implementation of robots by firms is to become more widespread, it seems particularly important that decisions about their implementation include those who invest their persons in these firms. Indeed, from the perspective of fostering the democratic capability to make choices about one's own future, identifying ways to ensure that those decisions will be made by the people whose lives will be affected by them is crucially important. Economic Bicameralism is a way to ensure that labor investors have voice in the government of the firm, and can help to orient its future investment decisions regarding the robot/human trade-off. In the years to come, given advances in artificial intelligence and robotization, it should be made clear that when firms hire labor, they are making a deliberate choice to prefer humans over robots. Hence, it would be difficult – and indeed contradictory – to argue that human labor power should be governed as if it were robotic, within a power structure designed to represent instrumental rationality alone. Advances in robotization are a formidable opportunity to highlight the unique qualities of investors "in person" in a firm, and to offer them a fitting environment in which to work. This requires an institutional power structure that gives voice to their specific – expressive – rationality. Here again, the growing need for bicameral firms is visible, in this case, as an institutional structure able to guarantee a productive compromise between instrumental and expressive rationalities.

25. It hardly seems wise to return to bicameralism in an era when political bicameralism seems to be failing our nation-states.

While it is true that the analogy we drew between firms and nations has been a useful one, it has its limits (Landemore and Ferreras 2016). The contemporary state was cast in a parliamentary and bicameral mold that focused on class. Today, states still fail to live up to their democratic ideals. They are even in crisis. A study of the principle of bicameralism shows there is every reason to think that the bicameral model, which was created to force social compromise and to guarantee prosperous social cohesion, and which effectively initiated the movement of democratization of society, is particularly adapted to the corporate firm in its current state in the capitalist economy. But indicates how primitive the level of institutional development in the economic field really is. Since their ongoing mission is to further the democratic ideal, it seems necessary to renew the democratic institutions currently governing our political communities as well, and to innovate in favor of improved forms of representation and participation that are better adapted to deepening the project of the democratic society[2]. Democratizing firms – indeed, this is already a classic argument (Pateman 1970) – is one obvious way to renew and reinvigorate our societies' democratic capabilities and political institutions.

[2] A whole field has emerged that highlights and debates the limits of political representation from different angles, underscoring the need for renewing its perspective through, e.g., direct participation (Pateman), associative democracy (Cohen and Rogers), deliberation (Cohen), directly deliberative polyarchy (Cohen and Sabel), institutional innovation (Unger), and experimentation (Fung and Olin Wright), social dialogue (De Munck, Didry, Ferreras, and Jobert), or random selection of representatives (Landemore).

Bibliography

Abdelal, R. 2007. *Capital Rules: The Construction of Global Finance*. Cambridge, MA: Harvard University Press.

Aglietta, Michel and Antoine Rebérioux. 2005. *Corporate Governance Adrift: A Critique of Shareholders Value*. London: Edward Elgar.

Alchian, Armen. 1975. "Corporate Management and Property Rights." Pp. 133–50 in *The Economics of Property Rights*, edited by E. Furubotn and S. Pejovis. Cambridge, MA: Ballinger Publishing Co.

Archambault, Paul. 1967. "The Analogy of the 'Body' in Renaissance Political Literature." *Bibliothèque d'Humanisme et Renaissance* (29): 21–53.

Arcq, Etienne and Pierre Blaise. 1999. "Les syndicats en Belgique." P. 49 in *Dossiers du CRISP*. Brussels.

Arendt, Hannah. 1958. *The Human Condition*. Chicago: University of Chicago Press.

Aristotle. 350 BC. *Politics*, Benjamin Jowett trans. Online: http://classics.mit.edu/Aristotle/politics.html.

Auroux, Jean. 1981. *Les droits des travailleurs. Rapport au Président de la République et au Premier Ministre*. Paris: La Documentation française.

Bandelj, Nina (ed.). 2009. "Economic Sociology of Work." *Research in the Sociology of Work*. Vol 18. Bingley, UK: Emerald Group Publishing Limited.

Barbier, Jean-Claude and Henri Nadel. 2000. *La flexibilité du travail et de l'emploi*. Paris: Flammarion.

Barreto, Thomas. 2011. "A Theoretical Approach to Co-Op Firms: Beyond Mainstream Reductionism." *Annals of Public and Cooperative Economics* 82 (2): 187–216.

Barth, Erling, Alex Bryson, James Davis, and Richard Freeman. 2014. " It's Where You Work: Increases in Earnings Dispersion across Establishments and Individuals in the U.S." *NBER Working Paper* n°20447.

Beckert, Jens. (2016) *Imagined Futures. Fictional Expectations and Capitalist Dynamics*. Cambridge, MA: Harvard University Press.

Bebchuk, Lucian. 2005. "The Case for Increasing Shareholder Power." *Harvard Law Review* 118 (3): 833–914.

Beffa, Jean-Louis. 2011. "Audition de M. J.-L. Beffa, Président du Conseil d'administration du groupe Saint-Gobin." Pp. 551–58 in *Rapport d''information N°227 fait au nom de la délégation sénatoriale à la prospective sur la prospective du pacte social dans l'entreprise*. Paris: Sénat français.

Bentham, Jeremy. 1997 (1814). *De l'ontologie*. Paris: Seuil.

Berger, Suzanne. 2005. *How We Compete. What Companies around the World Are Doing to Make It in Today's Global Economy*. New York City: Crown Business.

Berle, Adolf A. 1947. "The Theory of Enterprise Entity." *Columbia Law Review* 47 (3): 343–358.

Berle, Adolf and Gardiner Means. 1932. *The Modern Corporation and Private Property*. New York City: Transaction Publishers.

Berlin, Isaiah. 1969. "Two Concepts of Liberty." in *Four Essays on Liberty*, edited by I. Berlin. Oxford: Oxford University Press.

Bernard, Elaine. (1996) *Why Unions Matter*. New Jersey: Open Magazine Pamphlet Series, 1–5.

Biondi, Yuri, Arnaldo Canziani, and Thierry Kirat. 2007. *The Firm as an Entity: Implications for Economics, Accounting and Law*. London and New York: Routledge, 266–291.

Bloch-Lainé, François. 1963. *Pour une réforme de l'entreprise*. Paris: Seuil.

Bloch-Lainé, F. 2000. "Au coeur de l'état." *Annales des Mines. Paris* (Juin): 4–12.

Blondel, Jean and alii. 1970. "Legislative Behaviour: Some Steps Towards Cross-National Measurement." *Government and Opposition* 5 (1): 67–85.

Boltanski, Luc and Laurent Thévenot. 1989. *Justesse et justice dans le travail*. Paris: Presses universitaires de France.

Boltanski, Luc and Laurent Thévenot. 1991. *De la justification: les économies de la grandeur*. Paris: Gallimard.

Boltanski, Luc and Ève Chiapello. (2006) *The New Spirit of Capitalism*. London: Verso Books.

Boltanski, Luc. 2008. "Institutions et critique sociale. Une approche pragmatique de la domination." *Tracés. Revue des sciences humaines* (8):17–43.

Bryson Alex and Richard Freeman. 2006. "Worker Needs and Voice in the US and the UK." *NBER Working Paper* n°12310 June.

Caniëls, Marjolein. C. J. and Adriaan Roeleveld. 2009. "Power and Dependence Perspectives on Outsourcing Decisions." *European Management Journal*, 27 (6): 402–417.

Carley, Mark. 2010. *Developments in Industrial Action 2005–2009*. Dublin: European Foundation for the Improvement of Living and Working Conditions.

Carney, Brian and Isaac Getz. 2009. *Freedom Inc.: Free Your Employees and Let Them Lead Your Business to Higher Productivity, Profits, and Growth*. New York City: Crown Business.

Carpenter, Daniel and David A. Moss (eds). 2013. *Preventing Regulatory Capture. Special Interest Influence and How to Limit It*. Cambridge: Cambridge University Press.

Carpenter, O. F. 1921. "From Political to Industrial Government." Pp. 87–109 in *Industrial Government*, edited by J. R. Commons. New York: MacMillan.

Cassiers, Isabelle. (ed.) (2015) *Redefining Prosperity*. Oxford: Routledge. Routledge Studies in Ecological Economics.

Magna Carta. 1215. Online: http://Www.Aidh.Org/Biblio/Text_Fondat/Gb_01.Htm.

Castoriadis, Cornelius. 1999. (first ed. 1975). *L'institution imaginaire de la société*. Paris: Seuil.

Chandler, Alfred J. 1977. *The Visible Hand. The Managerial Revolution in American Business*. Cambridge, MA: Harvard University Press.

Charest, Gilles. 2007. *La démocratie se meurt, vive la sociocratie !* Reggio Emilia: Esserci Edizioni.

Charles, Julien. 2016. *La participation en actes. Entreprise, ville, association*. Paris: Desclée De Brouwer.

Chassagnon, Virgile. 2008. "The Network-Firm as a Single Real Entity: Beyond the Aggregate of Distinct Legal Entities." DRUID 25th Celebration International Conference 2008 on *Entrepreneurship and Innovation: Organizations, Institutions, Systems and Regions*. Copenhagen, Denmark, pp. 22.

Chassagnon, V. 2011a. "The Law and Economics of the Modern Firm: A New Governance Structure of Power Relationships." *Revue d'Economie industrielle* 134 (1): 25–50.

Chassagnon, V. 2011b. "The Network Firm as a Single Real Entity: Beyond the Aggregate of Distinct Legal Entities." *Journal of Economic Issues* 45 (1): 113–136.

Chassagnon, V. 2014. "Consummate Cooperation in the Network-Firm: Theoretical Insights and Empirical Findings." *European Management Journal* 32: 260–74.

Chassagnon, Virgile and Xavier Hollandts. 2014. "Who Are the Owners of the Firm: Shareholders, Employees or No One?" *Journal of Institutional Economics* 10: 47–69.

Collins, Chuck and Josh Hoxie, "Billionaire Bonanza: The Forbes 400 and the Rest of Us," *Institute for Policy Studies, Special Report*, December.

Ciepley, David. 2013. "Beyond Public and Private: Toward a Political Theory of the Corporation," *American Political Science Review* 107 (1) 139–158.

Clot, Yves. 2001. "Psychopathologie du Travail et Clinique de l'activité." *Éducation Permanente* 1 (146): 35.

Coase, Ronald. 1937. "The Nature of the Firm." *Economica* 4 (16): 386–405.

Coase, Ronald. 1960. "The Problem of Social Cost." *Journal of Law and Economics* 3: 1–44.

Cohen, G. A. 1982. "The Structure of Proletarian Unfreedom." *Philosophy and Public Affairs* 12: 3–33.

Cohen, Joshua and Charles Sabel. 1997. "Directly-Deliberative Polyarchy." *European Law Journal* 3 (4): 313–42.

Cohen, Joshua and Joel Rogers. 1983. *On Democracy. Toward a Transformation of American Society*. New York: Penguin Books.

Cohen, Joshua. 1989. "The Economic Basis of Deliberative Democracy." *Social Philosophy and Policy* 6 (2): 25–50.

Cohen, Joshua. 1997. "Procedure and Substance in Deliberative Democracy."
  Pp. 407–37 in *Deliberative Democracy. Essays on Reason and Politics*, edited
  by J. Bohman and W. Regh. Cambridge, MA: MIT Press.
Cohen, Joshua. 2009. *Philosophy, Politics, Democracy.* Cambridge, MA: Harvard
  University Press.
Cohen, Morris R. 1927. "Property and Sovereignty." *The Cornell Law Quarterly*
  13: 8–30.
Coker, F. W. 1910. *Organismic Theories of the State. Nineteenth Century Interpre-
  tations of the States as Organism or as Person.* New York: Columbia University
  Press.
Collins, Hugh. 1990. "Ascription of Legal Personality to Groups in Complex Pat-
  terns of Economic Integration." *The Modern Law Review*, 53(6): 731–744.
Collins, Randall. (ed.). 1994. *Four Sociological Traditions. Selected Readings.*
  Oxford: Oxford University Press.
Commons, John R. (ed.). 1921. *Industrial Government.* New York: MacMillan.
Compa, Lance. 2014. "An Overview of Collective Bargaining in the United
  States." Pp. 91–98 in *El Derecho a La Negociacion Colectiva: Monografías
  De Temas Laborales*, edited by J. G. Hernández. Seville: Consejo Andaluz de
  Relaciones Laborales.
Constant, Benjamin. 1819. "De la liberté des anciens comparée à celle des mod-
  ernes." Discours prononcé à l'Athénée royal de Paris. Online: http://www
  .panarchy.org/constant/liberte.1819.html.
Corcuff, Philippe. 2009. "Renaissance de l'anticapitalisme en France." Institute
  of French Studies, New York City. Manuscript. Online: http://www.mediapart
  .fr/club/blog/philippe-corcuff/200409/renaissance-de-l-anticapitalisme-en-
  france.
Coutant, Hadrien. (2016) *Un capitalisme d'ingénieurs: construire un groupe aéro-
  nautique après une fusion.* PhD Dissertation. Paris: Sciences Po-Institut d'études
  politiques. Centre de sociologie des organisations (CSO)
Crouch, Colin. 2004. *Post-Democracy.* London: Polity Press.
Crouch, Colin. 2011. *The Strange Non-Death of Neoliberalism.* London: Polity
  Press.
Dahl, Robert A. 1957. "The Concept of Power." *Behavioral Science* 2 (3): 201–
  215.
Dahrendorf, R. 1957. *Class and Class Conflict in Industrial Society.* Stanford:
  Stanford University Press.
Defourny, Jacques and Nyssens, Marthe. (2014) "Social Coops: When Social
  Enterprises Meet the Cooperative Tradition." *Journal of Entrepreneurial and
  Organizational Diversity.* 2 (2): 11–33.
De Munck, Jean and Isabelle Ferreras. 2012. "The Democratic Exchange as the
  Combination of Deliberation, Bargaining, and Experimentation." Pp. 149–169
  in *Renewing Democratic Deliberation in Europe. The Challenge of Social and
  Civil Dialogue*, edited by J. De Munck, C. Didry, I. Ferreras and A. Jobert.
  Oxford-Brussels: Peter Lang Press.
De Munck, Jean and Isabelle Ferreras. 2013. "Restructuring Processes and Capa-
  bility for Voice: Case Study of Volkswagen, Brussels." *International Journal of
  Manpower* 34 (4): 397–412.

De Munck, Jean, Isabelle Ferreras, and Sabine Wernerus. 2010. "Capacité à délibérer et restructuration industrielle. La restructuration de l'usine VW-Audi de Forest-Bruxelles 2006–2007." *CriDIS Working Paper Series* 19: pp. 30.

De Munck, Jean. 2000. "Procéduralisation du droit et négociation collective." Pp. 261–311 in *Démocratie et procéduralisation du droit, Vol. XXX, Bibliothèque de la faculté de droit de l'université catholique de Louvain*, edited by P. Coppens and J. Lenoble. Bruxelles: Bruylant.

De Munck, Jean. Claude Didry, Isabelle Ferreras, and Annette. Jobert (eds), *Renewing Democratic Deliberation in Europe, the Challenge of Social and Civil Dialogue*. Brussels-Oxford: Peter Lang Press.

Dehousse, Renaud. 1990. "Le paradoxe de Madison: réflexions sur le rôle des Secondes Chambres dans les systèmes fédéraux." *Revue du droit public* 3: 643–76.

Dejours, Christophe. 1993. "De la psychopathologie à la psychodynamique du travail." in *Travail: usure mentale. Addendum à la 2ième édition*, Vol. 1. Paris: Bayard.

Delpérée, Francis. 2004. "Les Secondes Chambres parlementaires." *XIXè Session de l'Académie internationale de Droit constitutionnel portant sur les Secondes Chambres parlementaires* XIII: 1–13.

Demsetz, Harold. 1967. "Toward a Theory of Property Rights." *American Economic Review* 57: 347–59.

Desmond, Matthew. 2016. *Evicted: Poverty and Profit in the American City*. New York City: Penguin Random House.

Doeringer, Peter B. and Michael J. Piore. 1971. *Internal Labor Markets and Manpower Analysis*. Lexington, MA: Heath.

Doria, Giancarlo. 2006. "The Paradox of Federal Bicameralism." *European Diversity and Autonomy Papers* 5: 41.

Dow, G. K. 2003. *Governing the Firm: Workers' Control in Theory and Practice*. Cambridge: Cambridge University Press.

Dubet, François. 2006. *Injustices. L'expérience des inégalités au travail*. Paris: Seuil.

Dunlop, John T. 1993. *Industrial Relations Systems*. Boston, MA: Harvard Business School Press.

Durkheim, Emile. 1893. *De la division du travail social*. Paris: Presses universitaires de France.

Ebert, Robert R. and Shea L. Monschein. "Paternalism, Industrial Democracy, and Unionization in the Cleveland Garment Industry, 1900–1935: The Case of the Printz-Biederman and Joseph and Feiss Companies." *The Baldwin-Wallace College Journal of Research and Creative Studies* 2 (2): 18–34.

Ellerman, David. 1988. "The Legitimate Opposition at Work: The Union's Role in Large Democratic Firms." *Economic and Democracy* 9: 437–53.

Ellerman, David. 1992. *Property & Contract in Economics. The Case for Economic Democracy*. Cambridge, MA, Oxford: Blackwell.

Ellerman, David. 2010. "Inalienable Rights: A Litmus Test for Liberal Theories of Justice." *Manuscript*.

Ellerman, David. 2015. "On the Renting of Persons: The Neo-Abolitionist Case Against Today's Peculiar Institution." *Economic Thought* 4 (1): 1–20.

Ellul, Jacques. 1961. *Histoire des Institutions. 1–2/ L'Antiquité*. Paris: Presses universitaires de France.

Elster, Jon. (2012) *Preventing Mischief*. Manuscript.

Endenburg, G. 2002. *Sociocratie: Het Organiseren Van De Besluitvorming*. Delft: Eburon Editie.

Erdal, David. 2011. *Beyond the Corporation. Humanity Working*. London: The Bodley Head.

Fama, Eugene. 1980. "Agency Problems and the Theory of the Firm." *Journal of Political Economy* 88: 288–307.

Fannion, Robert. 2006. *The Pin Maker and the Entrepreneur*. PhD Dissertation. Department of Government. Cambridge, MA: Harvard University.

Favereau, Olivier. 1994. "Règle, organisation et apprentissage collectif: un paradigme non standard pour trois théories hétérodoxes." in *Analyse économique des conventions*, edited by A. Orléan. Paris: Presses universitaires de France.

Favereau, Olivier. 1996. "Contrat, compromis, convention: point de vue sur les recherches en matière de relations industrielles." Pp. 487–507 in *L'état des relations professionnelles. traditions et perspectives de recherches*, edited by G. Murray, M.-L. Morin and I. Da Costa. Toulouse: Octares & Presses de l'Université de Laval.

Favereau, Olivier. 1998. "Décisions, situations, institutions." Pp. 245–56 in *Décisions économiques*, edited by F.O.R.U.M. Paris: Economica.

Ferreras, Isabelle. 2004. *On Economic Bicameralism*. MSc Thesis, MIT Department of Political Science. Cambridge, MA: Massachusetts Institute of Technology.

Ferreras, Isabelle. 2006. "Le Conflit ... Mais quel conflit?" *La Revue Nouvelle* 7/8: 30–35.

Ferreras, Isabelle. 2007. *Critique politique du travail. Travailler à l'heure de la société des services*, Paris: Presses de Sciences Po.

Ferreras, Isabelle. 2007b. "Mouvements syndical et alter-mondialiste: La nouvelle donne." *Recherches sociologiques et anthropologiques* 38 (1): 111–26.

Ferreras, Isabelle. 2012. *Gouverner le capitalisme? Pour le bicamérisme économique*. Paris: Presses universitaires de France.

Ferreras, Isabelle. 2012b. "The Collective Aspects of Individual Freedom. A Case Study in the Service Sector." Pp. 101–18 in *Democracy and Capabilities for Voice. Welfare, Work, and Public Deliberation in Europe*, edited by S. Negrelli, O. de Leonardis and R. Salais. Brussels-Oxford: Peter Lang Press.

Ferreras, Isabelle. 2012c. "La société des services donne un sens politique au travail" Pp. 71–86. in *Sens politiques du travail*, edited by I. Sainsaulieu and M. Surdez. Paris: Armand Colin.

Flauss, Jean-François. 1997. "La Seconde Chambre dans les Etats fédérés." Pp. 135–50 in *Le Bicamérisme*, edited by Association française de droit constitutionnel. Paris: Economica.

Fligstein, Neil. 2001. *The Architecture of Markets*. Princeton, NJ: Princeton University Press.

Ford, Martin. 2015. *Rise of the Robots. Technology and the Threat of a Jobless Future*. New York City: Basic Books.

François, Pierre and Claire Lemercier. 2016. "Une financiarisation à la française (1979–2009). Mutations des grandes entreprises et conversion des élites." *Revue française de sociologie* 57 (2): 269–320.

Franks, Julian, Colin Mayer, Paolo Volpin, and Hannes F. Wagner. 2010. "The Life Cycle of Family Ownership: International Evidence." *Manuscript* October Pp. 27.

Fraser, Nancy and Axel Honneth. 2003. *Redistribution or Recognition? A Political-Philosophical Exchange*. London: Verso.

Fraser, Nancy. 1992. "Rethinking the Public Sphere: A Contribution to the Critique of Actually Existing Democracy." Pp. 109–42 in *Habermas and the Public Sphere*, edited by C. Calhoun. Cambridge, MA: MIT Press.

Freeman, Richard and Edward Lazear. 1995. "An Economic Analysis of Works Councils." Pp 27–50 in *Works Councils. Consultation, Representation, and Cooperation in Industrial Relations*, edited by R. Joel and W. Streeck. Chicago: University of Chicago Press.

Freeman, Richard B. and James L. Medoff. 1984. *What Do Unions Do?* New York City: Basic Books.

Freeman, Richard B. and Joel Rogers. 2006. *What Workers Want*. Ithaca, New York: ILR Press/Russell Sage Foundation.

Freeman, Richard B. and Kelsey Hilbrich. 2013. "Do Labor Unions Have a Future in the United States?" in *The Economics of Inequality, Poverty, and Discrimination in the 21st Century*, edited by R. S. Rycroft. Santa Barbara, CA.: Praeger.

Frère, Bruno. 2009. *Le Nouvel Esprit Solidaire*. Paris: Desclée De Brouwer.

Freundlich, Frederick. 2009. *Generational Perspectives on Employee Ownership: The Relationship between Age and Satisfaction with Cooperative Ownership in Mondragon*, Ed.D. Dissertation, Graduate School of Education, Harvard University.

Frey, Carl Benedikt and Micahel A. Osborne. 2013. "The Future of Employment: How Susceptible are Jobs to Computerisation?" *Oxford Martin School Working Papers*, September.

Friedman, Milton. 1962 (2002). *Capitalism and Freedom*. Chicago: The University of Chicago Press.

Friedmann, Georges. 1956. *Le travail en miettes*. Paris: Gallimard.

Fukuyama, F. 1992. *The End of History and the Last Man*. New York: Free Press.

Fung, Archon and Erik Olin Wright. 2001. "Deepening Democracy: Innovations in Empowered Participatory Governance." *Politics and Society* 29 (1).

Fung, Archon and Erik Olin Wright. 2003. *Deepening Democracy. Institutional Innovations in Empowered Participatory Governance*. London: Verso.

Fung, Archon, Tessa Hebb, and Joel Rogers. 2001. *Working Capital. The Power of Labor's Pensions*. Ithaca, New York: ILR Press.

Gabaix, Xavier and Augustin Landier. 2008. "Why Has CEO Pay Increased So Much?" *The Quarterly Journal of Economics* 123 (1): 49–100.

Gadrey, Jean. 2003. *Socio-économie des services*. Paris: La Découverte.

Gamillscheg, Franz. 1979. "La cogestion des travailleurs en droit allemand. Bilan à la lumière du jugement du Tribunal constitutionnel fédéral du 1er Mars 1979." *Revue internationale de droit comparé* 32 (1): 57–74.

George, Suzanne. 2012. *Shadow Sovereigns: How Global Corporations Are Seizing Power*. London: Polity Press.

Gierke, Otto. 1900. *Political Theories of the Middle Ages*. Translated by F. W. Maitland. Cambridge: Cambridge University Press.

Gindis, David. 2007. "Some Building Blocks for a Theory of the Firm as a Real Entity." In *The Firm as an Entity: Implications for Economics, Accounting and Law*, edited by Y. Biondi, A. Canziani, and T. Kirat. London, New York: Routledge.

Giraud, Olivier, Michèle Tallard, and Catherine Vincent. 2007. "Processus d'institutionnalisation de la démocratie industrielle et crises sociales en France et en Allemagne à la fin des années 1960." *Travail et Emploi* 111 (Juillet-Septembre): 39–52.

Gorz, André. 1964. *Stratégie ouvrière et néo-capitalisme*. Paris: Seuil.

Gorz, André. 1988. *Métamorphoses du travail. Quête du sens. Critique de la raison économique*. Paris: Galilée.

Gorz, André. 1998. "Le travail fantôme." Pp. 30–39 in *Le monde du travail*, edited by J. Kergoat, J. Boutet, H. Jacot, and D. Linhart. Paris: La Découverte.

Gosseries, Axel. 2012. "La propriété peut-elle justifier la primauté actionnariale?" Pp. 439–468 in *L'entreprise: formes de la propriété et responsabilités sociales*, edited by B. Roger. Paris: Lethielleux.

Gourevitch, Alex. 2014. *From Slavery to the Cooperative Commonwealth: Labor and Republican Liberty in the Nineteenth Century*. Cambridge: Cambridge University Press.

Green, Jim. 2000. *Taking History to Heart: The Power of the Past in Building Social Movements*. Amherst, MA: University of Massachusetts Press.

Green, Jim. 2007. *Death in the Haymarket: A Story of Chicago, the First Labor Movement and the Bombing that Divided Gilded Age America*. New York: Pantheon.

Grewal, D. S. 2008. *Network Power: The Social Dynamics of Globalization*. New Haven, CT: Yale University Press.

Guélaud, François. 1991. "Les diverses formes de la gestion de la flexibilité dans les hypermarchés." *Formation-Emploi* (35): 3–13.

Habermas, Jurgen. 1971. *Knowledge and Human Interests*. Translated by J. J. Shapiro. Boston: Beacon Press.

Habermas, Jurgen. 1989. *The Structural Transformation of the Public Sphere. An Inquiry into a Category of Bourgeois Society*. Cambridge, MA: MIT Press.

Hale, David G. 1971. *The Body Politic: A Political Metaphor in Renaissance English Literature*. The Hague: Mouton.

Hall, Peter and David Soskice. 2001. *Varieties of Capitalism. The Institutional Foundations of Comparative Advantage*. Oxford: Oxford University Press.

Hallett, Graham. 1973. *The Social Economy of West Germany*. London: The Macmillan Press.

Hans-Bockler-Stiftung. 2007. "Résultats de la Commission Biedenkopf. Commission gouvernementale pour la modernisation du système allemand de codétermination au niveau de l'entreprise." Online: http://www.boeckler.de/: 7.

Hayek, Friedrich A. von. 1967. *Studies in Philosophy, Politics and Economics*. London: Routledge & Kegan Paul.

Hayek, Friedrich A. von. 1948. *Individualism and Economic Order*. Chicago: The University of Chicago Press.

Hayek, Friedrich A. von. 1960 (2007). "L'entreprise dans une société démocratique: dans l'intérêt de qui devrait-elle et sera-t-elle dirigée?" Pp. 433–49 in *Essais de philosophie, de science politique et d'économie*, F. A. von Hayek. Paris: Les Belles lettres.

Hirst, Derek. 1975. *The Representative of the People? Voters and Voting in England under the Early Stuarts*. Cambridge: Cambridge University Press.

Hochschild, Arlie R. 1983. *The Managed Heart. Commercialization of Human Feelings*. Berkeley: University of California Press.

Hochschild, A. R. 2016. *Strangers in Their Own Land: Anger and Mourning on the American Right*. New York City: The New Press.

Honegger, Claudia, Sighard Neckel, and Chantal Magnin. 2010. *Strukturiete Verantwortungslosigkeit. Berichte Aus Der Bankenwelt*. Berlin: Suhrkamp.

Humbert, Michel. 2007. *Institutions politiques et sociales de l'Antiquité*. Paris: Dalloz.

Jaumotte, Florence and Carolina Osorio Buitron. 2015. "Inequality and Labor Market Institutions." *International Monetary Fund Research Department, IMF Staff Discussion Note*, SDN/15/14, July, 31 pp.

Jensen, Michael C. and William H. Meckling. 1976. "Theory of the Firm: Managerial Behavior, Agency Costs and Ownership Structure." *Journal of Financial Economics* 3: 305–60.

Jung, Jiwook and Frank Dobbin. 2016. "Agency Theory as Prophecy: How Boards, Analysts, and Fund Managers Perform Their Roles." *Seattle University Law Review* 39: 291–320.

Juster, Thomas F. 1986. "Preferences for Work and Leisure." *Economic Outlook USA* First Quarter: 15–17.

Kalberg, Stephen. 1980. "Max Weber's Types of Rationality: Cornerstones for the Analysis of Rationalization Processes in History." *The American Journal of Sociology* 85 (5): 1145–79.

Kirsch, Stuart. 2014. *Mining Capitalism: The Relationship between Corporations and Their Critics*. Oakland, CA: University of California Press.

Knight, Frank. 1922. "Ethics and the Economic Interpretation." *Quarterly Journal of Economics* 36 (3): 454–81.

Kruse, Douglas, Richard Freeman, and Joseph Blasi. 2010. *Shared Capitalism at Work: Employee Ownership, Profit and Gain Sharing, and Broad-Based Stock Options*. Chicago: The University of Chicago Press.

Laloux, Frédéric. 2014. *Reinventing Organizations. A Guide to Creating Organizations Inspired by the Next Stage of Human Consciousness*. Brussels: Nelson Parker.

Lamine, Auriane. 2016. *Accords d'entreprise transnationaux en quête d'effectivité. Etude juridique et prospective d'une norme collective du travail*. Doctoral Dissertation. Louvain Law School. Université Catholique de Louvain.

Landemore, Hélène. 2013. "Deliberation, Cognitive Diversity, and Democratic Inclusiveness: An Epistemic Argument for the Random Selection of Representatives." *Synthese* 190 (7): 1209–1231.

Landemore, Hélène. 2008. "Democratic Reason: The Mechanisms of Collective Intelligence in Politics." *Paper presented at Collective Wisdom: Principles and Mechanisms.* Conference. Paris: Collège de France. May 22–23.

Landemore, Hélène. 2012. *Democratic Reason: Politics, Collective Intelligence, and the Rule of the Many.* Princeton, NJ: Princeton University Press.

Landemore, Hélène and Jon Elster (eds). 2012. *Collective Wisdom: Principles and Mechanisms.* Cambridge: Cambridge University Press.

Landemore, Hélène and Isabelle Ferreras. 2016. "In Defense of Workplace Democracy. Toward a Justification of the Firm-State Analogy." *Political Theory* 44 (1): 53–81.

Lane, Robert E. 1992. "Work as 'Disutility' and Money as 'Happiness': Cultural Origins of a Basic Market Error." *The Journal of Socio-Economics* 21 (1): 43–64.

Laville, Jean-Louis. (ed). 1994. *L'économie solidaire. Une perspective internationale.* Paris: Desclée De Brouwer.

Laville, Jean-Louis. 2010. *Politique de l'association.* Paris: Seuil.

Leitch, John. 1919. *Man to Man: The Story of Industrial Democracy.* New York: Forbes.

Lester, Richard K. and Michael J. Piore. 2004. *Innovation. The Missing Dimension.* Cambridge, MA: Harvard University Press.

Lewis, Ewart. 1938. "Organic Tendencies in Medieval Political Thought." *American Political Science Review* (32): 849–76.

Lincoln, Abraham. 1861. "First Annual Message," December 3. *The American Presidency Project.* Online: http://www.presidency.ucsb.edu/ws/?pid=29502

Lipset, Seymour Martin and Stein Rokkan. 1967. *Party Systems and Voter Alignments: Cross-National Perspectives.* New York City: The Free Press.

Livy, *The History of Rome, Book II.* Online: http://www.loebclassics.com/view/livy-history_rome_2/1919/pb_LCL114.323.xml

Locke, Richard M. 2013. *The Promise and Limits of Private Power: Promoting Labor Standards in a Global Economy.* Cambridge: Cambridge University Press.

Lordon, Frédéric. 2000. *Fonds de pension, piège à con.* Paris: Liber/Raisons d'agir.

Lyon-Caen, Gérard and Arnaud Lyon-Caen. 1978. "La 'doctrine' de l'entreprise." Pp. 570–602 in *Dix ans de droit de l'entreprise,* edited by de Y. Guyon, J. Boucourechliev, A. Jauffret, J. Hémard. Paris: Librairie technique.

Mabille, Xavier. 2000. *Histoire politique de la Belgique.* Bruxelles: CRISP.

Mackin, Christopher. 2015. "Defining Employee Ownership: Four Meanings and Two Models." *Annual Meeting of the American Economic Association.* Boston. Manuscript.

Macpherson, C. B. (1977) The Life and Times of Liberal Democracy. Oxford: Oxford University Press.

Mallet, Serge. 1963. *La nouvelle classe ouvrière.* Paris: Seuil.

Mandel, Ernest. 1973. *Autogestion, occupations d'usines et contrôle ouvrier.* Paris: Maspero.

Manin, Bernard. 1995. *Principes du gouvernement représentatif.* Paris: Calmann-Lévy.

March, James. 1962. "The Business Firm as a Political Coalition." *The Journal of Politics* 24: 662–78.

Mario Turchetti. 2008. "'Despotism' and 'Tyranny' Unmasking a Tenacious Confusion." *European Journal of Political Theory* 7 (2): 159–182.

Marshall, T. H. 1950. *Citizenship and Social Class, and Other Essays.* Cambridge: Cambridge University Press.

Martuccelli, Danilo. 2002. *Grammaires de l'individu.* Paris: Gallimard.

Marx, Karl. 1845. *Thesis on Feuerbach,* Cyril Smith trans. Online: https://www .marxists.org/archive/marx/works/1845/theses/

Marx, Karl. 1847. "The Poverty of Philosophy." Pp. 218–19 in *The Marx-Engels Reader,* edited by R. C. Tucker. New York, London: Norton.

Marx, Karl. 1968. *Oeuvres. Economie II* Paris: Gallimard.

Massaro, Kerry. 2003. "Getting Them to Stay When You Can't Pay." *Wall Street & Technology* August 1: 14.

McKean, Benjamin. 2013. "Disposing Individuals to Solidarity in the Theory and Practice of Global Justice." *American Political Science Association 2013 Annual Meeting*, Manuscript.

Méda, Dominique. (1998) *Le travail. Une valeur en voie de disparition?* Paris: Aubier.

Méda, Dominique and Vendramin, Patricia (2017) *Reinventing Work in Europe. Value, Generations and Labour.* London: Palgrave Macmillan.

Milano, Serge. 1996. *Allemagne, la fin d'un modèle.* Paris: Aubier.

Milanovic, Branko. 2016. *Global Inequality: A New Approach for the Age of Globalization.* Cambridge, MA: Harvard University Press.

Miliband, Ralph. 1969. *The State in Capitalist Society.* London: Weidenfeld and Nicolson.

Mill, John Stuart. 1861 (1998). "Considerations on Representative Government." in J. S. Mill. *Liberty and Other Essays.* Oxford: Oxford University Press.

Miller, Arthur S. 1978. "Toward 'Constitutionalizing' the Corporation: A Speculative Essay." *West Virginia Law Review* 80 (2–3): 187–208.

Mirowski, Philip and Dieter Plehwe. 2009. *The Road from Mont Pélerin: The Making of the Neoliberal Thought Collective.* Cambridge, MA: Harvard University Press.

Montesquieu, Charles de Secondat. 1995 (orig.ed. 1748). *De l'esprit des Lois.* Paris: Gallimard.

Muirhead, Russell. (2004) *Just Work.* Cambridge, MA: Harvard University Press.

Müller-Jentsch, Walther. 2008. "Industrial Democracy: Historical Development and Current Challenges." *Management Revue* 19 (4): 260–73.

Nachi, Mohammed and Matthieu de Nanteuil. 2005. *Eloge du compromis. Pour une nouvelle pratique démocratique.* Louvain-la-Neuve: Academia-Bruylant.

Néron, Pierre-Yves. 2010. "Business and the Polis: What Does It Mean to See Corporations as Political Actors?" *Journal of Business Ethics* 94: 339–345.

Néron, Pierre-Yves. 2013. "Toward A Political Theory of the Business Firm? A Comment on *Political CSR.*" *Business Ethics Journal Review* 1 (3): 14–21.

Norton, Philippe. 1984. "Parliament and Policy in Britain: The House of Commons as a Policy Influencer." *Teaching Politics* 13 (2): 198–221.

Norton, Philippe. 2010. "La nature du contrôle parlementaire." *Pouvoirs* 3: 134–194.

Nyssens, Marthe and Defourny, Jacques. (2017) "Fundamentals for an International Typology of Social Enterprise Models." *International Journal of Voluntary and Non-profit Organizations*. 1: 1–60.

Offe, Claus and Helmut Wiesenthal. 1985. "Two Logics of Collective Action." Pp. 170–220 in *Disorganized Capitalism*, edited by C. Offe. Cambridge: Polity Press.

Olin Wright, Erik. 2006. "Compass Points." *New Left Review* 41: 93–125.

Olin Wright, Erik. 2010. *Envisioning Real Utopias*. London: Verso.

Olin Wright, Erik and Joel Rogers. 2015. *American Society: How it Really Works*. New York City: W. W. Norton.

Olson, John F. 2008. "Is the Sky Really Falling? Shareholder-Centric Corporate Governance vs. Director-Centric Corporate Governance." *Transaction: The Tennessee Journal of Business Law*. 9: 295–304.

Orwell, George. 1946. *Animal Farm: A Fairy Story*. New York: Harcourt, Brace and Company.

O'Sullivan, Mary. 2000. *Contests for Corporate Control: Corporate Governance and Economic Performance in the United States and Germany*. Oxford: Oxford University Press.

Pacces, Alessio M. 2010. *The Law and Economics of Corporate Governance: Changing Perspectives*. Cheltenham, UK, Northampton, MA, USA: Edward Elgar.

Pateman, Carol. 1970. *Participation and Democratic Theory*. Cambridge: Cambridge University Press.

Pech, Thierry. 2007. "Le syndicalisme à l'épreuve du capitalisme séparateur." *La vie des idées* Online: http://www.laviedesidees.fr/Le-syndicalisme-a-l-epreuve-du.html#nh3.

Pettit, Philip. 2013. *On the People's Terms: A Republican Theory and Model of Democracy*. Cambridge: Cambridge University Press.

Phillips, Michael J. 1994. "Reappraising the Real Entity Theory of the Corporation." *Florida State University Law Review*. 21 (4): 1061–1122.

Picoche, Jacqueline. 1983. *Dictionnaire étymologique du français*, Paris: Le Robert.

Pierré-Caps, Stéphane. 2004. "Deuxième Chambre et représentation." *XIXè Session de l'Académie internationale de droit constitutionnel portant sur les Secondes Chambres parlementaires* XIII: 358–403.

Piketty, Thomas. 2013. *Le capital au XXIe siècle*. Paris: Seuil.

Pink, Daniel. 2009. *Drive: The Surprising Truth About What Motivates Us*. New York City: Riverhead.

Pinto, Sanjay. Forthcoming. "Worker Cooperatives and Other Alternative Forms of Business Organization." in *Handbook of the International Political Economy of the Corporation*, edited by Christian May and Andreas Noelke, Cheltenham, UK: Edward Elgar.

Piore, Michael J. and Charles F. Sabel. 1984. *The Second Industrial Divide. Possibilities for Prosperity*. New York: Basic Books.

Piore, Michael J. and Sean C. Safford. 2006. "Changing Regimes of Workplace Governance, Shifting Axes of Social Mobilization, and the Challenge to

Industrial Relations Theory." *Industrial Relations: A Journal of Economy and Society* 45 (3): 299–325.

Pizzorno, Alessandro. 1978. "Political Exchange and Collective Identity in Industrial Conflict." Pp. 277–98 in *The Resurgence of Class Conflict in Westen Europe since 1968*, edited by C. Crouch and A. Pizzorno. New York: Holmes & Meier.

Pleyers, Geoffrey. (2010) *Alter-Globalization. Becoming Actors in the Global Age.* Cambridge: Polity Press.

Polanyi, K. 2001 (orig. ed. 1944). *The Great Transformation. The Political and Economic Origins of Our Time.* Boston: Beacon Press.

Polsby, Nelson. 1975. "Legislatures." Pp. 257–319 in *Handbook of Political Science: Governmental Institutions and Processes. Reading*, Vol. 5, edited by N. Polsby and F. Greenstein. Boston: Addison-Wesley.

Rebérioux, Antoine. 2003. "Gouvernance d'entreprise et théorie de la firme: Quelle(S) alternative(s) à la valeur actionnariale?" *Revue d'économie industrielle* 4 (104): 85–110.

Reman, Pierre. 1994. "Du pacte social de 1944 au plan global de 1993." Pp. 125–35 in *Pour Un Nouveau Pacte Social*, edited by EVO. Charleroi.

Renault, Emmanuel. 2004. *Reconnaissance et clinique de l'injustice.* Paris: La Découverte.

Riboud, Frank. 2007. "Le projet économique et social de Danone." *Compte-rendu de l'Observatoire du management alternatif d'HEC Paris.* 28 pp.

Robé, Jean-Philippe. 1999. *L'entreprise et le droit.* Paris: Presses universitaires de France.

Robé, Jean-Philippe. 2001. "L'entreprise oubliée par le droit." *Journal de l'Ecole de Paris* 32: 29–37.

Robé, Jean-Philippe. 2011. "The Legal Structure of the Firm." *Accounting, Economics, and Law* 1 (5): 86 pp.

Robé, Jean-Philippe. 2012. "Being Done with Milton Friedman." *Accounting, Economics, and Law* 2 (2): (Online) 2152–2820.

Robé, Jean-Philippe. 2012b. "L'entreprise et la constitutionalisation du système-monde de pouvoir." Pp. 281–354 in *L'entreprise: formes de propriété et responsabilités sociales*, edited by B. Roger. Paris: Lethielleux.

Robé, Jean-Philippe, Antoine Lyon-Caen and Stéphane Vernac (eds). (2016) *Multinationals and the Constitutionalization of the World Power System.* Oxford: Routledge.

Rogers, Joel and Wolfgang Streeck. 1995. *Works Councils. Consultation, Representation, and Cooperation in Industrial Relations.* Chicago: University of Chicago Press.

Rogers, Joel. 1995. "United States: Lessons from Abroad and Home." Pp. 375–410 in *Works Councils. Consultation, Representation, and Cooperation in Industrial Relations*, edited by J. Rogers and W. Streeck. Chicago: University of Chicago Press.

Rogers, Joel. 1995b. "A Strategy for Labor." *Industrial Relations* 34 (3): 367–81.

Rogers, Joel. 2012. "Productive Democracy." Pp. 71–92 in *Renewing Democratic Deliberation in Europe, The Challenge of Social and Civil Dialogue*, edited by J. De Munck, C. Didry, I. Ferreras, and A. Jobert. Brussels: Peter Lang.

Rosanvallon, Pierre. 1976. *L'âge de l'autogestion*. Paris: Le Seuil.

Rosanvallon, Pierre. 1989. *Le libéralisme économique. Histoire de l'idée de marché*. Paris: Seuil.

Rouilleault, Henri. 2010. *Où va la démocratie sociale? Diagnostic et propositions*. Paris: Editions de l'Atelier.

Roundtable Institute for Corporate Ethics Report. 2006. "Breaking the Short-Term Cycle."

Sabel, Charles F. 1994. "Learning by Monitoring: The Institutions of Economic Development." Pp. 138–65 in *The Handbook of Economic Sociology*, edited by N. J. Smelser and R. Swedberg. Princeton, NJ: Princeton University Press.

Sabel, Charles F. 2006. "A Real-Time Revolution in Routines." Pp. 107–56 in *The Firm as a Collaborative Community. Reconstructing Trust in the Knwoledge Economy*, edited by C. Heckscher and P. S. Adler. Oxford: Oxford University Press.

Sabel, Charles. 2012. "Dewey, Democracy, and Democratic Experimentalism." *Contemporary Pragmatism*. 9 (2): 35–55.

Santos, Boaventura De Sousa. (2014) *Epistemologies of the South. Justice Against Epistemicide*. Boulder, CO: Paradigm.

Sassen, Saskia. 2006. *Territory, Authority, Rights. From Medieval to Global Assemblages*. Princeton, NJ: Princeton University Press.

Sassen, Saskia. 2014. *Expulsions: Brutality and Complexity in the Global Economy*. Cambridge, MA: Harvard University Press.

Schumpeter, Joseph A. 1943. *Capitalism, Socialism, and Democracy*. New York: Harper and Brothers.

Segrestin, Blanche and Armand Hatchuel. 2011. "L'entreprise comme dispositif de création collective: vers un nouveau type de contrat collectif." Pp. 219–272 in *L'entreprise: formes de la propriété et responsabilités sociales*, edited by B. Roger. Paris: Lethielleux.

Segrestin, Denis. 1992. *Sociologie De L'entreprise*. Paris: A. Colin.

Semler, Ricardo. 1999. *Maverick! The Success Story Behind the World's Most Unusual Workplace*. London: Arrow Books.

Sen, Amartya. 1999. "Democracy as a Universal Value." *Journal of Democracy* 10 (3): 3–17.

Sen, Amartya. 2006. *La démocratie des autres*. Paris: Payot & Rivages.

Serres, Michel. 2009. *Temps des crises*. Paris: Le Pommier.

Shell, Donald. 2001. "The History of Bicameralism." *The Journal of Legislative Studies* 7 (1): 5–18.

Silva, Stephen J. 2013. *Holding the Shop Together: German Industrial Relations in the Postwar Era*. Ithaca, NY: Cornell University Press.

Smith, Adam. 2000 (orig. ed. 1776). *The Wealth of Nations. An Inquiry into the Nature and Causes of the Wealth of Nations*. New York: Modern Library.

Stirner, Max. 1845. *L'unique et sa propriété*. Online: http://classiques.uqac.ca/classiques/stirner_max/stirner_max.html

Streeck, Wolfgang. 1992. "National Diversity, Regime Competition and Institutional Deadlock." *Journal of Public Policy* 12: 301–30.

Streeck, Wolfgang. 2001. "La transformation de l'organisation de l'entreprise en Europe: une vue d'ensemble." Pp. 175–230 in *Institutions et croissance, les chances d'un modèle économique européen*, edited by R. Solow. Paris: Albin Michel.

Streeck, Wolfgang. 2013. *Buying Times: The Delayed Crisis of Democratic Capitalism*. London: Verso.

Sudreau, Pierre, sld. 1975. *La réforme de l'entreprise*. Paris: La documentation française.

Supiot, Alain. 2002. *Critique du droit du travail*. Paris: Presses universitaires de France.

Swift, Elaine K. 1996. *The Making of an American Senate: Reconstitutive Change in Congress, 1787–1841*. Chicago: University of Michigan.

Touraine, Alain. 1966. *La conscience ouvrière*. Paris: Seuil.

Touraine, Alain. 1973. *Production de la société*. Paris: Seuil.

Unger, Roberto Mangabeira. 1998. *Democracy Realized: The Progressive Alternative*. London and New York: Verso.

Urban, Greg., ed. 2014. *Corporations and Citizenship*. Philadelphia: University of Pennsylvania Press.

Van Parijs, Philippe and Yannick Vanderborght. (2017) *Basic Income. A Radical Proposal for a Free Society and a Sane Economy*. Cambridge, MA: Harvard University Press.

Webb, Sidney and Beatrice Webb. 1902. *Industrial Democracy*. London, New York, Bombay: Longmans, Green & Co.

Weber, Max. 1958. *The Protestant Ethic and the Spirit of Capitalism*. Translated by T. Parsons. New York: Charles Scribner's Sons.

Weber, M. 1971. *From Max Weber: Essays in Sociology*. New York: Oxford University Press.

Weick, Karl E. 1976. "Educational Organizations as Loosely Coupled Systems." *Administrative Science Quarterly*. 21: 1–19.

Weil, David. 2014. *The Fissured Workplace. Why Work Became So Bad for So Many and What Can Be Done to Improve It*. Cambridge, MA: Harvard University Press.

Weiler, Paul. 1990. *Governing the Workplace. The Future of Labor and Employment Law*. Cambridge, MA: Harvard University Press.

Weitzman, Martin and Douglas Kruse. 1996. "Profit Sharing and Productivity." Pp. 288–96 in *The Economic Nature of the Firm*, edited by L. Putterman and R. S. Kroszner. Cambridge: Cambridge University Press.

Whelan, Glen. 2012. "The Political Perspective on Corporate Social Responsibility: A Critical Agenda." *Business Ethics* 22 (4): 709–737.

Whyte, William F. and Kathleen K. Whyte. 1991 *Making Mondragon. The Growth and Dynamics of the Worker Cooperative Complex*. New York: ILR Press.

Williamson, O. 1985. *The Economic Institutions of Capitalism*. New York: Free Press.

Withford, Josh. 2005. *The New Old Economy. Networks, Institutions and the Organizational Transformation of American Manufacturing*. Oxford: Oxford University Press.

Wormser, Maurice. 1912. "Piercing the Veil of Corporate Entity." *Columbia Law Review* 12 (6): 496–518.

Yeoman, Ruth. 2014. *Meaningful Work and Workplace Democracy: A Philosophy of Work and a Politics of Meaningfulness*. London: Palgrave Macmillan.

Zinn, Howard. 2001. *A People's History of the United States: 1492-Present*. New York City: HarperCollins.

Index

Bryson, Alex, 128
Buitron, Carolina Osorio, 37
bureaucratization, 82

Caniëls, Marjolein, 104
Canziani, Arnaldo, 108
capital investors
  despotic power, 1
  firm as instrument of, 66–70
  optimal guarantors of instrumental
    rationality, 70–72, 79–81
  ownership of shares in the corporation
    not the firm, 65–66
  power based on questionable logic,
    113–16
  power compared to absolute monarchy,
    113–16
  power sharing, 8
capitalism, 120
  contradiction with democracy, 3,
    160–63
  creation of the proletariat, 25
  invention of wage labor, 26–27
  separation of home and work,
    26–27
capitalist despotism
  United States, 3
capitalist firm
  labor investors' participation in
    governing, 58–61
  mistaken for the corporation, 137–40
  motivating employees, 58–61
capitalist institutional innovations
  ambiguities, 56–57
  Collins, Randall, 18, 53, 110
  co-management, 48–53
  labor participation options, 40–42
  participating in management, 42–48
  post-Second World War period,
    39–40
  union reactions, 53–56
Carley, Mark, 135
Carney, Brian, 47, 59, 114, 150
Carpenter, O.F., 42, 43, 110
Cassiers, Isabelle, 106
Castoriadis, Cornelius, 16, 92
Catholic social teaching, 55–56
Césaire, Aimé, vi
Chandler, Alfred, 53, 101
Chaplin, 144
Charest, Gilles, 150

Charles, Julien, 60
Chassagnon, Virgile, 102, 103–05, 108
Chiapello, Eve, 114
Chief Executive Officer, 137
Christian labor movement, 53, 55–56
Ciepley, David, 6
Citizens United ruling, 3
class compromise, 126
class conflict (Marx), 120
Clinton administration, 17
Coase, Ronald, 68
Cohen, G.A., 67
Cohen, Joshua, 2, 4, 23, 42, 66, 129, 156,
  188
Cohen, Morris R., 57, 77, 82, 103, 105,
  154
Coker, F.W., 120
Cold War, 39
collective bargaining
  and the democratic ideal, 33–38
co-management
  Mitbestimmung in Germany, 48–53
Commons, John, 42
Communism, 39
communitarian view of the firm, 99
Compa, Lance, 36
Constant, Benjamin, 28–30
contractualism, 27
contradiction between capitalism and
  democracy, 3, 160–63
cooperatives, 58
Corcuff, Philippe, 161
corporate citizenship, 47
corporate investors
  distinction between ownership and
    control, 95–99
corporate law, 95–99
corporate social responsibility, 47, 106
corporation
  capitalist firm mistaken for, 137–40
  confusion between firm and corporation,
    65–66
  definition, 19
  distinguishing firm from, 95–99
  relationship to the firm, 107–09
  role in financial globalization, 19–20
Coutant, Hadrien, 84
critical intuition of democratic justice,
  91
Cromwell, Oliver, 122
Crouch, Colin, 165

Olin Wright, Erik, 4, 58, 157, 161, 165,
171, 182, 188
Olson, John, 98
Orwell, George, 1
Osborne, Michael A., 10, 186
Occupy Wall Street, 160
oligarchy, 14
Owen, Robert, 58

papal encyclical *Rerum Novarum* (1891),
56
Parsons, Talcott, 121
Pateman, Carol, 55, 75, 188
Pech, Thierry, 151, 176
Pettit, Philip, 28
Philadelphia Constitutional Convention,
124
Philipps, Michael J., 108
Picoche, Jacqueline, 21
Pierre-Caps, Stéphane, 130
Piketty, Thomas, 2, 37, 166
Pink, Daniel, 59, 84, 150
Pinto, Sanjay, 59, 174, 179
Piore, Michael J., 38, 43, 105, 185
Pizzorno, Alessandro, 43
Plato, 106
Plehwe, Dieter, 17
Pleyers, Geoffrey, 157
plutocracy, 138
Pocock, 28
Polanyi, Karl, 16–17, 18, 19, 20
political influence of the firm
regulatory capture, 110–11
political logic of work, 88–90
political theory of the firm, 78–79
descriptive account of the firm, 94–111
dimensions of, 5–6
substantive account of the firm, 79–93
Polsby, Nelson, 131, 144
populist revolt against the establishment,
3
power relationships
authority, 104–05
de facto power, 104–05
de jure power, 104–05
within and between firms, 103–05
power sharing 8
principal–agent relations, 68, 70, 98
Pro-Brexit campaign, 19
progressive approach to democracy,
155–58

proletariat
constraints which require working for
pay, 136
emergence with the industrial revolution,
25–26
Proudhon, Pierre-Joseph, 58
public character of work, 85–87
purposive rationality, 69

Rancière, Francis, 92
rational choice theory, 68
rational representation, 126
Reagan, Ronald, 17
realist approach to democracy, 155–58
Rebérioux, Antoine, 67, 68, 72, 105
Reductio ad Corporationem, 5, 68, 98
regulatory capture
political influence of the firm, 110–11
Reman, Pierre, 39
Renaissance
rise of the merchant class, 25
Renault, Emmanuel, 92
Riboud, Frank, 47
Robé, Jean-Philippe, 66, 69, 95, 96, 97, 98,
102, 103, 107, 109, 110, 152, 164
Rocard, Michel, 46, 55
Roeleveld, Adriaan, 104
Rogers, Joel, 4, 23, 35, 36, 37, 39, 42, 43,
51, 53, 66, 92, 150, 156, 157,
165, 188
Rokkan, Stein, 120
Roosevelt administration, 43
Rosanvallon, Pierre, 27–28, 54, 55
Rouilleault, Henri, 39, 40
Rousseau, Jean-Jacues, 27

Sabel, Charles F., 43, 101–03, 105, 106,
128, 157, 165, 188
Safford, Sean C., 38
Santos, Boaventura De Sousa, 16
Sassen, Saskia, 110
Schillinger, 44
Schroëder, Gerhard, 50
Schumpeter, Joseph, 152
scientific management, 75
Second World War, 39
Segrestin, Denis, 100, 147
self-managed companies, 58
Semco
workers' self-regulation, 59–60
Semler, Ricardo, 59, 114

For EU product safety concerns, contact us at Calle de José Abascal, 56–1°,
28003 Madrid, Spain or eugpsr@cambridge.org.